STALINGRAD
Day by Day

STALINGRAD
Day by Day

Jason Turner

WINDMILL BOOKS

This edition published in 2012

ISBN: 978-1-78121-000-0

Produced by
Windmill Books Ltd
First Floor
9-17 St. Albans Place
London N1 ONX

In the preparation of this book extensive use has been made of U.S. Department of Defense analyses of both German and Russian planning, logistics and combat methods on the Eastern Front. This material is probably the best ever assembled and was based on long, indepth interviews with German officers and men who fought at Stalingrad and who had to make command decisions during the battle. These excellent descriptions are supplemented by interviews with veterans and other first-hand accounts of the Stalingrad campaign in 1942–43.

Project Editor: Peter Darman
Designer: Jerry Udall
Index: Indexing Specialists (UK) Ltd
Editorial Director: Lindsey Lowe

Printed in Indonesia

Pages 2–3: Red Army soldiers in Stalingrad in January 1943.

Contents

▼ *German reinforcements arrive on the Eastern Front in the spring of 1942, ready to participate in Operation Blue, the Wehrmacht's summer offensive into the Caucasus.*

Phase I: Planning and preparation

The German Army had suffered a major setback on the Eastern Front at the end of 1941 when it had failed to capture Moscow and defeat the Soviet Union. Worse, the Red Army's counteroffensive in December 1941 had nearly shattered the German frontline. But the front had held and Hitler had begun to conceive of a new offensive on the Eastern Front in 1942. Lacking the strength to launch an attack along the whole front, The Führer was determined to launch his armies south into the Caucasus to seize the oil fields located there. In his initial plans, the city of Stalingrad on the River Volga was a mere footnote and not a strategic priority.

DECEMBER 20, 1924

GERMANY, *POLITICS*
Hitler is released from his confinement in Landsberg prison, where he has served just nine months of the five-year sentence imposed for organizing the failed Munich putsch of 1923. While in prison, he has written the book *Mein Kampf* ("My Struggle"), which lays out clear guidelines for how he believes Germany should conduct its foreign policy in the future. He describes how Germany needs *Lebensraum* ("living space") and the method to obtain this "has to lie in the acquisition of land in the East at the expense of Russia". The book is enormously successful, and sells hundreds of thousands of copies. Hitler makes over one million marks from the royalties.

▶ German dictator Adolf Hitler was determined to attack the Soviet Union in his quest for "living space" for the German people.

NOVEMBER 5, 1937

GERMANY, *STRATEGY*
Hitler tells his senior military commanders that he expects to have seized the Soviet Union by 1943 in the search for *Lebensraum* for the German people.

AUGUST 23, 1939

GERMANY, *DIPLOMACY*
The German and Soviet foreign ministers, Ribbentrop and Molotov, sign a Nazi-Soviet Non-Aggression Pact that seals the fate of Poland. Germany invades Poland on September 1, and the Red Army moves into eastern Poland on September 17.

FEBRUARY 11, 1940

GERMANY, *DIPLOMACY*
Germany and the Soviet Union agree a trade pact, under which vast quantities of raw materials are to be shipped to the Third Reich. This raw material services much of the German armaments industry – Soviet oil fuels the German military machine and Soviet metal is used to build German aircraft and tanks.

JULY 31, 1940

GERMANY, *STRATEGY*
In spite of the close trading links between Nazi Germany and the Soviet Union, Adolf Hitler plans for war. He notes that the oil fields at Baku in the Soviet Caucasus will be a major target for any German invasion of the Soviet Union.

▲ German Foreign Minister Joachim von Ribbentrop (centre) and Joseph Stalin (right) following the signing of the Nazi-Soviet Non-Aggression Treaty in Moscow in August 1939.

AUGUST 5, 1940

GERMANY, *STRATEGY*
General Franz Halder, Germany's chief of staff, inspects the plans for an invasion of the Soviet Union.

DECEMBER 18, 1940

GERMANY, *STRATEGY*
Hitler's Directive No 21 explains how Operation Barbarossa, the invasion of the Soviet Union, will take place in May 1941 and will involve the conquest of the Caucasus. German forces will aim to establish a line from the Volga River in the south up to Archangel in the north.

JUNE 11, 1941

GERMANY, *STRATEGY*
Directive No 32 is circulated to Germany's armed forces. It describes a drive through the Caucasus to take over Iran.

JUNE 22, 1941

USSR, *LAND WAR*
Operation Barbarossa, the German invasion of the Soviet Union, begins. Army Group South pushes east into the Ukraine.

NOVEMBER 20, 1941

SOUTHERN USSR, *LAND WAR*
Units of the First Panzer Group (part of Army Group South) are fighting in the city of Rostov. Rostov is strategically vital, as it sits at the mouth of the River Don, on the Sea of Azov. Its fall will open the way to Stalingrad and the Caucasus.

NOVEMBER 22, 1941

SOUTHERN USSR, *LAND WAR*
Hitler orders an infantry division to be prepared for an invasion of the Caucasus.

NOVEMBER 24, 1941

SOUTHERN USSR, *LAND WAR*
Under flank attacks from the Soviet Thirty-Seventh Army, German forces pull back from Rostov.

NOVEMBER 28, 1941

SOUTHERN USSR, *LAND WAR*
The Red Army reoccupies Rostov and Field Marshal Gerd von Rundstedt pulls Army Group South back to the line of the river Mius. Hitler immediately sacks von Rundstedt but reluctantly permits his successor, Walter von Reichenau, to go on the defensive rather than attack towards Rostov again.

APRIL 5, 1942

GERMANY, *STRATEGY*
Hitler's Directive No 41 is issued, detailing his strategy for the Eastern Front in the summer of 1942. It describes how there would be offensives by Army Group North to capture Leningrad and by Army Group South to penetrate into the Caucasus, while Army Group Centre remained on the defensive. Stalingrad would be a major objective of Army Group South.

▲ Field Marshal Gerd von Rundstedt was the scapegoat for the setback at Rostov in November 1941.

◄ A German soldier watches a Russian house burn during the latter stages of Operation Barbarossa. Despite a string of victories against the Red Army, by the end of 1941 the Wehrmacht had failed to achieve victory on the Eastern Front and faced another campaigning season in the Soviet Union.

The Eastern Front, 1942

Failure to defeat the Soviet Union in 1941 had created a dilemma for the Germans on the Eastern Front in 1942, for they were not strong enough to mount a new offensive along the whole front.

To Hitler, the oil of the Caucasus had always been one of the foremost attractions of Russia. He had mentioned the necessity of seizing the Baku oil fields as early as July 31, 1940, during one of the initial discussions of his plan to invade the Soviet Union. In the spring of 1941 the Armed Forces High Command (OKW) activated the so-called Oil Detachment Caucasus for the purpose of taking over the oil fields. The next step in this direction was the preparation of Directive No. 32, circulated by the Armed Forces High Command (OKH) among the three services on June 11, 1941, some 11 days before the start of Operation Barbarossa. This directive envisaged a drive from the Caucasus across Iran as a part of the plan for the continuation of operations against the British Empire following the defeat of the Soviets.

A few days later, on June 16, 1941, German counterintelligence submitted to OKH a plan for securing the Caucasus oil fields as soon as the disintegration of the Soviet Union occurred. A nucleus of 100 Georgians, trained by German counter-intelligence agents in sabotage and insurgency tactics, was in existence in Romania. These Georgians would have to be brought to the oil fields by sea or air transport as soon as the German ground forces approached the Caucasus region.

With regard to the Caucasus, it was anticipated that the British would seize and block this area as soon as the Germans approached the Sea of Azov. The first British troop concentrations were believed to be taking place along the northern and eastern border of Iraq. Because of terrain difficulties, a German offensive from the southern slopes of the Caucasus across Iran into Iraq could not be carried out before the spring of 1942. Meanwhile, data regarding the Caucasus were to be collected. A list of German tourists who had climbed the Caucasus Mountains during recent years and knew the terrain and weather conditions was drawn up, and books dealing with the same subjects were scrutinized.

At the beginning of August 1941, the German Naval Operations Staff submitted an estimate of the probable reaction of the Soviet Black Sea Fleet in the event of a German penetration into the Caucasus. It was believed that the fleet could seriously hamper operations by keeping the coastal road and railroad between Tuapse and Sukhumi under fire. Among the Soviet ships suitable for such operations were one battleship, six cruisers and 15 modern plus five outdated destroyers. In the Black Sea area the German Navy had no units capable of stopping or disturbing the movements of the Soviet fleet.

In late September reports from agents and radio intercepts indicated that the Russians had from five to six divisions in the Caucasus and three in Iran. It was estimated that British troops entering the Soviet Union would take three weeks to get from Iran to the Caucasus and four weeks to the Crimea.

In October 1941 the Operations Division of the Army High Command drew up the first detailed plan for a Caucasus operation. The scope of the offensive was limited to seizing the oil of the Caucasus and reaching the Iranian and Iraqi border passes for a possible further advance towards Baghdad. The operation was to be executed in six separate phases, extending from November 1941 to September 1942. These phases were outlined as follows:

1. Seizure of the approaches to the northern Caucasus, starting in November 1941.
2. A series of preliminary attacks leading to the seizure of favourable jump-off areas by May 1942.

◀ *German troops, ill equipped for fighting in the Russian winter, stand shivering in the snow after being captured during the Russian counteroffensive of December 1941.*

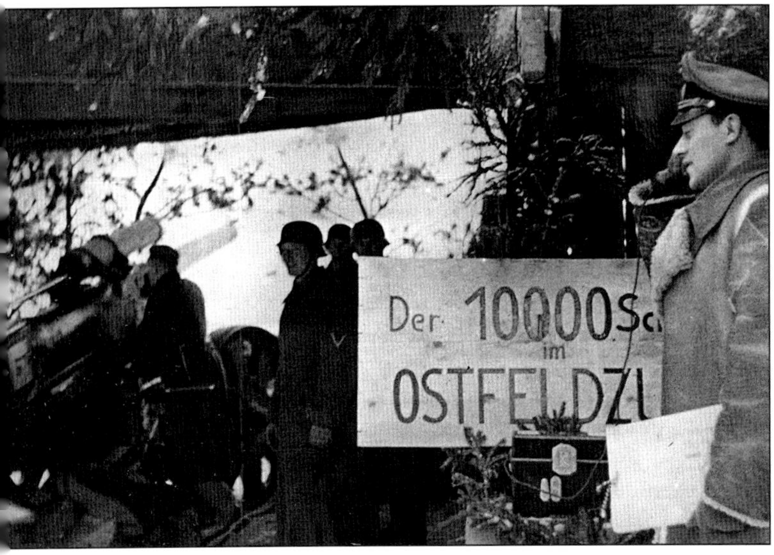

▲ ***A sign at the beginning of 1942 celebrates the fact that this German howitzer has fired 10,000 shells thus far on the Eastern Front.***

3. Launching the offensive across the Caucasus Mountains in two different stages in June 1942.
4. The advance across Transcaucasia towards the Turkish and Iranian borders.
5. Seizure of favourable jump-off areas within Iran.
6. Capture of the border passes leading into Iraq.

The last three phases were to take place in the period July–early September 1942. The feasibility of the entire offensive would depend on the course taken by current operations in the Russian theatre. The second and third phases could be executed only if German troops reached the lower Volga during the winter of 1941–42. The scope of the preliminary attacks to be launched during the second phase would depend on the overall plan adopted for the offensive across the Caucasus. The latter could be launched via the two roads following the Black and Caspian Sea coasts respectively, and over the mountain road leading to Tiflis. The interior roads crossed the mountains over passes more than 3048m (10,000ft) in altitude. These roads could be negotiated only by mountain divisions. The movement along the Caspian coastal road would be easier because only a few outdated Russian destroyers were liable to interfere.

During the first stage of the offensive proper, two motorized and two mountain corps were to be employed, driving towards Sukhumiand Kutaisi in the west, Tiflis in the centre and Baku in the east, respectively. As soon as any one of these forces had achieved a breakthrough, one additional motorized corps that was being held in reserve was to move up and launch the pursuit. The commitment of this reserve force would determine where the point of main effort was to be placed during the second stage of the offensive. The employment of two corps in the west during the first stage would be necessary due to the vulnerability of the lines of communications along the Black Sea. Moreover, the west was the only opening for launching an enveloping drive, since unfavourable terrain prevented any such manoeuvre elsewhere. During the second stage of the offensive, the penetration into the mountains would have to be exploited by the reserve corps. The latter could advance either via the Black Sea coastal road to Batumi and from there via Tiflis to Baku; or across the mountains to Tiflis and from there to either Batumi or Baku; or along the Caspian shore to Baku and

▶ ***Germans retreat west after the failure of Operation Typhoon, the German attack on Moscow in 1941. Hitler had failed to defeat the Soviets in one campaign.***

from there to Tiflis. While the offensive was in progress, German naval contingents would have to protect Novorossisk and Tuapse by taking over captured coastal batteries. In addition, some submarines would have to keep the Russian Black Sea Fleet under control, and the navy would also have to make available the shipping space needed for carrying supplies from Novorossisk to Batumi once the Russian fleet had been eliminated.

The Luftwaffe's tasks were as follows: to protect and support the ground forces; battle the Red Navy and its ports; commit airborne troops to capture the major cities; use dive-bombers against the pass strongpoints; and prepare transport planes to airdrop supplies. This plan met with general approval at an exploratory conference held at OKH headquarters on October 24, 1941. An attack across the Caucasus was also considered the quickest solution to Germany's Middle Eastern problems. The effect of such an offensive would induce Turkey to join the Axis, and British forces that would otherwise oppose General Rommel in North Africa would be tied down in Iran. An offensive launched in the spring of 1942 would first lead to the seizure of the Caucasus oil fields, then open the passes from Iran to Iraq, and finally permit the capture of the Iraqi oil fields in the autumn of 1942, when the weather favoured the

▲ *Some of the hundreds of thousands of Soviet captives netted in 1941. At Kiev alone, 600,000 surrendered in September 1941.*

commitment of large ground forces. The essential prerequisite for such far-reaching operations was the seizure of the west bank of the lower Volga from Stalingrad to Astrakhan. This realization implied that if, for example, the Germans failed to take Stalingrad, a complete re-evaluation of the plans for an offensive against the Caucasus would become necessary. Among the essential preparations for a Caucasus operation discussed at this conference were the production of military maps and tropical clothing, as well as the activation and equipment of special mountain troops.

Caucasus planning, November 1941

In a conversation with Field Marshal von Brauchitsch, Army Commander-in-Chief, on November 7, Hitler mentioned that the seizure of the oil fields would have to be delayed until the following year. This delay had actually been anticipated by the Operations Division of OKH. However, a new point was brought up by the Führer when he added that he had no intention of going beyond the Soviet border. The scope of the offensive was thus limited to the

▲ Red Army tankmen during Zhukov's Moscow counteroffensive in December 1941, which temporarily halted German planning for 1942 on the Eastern Front.

Caucasus. This change in plans was probably due to the slowdown in the 1941 advance caused by the muddy season. According to all available intelligence, the Red Army intended to put up stiff resistance in the Caucasus. By November 9, German intercept units had identified five army headquarters in the area. If exact, this information would imply the presence of at least 15 divisions whereas prior to that time the presence of only five divisions had been assumed. It seemed improbable that the Russians would move sizeable forces across their border into Iran. And it seemed even more unlikely that the British would send strong forces northwards into the Caucasus.

In a conversation with General Halder, Chief of the Army General Staff, on November 19, Hitler stated that the first objective for 1942 would be the Caucasus. An offensive launched for this purpose in March–April 1942 would bring German forces to the Soviet border with Iran. Depending on the situation at the end of 1941, offensives in the centre could subsequently be launched beyond Moscow towards Vologda or Gorki by the end of May 1942. Other objectives for 1942 could not yet be designated; their scope would depend mainly on railroad capacity. Hitler thus revealed a number of interesting facts. Even as late as November 19 he seemed convinced that the Germans would be able to capture Moscow before the end of 1941. Furthermore, he seemed to believe that the Caucasus offensive across difficult mountain terrain could be successfully executed within a few weeks in April and May, as a kind of southern interlude prior to another offensive farther north. Three days later, on November 22, 1941, Halder ordered a light infantry division organized for the Caucasus operation and mountain personnel withdrawn from combat. As late as 16 days before the turning of the tide in front of Moscow the atmosphere at OKH headquarters appeared definitely optimistic.

Effects of the Moscow setback

An order dated December 10, 1941, five days after Zhukov's counteroffensive before Moscow, and signed by Hitler underlined the newly imposed material limitations – if not the change in scope – of the 1942 operations. In the introductory paragraph Hitler stated that the long-range strategic plans remained unchanged, but the army would be given even more than its ordinary share of manpower and armaments so that it could accomplish its mission

▲ *Field Marshal Walter von Brauchitsch, Army Commander-in-Chief (right), and General Franz Halder, Chief of OKH, were both involved in planning for 1942.*

for 1942. In effect, the army was to have top priority on armament production. Wherever shortages of raw materials developed, the navy and Luftwaffe would have to take the cuts. Greater standardization, the introduction of more substitutes, and the increased use of captured munitions were recommended as a means to overcome production bottlenecks. The ground forces were to be ready for offensive commitment by May 1, 1942, no matter what. Supplies for at least four months of continuous operations would have to be accumulated by that time. The units taking part in the offensive would have to be amply provided with supply and service troops as well as motor vehicles (those forces along the Atlantic Coast were to be stripped of trucks). Ammunition supplies for all weapons used in the Russian theatre would have to be built up to one month's expenditure, in addition to the standard load.

German weaknesses

Among the German military-economic programmes, oil had first priority. The railroad transportation, signal and other programmes were to be carried on along the same lines as before, whereas motor vehicle production was to be increased. Military manpower requirements were to be coordinated with the industrial ones. Perhaps the most striking note in this order was its pessimistic undertone. Written at a time when the Germans were desperately trying to stem the Russian tide west of Moscow, the order showed the many weaknesses in the German war machine, which had become manifest after less than seven months of fighting in Russia. During the following weeks further planning for the summer offensive came to a standstill, probably because of the life-and-death struggle that raged along Army Group Centre's front.

Preparatory orders, February 1942

By February 1942, with the acute danger past at the front, the military planners were able to pursue more actively the preparations for a summer offensive. On February 12, 1942, the Operations Division of OKH issued a directive for the conduct of operations after the end of the winter. An introductory statement anticipated that the Russian winter offensive would not succeed in destroying the German troops and their equipment. During the coming weeks the Germans would have to consolidate their lines, eliminate Russian forces that had penetrated into their rear areas, and attempt to seize the initiative. At the same time, they would have to prepare themselves for the muddy period following the spring thaw. The directive then went into great detail in describing the different aspects of the muddy season and the countermeasures to be taken. OKH intended to use this probable lull in operations to rehabilitate and regroup its forces. Army Group South was to hold its positions and make preparations for the planned offensive. First, the Russian penetration west of Izyum would have to be eliminated, then the Kerch Peninsula recaptured and Sevastopol seized, so that the forces stationed in the Crimea would become available for deployment elsewhere. Army Group Centre was to seize Ostashkov and shorten its frontline by eliminating various dents and penetrations. Army Group North was to hold its lines near Cholm, Staraya Russa, and north of Lake Ilmen. After the end of the muddy season all three army groups were to improve their frontlines and establish continuous defensive positions, if possible. However, because of the precarious supply situation, it seemed doubtful whether more than isolated strongpoints could be held along certain sectors of the front.

Papering over the cracks

During the spring of 1942, the German Army underwent a reorganisation. Units withdrawn from the frontline for rehabilitation would have to train their replacements on the basis of past experience in combat. Because of shortages of equipment, only a certain number of divisions could be fully rehabilitated. The ones selected for this purpose were the panzer and motorized divisions, as well as the army and corps troops of Army Group South, three panzer and three motorized infantry divisions, as well as some of the army and corps troops of Army Groups Centre and North. In the process of rehabilitation, each panzer division was to have three tank battalions, and each motorized infantry division one. The panzer divisions of Army Groups Centre and North that were not to be rehabilitated would have to

▼ Red Army infantrymen, well equipped for the Russian winter, march past German corpses in January 1942 during the continuing Russian offensive on the Eastern Front.

transfer some of their cadres to the south. Three panzer and six infantry divisions of Army Group Centre were to be moved to Western Europe without their equipment. There they were to be rehabilitated and re-equipped. The panzer and motorized infantry divisions remaining with Army Groups Centre and North would have to be rehabilitated in the line without being issued with any new equipment. These panzer divisions have only one tank battalion.

Around 500,000 replacements were supposed to arrive on the Eastern Front by the end of April 1942. A special rehabilitation area for Army Group South was to be established near Dnepropetrovsk, while for Army Group Centre similar areas would be set up near Orsha, Minsk, Gomel and Bryansk. Those few units of Army Group North that were to be rehabilitated would probably be transferred to the Zone of Interior. Rehabilitation was to begin in mid-March at the latest. After the muddy season, the fully rehabilitated units of Army Group Centre were to be transferred to Army Group South.

Lack of specialists

The exigencies of the previous few months had led to the commitment of a great number of technical specialists as infantrymen. The overall personnel situation and the shortage of technically trained men made it imperative either to return all specialists to their proper roles, or to use them as cadres for newly activated units. The future combat efficiency of the army would depend upon the effective enforcement of this policy. The high rate of materiel attrition and the limited capacity of the armament industry were compelling reasons for keeping weapons and equipment losses at a minimum. In the implementing order to the army groups and armies, the Organization Division of OKH directed on February 18 that those mobile divisions that were to be fully rehabilitated would be issued 50–60 percent of their prescribed motor vehicle allowance, and infantry divisions up to 50 percent.

Every infantry company was to be issued with four automatic rifles and four carbines with telescopic sights; armour-piercing rifle grenades were also to be introduced. Bi-monthly reports on manpower and equipment shortages, as well as on current training and rehabilitation of units, were to be submitted by all headquarters concerned.

▲ A German mortar team in action on the Eastern Front in February 1942. The winter fighting seriously reduced the manpower levels of German infantry divisions in the East.

In a summary dated February 20, 1942, the Eastern Intelligence Division of OKH stated that the Russians were anticipating a German offensive directed against the Caucasus oil wells. As a countermeasure the Red Army would have the choice between a spoiling offensive and a strategic withdrawal. If the Russians did attack, it was estimated that their offensive would take place in the south, where they could interfere with German attack preparations, reoccupy economically valuable areas, and land far to the rear of the German lines along the Black Sea coast. If they were sufficiently strong, the Soviets would also attempt to tie down German forces by a series of local attacks in the Moscow and Leningrad sectors. Numerous reports from German agents in Soviet-held territory indicated that the Red Army had been planning the recapture of the Ukraine for some time. At the earliest, the Russian attack could take place immediately after the muddy season, i. e. on May 1. The Soviet forces identified opposite Army Group South consisted of 83 infantry divisions, 12 infantry brigades, 20 cavalry divisions and 19 armoured brigades, plus newly organized units.

▲ *In 1941 Soviet partisans were a minor problem for the Germans, but from 1942 they would cause growing problems for Army Group Centre.*

On March 5, an order signed by Field Marshal Wilhlem Keitel, Chief of OKW, set forth the mission of each army group for the immediate future:

Army Group South

1) If the Crimea was to be seized with a minimum of delay, the Kerch Peninsula would have to be captured before starting the siege of Sevastopol. The Russian ports and Black Sea Fleet would have to be neutralized from the air before ground operations were started in the Crimea.

2) The next step was to eliminate the Izyum salient by first letting the Soviets exhaust their offensive power in that area and then cutting off the salient by thrusts directed from the shoulders. The armoured divisions of the First Panzer Army were to carry out these thrusts and were thus given top priority on tank and vehicle deliveries.

Army Group Centre

All forces available in the Army Group Centre area were to be assembled for a Ninth Army thrust in the direction of Ostashkov. This drive was to take place before the spring muddy period. The lines of communications that had been frequently fought over would have to be secured.

Army Group North

The airlift operations that had been initiated to bring the situation under control at Demyansk and Cholm were to be stepped up. More reinforcements were to be moved up to permit the consolidation of the situation at Demyansk and prevent an encirclement along the Volkhov River. Eventually, the Sixteenth Army was to attack from the Staraya Russa area in a movement that was to be coordinated with the Ninth Army drive towards Ostashkov. VIII Air Corps was to support this operation as well as the Volkhov manoeuvre.

Another directive, signed by Hitler on March 14, dealt with the problem of Allied assistance to the Soviet Union. It stated that British and American efforts to bolster Russia's power of resistance during the decisive months of 1942 would have to be curbed. For this purpose the Germans would have to strengthen their coastal defences in Norway to prevent Allied landings along the Arctic coast, particularly in the Petsamo nickel mine area in northern Finland. Moreover, the navy would have to intensify submarine operations against convoys crossing the Arctic Ocean. The Luftwaffe was to strengthen its long-range reconnaissance and bomber units in the far north and transfer the bulk of its torpedo planes to that area. The flying units were to keep the Russian ports along the Murmansk coast under constant attack, increase their reconnaissance activities and intercept convoys. Close interservice cooperation was essential.

Situation at the end of March 1942

The overall situation remained static during the month of March. The Russians showed signs of exhaustion, while the Germans were incapable of launching any major counterattacks. Like two groggy boxers, the opponents warily eyed each other, neither of them strong enough to land a knockout blow. The weakness of the Russians became manifest through a number of incidents. In the area around Velizh, for example, the Germans captured rifles, the butts of which were unfinished, indicating that the weapons had been issued before they were ready. The shortage of Soviet infantry weapons, though nothing new, seemed more acute than ever. Russian

▲ *A German memorial to those killed during Barbarossa. It states: "Men's worth will be reckoned by what they gave for their fatherland – and these gave their lives."*

prisoners stated that wooden rifles were being used for training recruits in the Zone of Interior. In another instance, the Russian cavalry divisions opposite Army Group South were so short of horses – their strength had dropped to approximately 60 horses per regiment – that the men had to be employed as infantry.

During March Army Group South was not engaged in any large-scale fighting, and Field Marshal von Bock, who had assumed command of the army group after General Walter von Reichenau's sudden death on January 17, 1942, used this lull to reinforce the wall around the Russian breach near Izyum.

Army Group Centre

In the Army Group Centre area the heavy fighting in the rear of the Fourth and Ninth Armies continued. The Russians did everything in their power to supply their forces fighting behind the German front, and they exerted constant pressure on Army Group Centre's only supply line, the Smolensk–Vyazma –Rzhev railroad. German efforts to keep this route open were handicapped by a shortage of troops. Also, in the Vitebsk-Velikiye Luki area there was a latent threat which the Germans were unable to eliminate. But they were fortunate that the Russians in this region had dispersed their forces over a wide area instead of concentrating them for a southwards drive.

South of Lake Ilmen, Army Group North had assembled a relief force to establish contact with the Demyansk Pocket. The situation along the Volkhov Front had deteriorated because a strong attack launched by the Russians northeast of Lyuban resulted in a deep breach, which, in conjunction with the Volkhov penetration, threatened to develop into a double envelopment of the German forces in that area. The Red Army was as yet unable to mount effective deep-penetration operations that could have taken advantage of German weaknesses. And the Wehrmacht was suffering major shortcomings, not withstanding the grandiose missives emanating from OKW and OKH. By the end of February 1942, for example, the German armed forces had lost 394,000 killed, 725,000 wounded, 414,000 captured, 46,000 missing (presumed dead) and 112,000 injured through illnesses since the start of Opeation Barbarossa in June 1941.

Opposing Forces

The Germans were masters of mobile mechanized warfare, but many of the divisions earmarked for Blue were understrength, and they faced a Red Army that had learned some valuable lessons.

Compared to the stripped-down divisions left holding the defensive front, the German southern attack forces that assembled for Operation Blue seemed sleek and powerful. However, this appearance was deceiving. The divisions assigned to Army Group South suffered from many deficiencies that compromised their offensive and defensive capabilities.

In May 1942, most of the infantry divisions in Army Group South stood at about 50 percent strength. Although brought nearly up to strength over the next six weeks, they had little time to assimilate their new troops. Only one-third of the infantry divisions committed to the upcoming attack could be taken out of the line in early spring for rehabilitation; the remaining divisions stayed in their old winter defensive positions and tried to train and integrate their replacements even as they fought desultory defensive battles against minor Russian attacks. As a result, the general training standards in the southern assault forces were far below those of the 1939–41 German armies. Losses in officers, noncommissioned officers (NCOs) and technical personnel during the 1941 winter battles had further sapped the combat abilities of German forces. In fact, many German units now regretted the use of artillerymen, signallers and other specialists as infantry during the winter months since they were so hard to replace. Also, even after stripping vehicles and equipment from the northern forces, Army Group South's divisions lacked their full complement of motor transport. According to an OKH study in late May, the spearhead forces (those divisions that would actually lead the attacks towards Stalingrad and the Caucasus) would start with only 80 percent of their vehicles, and the follow-on infantry divisions and supply columns would be slowed by shortages of both horses and vehicles. For all of the ruthless economies inflicted on their poorer relatives to the north, Army Group South would therefore be more clumsy, be less mobile, and have less logistical staying power than the German armies that had launched Barbarossa a year before.

◀ ***Despite the fame of the panzers, the backbone of the German Army was its infantry divisions. During Operation Blue the infantry were stripped of their vehicle support.***

Rehabilitation of units

The main problem facing the Organization Division of the Army High Command was the rehabilitation of units. Altogether, three panzer and five infantry divisions committed in the Russian theatre were selected to be exchanged for one panzer and nine infantry divisions stationed in the West. The troops to be withdrawn from the Russian theatre were to be deloused twice: first before entraining and then again after detraining.

Some of the army and corps troops, as well as the divisions, that were to be rehabilitated within theatre could not even be pulled out of the front. They were to be rehabilitated in situ, a very unsatisfactory procedure not propitious to raising the combat efficiency of the respective units. Leave was to be granted to all those men who had served uninterruptedly in theatre since the start of the campaign. Two leave trains per week were scheduled for each army group.

The panzer divisions complained about the continued shortage of technicians and the weakness of their cadres. Tank and truck drivers in particular were at a premium. Several orders were issued requesting field commanders to return technicians and specialists to the assignments for which they were trained. To relieve the manpower shortage within theatre, native units were to be activated from the prisoners of Tatar, Caucasian, Georgian, Armenian and Cossack nationality who would be captured during the summer offensive. These units were to assume some of the routine duties heretofore carried out by German troops, thus permitting a more judicious employment of the latter.

Construction of fortifications

On April 26, Halder issued an order calling for the establishment of a defence system in the East. In view of the general weakness of the frontlines, enemy breakthroughs could be prevented only by constructing fortifications, establishing switch positions and building specific fortified areas. The frontlines were to be fortified in depth. Switch positions were to protect the Bryansk-Kharkov line. Since there was not sufficient manpower to construct continuous lines in the rear, it would be necessary to establish fortified areas that could be held for prolonged periods by weak forces against superior enemy pressure. These fortified areas were to secure important supply and communications centres, such as Melitopol, Dnepropetrovsk, Poltava, Bryansk, Roslavl, Smolensk, Nevel, Luga, Gatchina and Pskov. By securing the most important road and rail junctions, and river crossings situated between the frontline and the fortified areas in the rear, the Germans could create a defence system capable of successfully withstanding any Soviet armoured elements that might break through the front. Engineer staffs were to be responsible for the construction of the fortifications. Only indigenous labour was to be used because of the shortage of German manpower.

The Oil Detachment Caucasus, formed in the spring of 1941, was expanded because of recent experiences with the Russian scorched-earth policy. Since the oil fields would be more severely damaged than originally presumed, the detachment was brought up to a strength of 10,794 men and redesignated Oil Brigade Caucasus. The brigade was issued with 1142 vehicles and six aircraft and ordered to stand by, ready to move into the Caucasus oil fields immediately behind the combat troops.

Casualties and replacements

At the end of the winter fighting, on April 30, 1942, total German casualties in the USSR, excluding sick, had reached 1,167,835 officers and men. A number of measures to save personnel had been introduced, such as lowering the paper strength of infantry divisions. Nevertheless, by October 31, 1942, the estimated shortage of replacements in the Russian theatre would amount to 280,000 men, even if all operations proceeded according to plan. The Organization Division believed that it would be impossible to provide sufficient replacements for all three army groups. The three solutions therefore taken under consideration at the end of April were as follows:

1. To give Army Group South its full complement of replacements, in which case the situation at Army Groups Centre and North would not be relieved until July 1942;
2. To fulfill only 80 percent of the Army Group South requirements, as a result of which the position of the other two army groups would improve quite considerably by July 1942;
3. To give Army Group South its full complement and accelerate the arrival of additional replacements during May and June by transferring to each of the two other army groups 100,000 men with only two months of training.

Halder chose the third solution, fully cognizant of the disadvantage incurred by committing replacements with only two months of training. Actually, he had little choice in the matter. The monthly report on the rehabilitation of units in the Army Group Centre area during April 1942 indicated that the

◀ ***The 105mm le FH 18/40 gun was the standard light divisional howitzer of the German Army throughout the war. Over 10,000 were built in total.***

▲ *The Panzer III Ausf J was armed with a 50mm main gun. Although outclassed by the T-34 from the end of 1941, many of this variant took part in Operation Blue.*

unabated intensity of the defensive fighting, as well as the withdrawal of divisions for transfer to the West, had almost completely obstructed the reorganization and rehabilitation of units that stayed in place. In general, the divisions which were to be rehabilitated in place would have only limited mobility and reduced combat efficiency, the shortage of motor vehicles and horses being their greatest handicap.

Participation of Germany's allies

During the summer of 1942, Germany's allies were to play a much more significant part in the Russian theatre than before. In an effort to intensify their participation in the struggle against the Soviet Union, Keitel had visited Hungary and Romania during the preceding winter and Hitler had made a personal appeal to Mussolini. OKW was to provide all the weapons and equipment it could spare for the allied contingents. The political differences were to be partly overcome by interspersing Italian corps or armies between Hungarian and Romanian ones. In compliance with requests received from Germany's allies, Hitler on April 15 ordered national units to fight under the command of their own army or at least corps headquarters. This decision was to cost the Germans dearly when their allies collapsed along the Don Front under the blows of the Russian counteroffensive in late 1942.

To ascertain smooth cooperation at different command levels, the German Army organized a number of liaison staffs to be attached to allied divisions, corps and army headquarters. Hitler showed his continued anxiety over the morale of the allied troops a few weeks later, when he stated that Italian and other allied achievements should be given proper credit in German news releases. He believed that fanatical loyalty on the part of the Germans would in turn inspire their allies with similar feelings.

On the other hand, Hitler was unable to satisfy the requests of General Erwin Rommel after his meeting with Mussolini at the beginning of April 1942. No motorized army artillery and engineer units could be made available for North Africa before the successful conclusion of the Caucasus offensive in the autumn of 1942. By June, however, Rommel's advance into Egypt seemed so promising that Hitler suddenly decided to divert to North Africa a number of tanks, trucks and weapons that had been reserved for the rehabilitation of two Russian-theatre divisions.

Aside from Germany's allies, a number of European states, even some of the recently vanquished ones, offered contingents of volunteers who desired to participate in the campaign against the Soviet Union – which for a time tended to assume the characteristics of a crusade against Bolshevism. But Hitler, distrusting his former enemies, reluctantly permitted only a limited number of Frenchmen to serve in national units up to regimental strength. Party political considerations induced him to transfer the responsibility for organizing foreign military volunteer units from army to Waffen-SS control.

▲ *The Nebelwerfer was a multi-barrelled rocket launcher that provided mass fire support. At the commencement of Operation Blue the army had six Nebelwerfer regiments.*

Anxious to secure the lines of communications of the combat forces, Halder decided that three German security divisions, plus Hungarian and Romanian troops, were to follow behind the advance. Each security division was to be composed of one infantry

and one security regiment, one motorized military police, one artillery and one signal battalion, as well as one Cossack troop. Military administrative headquarters and prisoner-of-war processing units were also to be formed.

Army Group South's defence line

One of the problems that constantly preoccupied Hitler during the preparatory period was the exposed flank that would extend from Voronezh to the area northeast of Kursk. The Führer ordered this defence line amply provided with anti-tank guns. A total of 350–400 self-propelled 75-mm anti-tank guns – more than half of them captured French weapons – and some 150 captured Russian 76mm guns were to be distributed along this front to repel Soviet tanks. Tractors and captured prime movers were to be employed to give a certain degree of mobility to those guns which were not self-propelled.

▲ ***Ju 87 Stuka dive-bombers en route to southern Russia in the spring of 1942, some of the 2690 aircraft that the Luftwaffe deployed to support Operation Blue.***

German deficiencies

Despite the planning of OKW and OKH, German forces still had major problems on the eve of Operation Blue:

Tanks. At the start of the summer offensive the Germans would have 3300 tanks in the Russian theatre against 3350 on June 22, 1941. That said, the 1942 tanks were better armed than the ones with which Germany invaded the Soviet Union the previous year.

Anti-tank weapons. A considerable number of 37mm and 50mm anti-tank guns had been lost during the winter fighting, but these losses would be compensated for by the use of heavier calibre captured French and Russian guns – hardly a satisfactory state of affairs.

Anti-aircraft units. Only the spearhead divisions would have organic anti-aircraft units. Although the commitment of corps and army flak battalions had improved overall anti-aircraft protection, with operations extending over wide areas, anti-aircraft units would have to be spread very thinly.

Ammunition. The retrenchment on ammunition production imposed during the summer of 1941 and the high rate of expenditure of the following winter had led to a shortage of heavy weapons, howitzer and anti-tank ammunition, which was expected to continue through the autumn of 1942. By August 1942 shortages might affect operations. In this estimate the possibility of increased expenditure before the outset of the offensive had not been taken into account. Expedients, such as imposing expenditure quotas and arranging for ammunition transfers from the West, had already been introduced.

Transportation. The heavy attrition of motor vehicles suffered during the winter battles – 75,000 vehicles lost against the arrival of only 7500 replacements for the period November 1, 1941–March 15, 1942 – complicated efforts to restore full mobility to the ground forces by the start of the summer offensive. Current production was insufficient for both replacing past losses and equipping new units. Only the spearhead divisions would therefore receive new vehicles. At the same time, most of the infantry divisions would be deprived of their motor vehicles and the motorized units in other sectors would be faced with a reduction in their organic vehicle allowance. As spare parts production and repair installations would be incapable of fully satisfying the demands made by far-reaching offensive operations, whatever stocks

◀ ***A German infantry squad in southern Russia in 1942. Note the captured PPSh submachine guns, which were highly prized by German soldiers on the Eastern Front.***

▲ *Romanian troops on the Eastern Front. Many German commanders had a low opinion of their Axis allies, believing them to be poorly educated and led.*

and facilities were available would have to be diverted to the spearhead units.

To make matters even worse, there was an acute shortage of horses. During the winter, 180,000 horses had died from hunger and exposure as well as enemy action, with only 20,000 replacements arriving in theatre. Although 109,000 horses had been shipped from the Zone of Interior by May 1 and another 118,000 had been requisitioned from occupied countries, the number of horses available by the start of the offensive would still be insufficient.

In summarizing the transportation picture, the army estimated that the spearhead divisions in the south would have 85 percent of their organic motor vehicle allowance by the time the offensive got under way. Infantry divisions would be restricted in their movements because of an almost complete lack of motor vehicles. Major operations in the other army group areas would be dependent on adequate rail capacity. In any event, the logistical support that could be given to Army Groups Centre and North during the summer would curtail operations.

No further reserves would be available in the Zone of Interior. The unavailability of trained manpower and up-to-date equipment would prevent the activation of new divisions. Any replacements, weapons and equipment that would become available during the course of the summer offensive would be needed to make up current losses. No further increase in the number of divisions was possible, since the 18-year olds had already been inducted. Additional motorized and panzer divisions could be activated only by disbanding existing infantry units.

Blueprint for a disaster

A full rehabilitation of German forces in the Russian theatre before the start of the 1942 offensive was not feasible. Personnel and material shortages hampered every effort to obtain greater mobility and raise combat efficiency. These shortages, as well as the wear and tear on man, beast and vehicle caused by the winter fighting, seemed to have reduced the stamina of the German Army.

Halder's report revealed that the German ground forces that were to launch the summer offensive of 1942 could not compare with the troops that had invaded Russia a year earlier. The spearhead units would be almost up to strength, but the follow-up infantry was weak and slow, and no reserves were available. No wonder the Army High Command felt apprehensive about executing Hitler's overambitious plans. An equally sombre note was struck by the Organization Division of OKH in its memorandum to the Chief of the Armed Forces Operations Staff, dated May 27, 1942.

In reporting on the composition and condition of the Army Group South units by the beginning of the summer offensive, the Organization Division repeated that only part of the personnel and material losses suffered during the winter could be replaced. For this reason, all available replacements had been channelled to the spearhead divisions. Two types of units had been created: highly effective attack forces and units having little punch or mobility.

Of the 65–67 German divisions that were to participate in the offensive in the south, only 21–23 were either being newly activated or fully rehabilitated behind the front, whereas the remaining 44 divisions were to be rehabilitated while committed at the front. Each of the fully rehabilitated infantry divisions would receive 1000 replacements with only two months of training. The mobility of these divisions would be limited because they were short of horses and lacked most of their organic motor transport. The reconnaissance battalions were now equipped with bicycles. Contrary to previous reports, the spearhead divisions would have only about 80 percent of their organic motor vehicles.

In revising the distribution of forces, greater consideration would have to be given to the unequal strength and mobility of the different divisions. Since no reserves of manpower or equipment were available, the rehabilitation of units would have to be accomplished with insufficiently trained men and untested equipment coming directly from the assembly lines. The possibility of forming strategic reserves before or during the course of the initial operations appeared unlikely.

The Red Army

As well as having to deal with their own material and manpower shortages, the Germans would also face a tenacious foe who had learned from the disasters of 1941. Once the Red Army halted and threw the invaders back from Moscow in December 1941, Soviet commanders began to revive their military organization and doctrine. Soviet factories made a phenomenal production effort in the spring of 1942, enabling General Yakov Fedorenko, Chief of the Armoured Forces Administration, to begin construction of new tank corps in April. By July, these corps had settled on an organization of one rifle and three tank brigades, plus supporting arms – a fairly tank-heavy force that the Soviets intended to use as the mobile exploitation unit for a field army. In the autumn of 1942, Fedorenko added mechanized corps, which were more infantry-heavy and therefore more expensive in manpower and trucks (truck production was a major problem in World War II, and the Soviets depended upon imported US wheeled vehicles to support their mobile units).

Unlike those of 1940, these 1942 Soviet corps were actually of division size or smaller. To conduct

▼ ***Trucks and motorcycles of the Romanian Third Army prior to Blue. Lacking training and equipped with obsolete weapons, the Romanians suffered greatly at Stalingrad.***

the deep exploitations of 150km (94 miles) or more envisaged in the 1920s, the Red Army needed a larger formation, the equivalent of a German panzer corps or panzer army. In May 1942, the Commissariat of Defence took the next logical step, uniting the existing tank corps into tank armies. The 1942 tank armies, however, were merely improvised combinations of armoured, cavalry and infantry divisions, combinations that lacked a common rate of mobility and doctrine of employment. Moreover, these armies rushed into battle against the Germans during the summer of 1942 and were largely destroyed before they had even trained together.

Not until January 1943 did the Soviets finally produce a coherent tank army; the six tank armies formed in 1943 were the spearheads of all Soviet offensives for the remainder of World War II. Each of these new tank armies was actually a corps-sized formation in Western terminology and, like the tank corps, was extremely tank-heavy. This was probably an appropriate response, both because of the open tank country of European Russia and because of the high Soviet tank losses against the Germans. Given the inexperience of most tank crews and junior leaders in the Red Army of 1941–43, it was inevitable that the better-trained German anti-tank and armour formations would inflict such disproportionate losses on the Reds. Thus, the Soviet Union's armoured forces remained much more tank-heavy than those of other armies. Yet throughout the war, the Soviets also maintained corps-sized formation of horse cavalry with limited tank and artillery support, for use in swamps, mountains and other terrain that did not favour heavily mechanized forces.

The new mechanized formations must be understood in the context of their accompanying doctrine. During 1942, the Soviets digested the lessons of the first year of war and issued a series of orders to

▼ The German Pak 38 anti-tank gun was introduced in 1941 to replace the 37mm gun. It could penetrate 56mm (2.2in) of armour at a range of 914m (3000ft).

correct their errors. These orders greatly increased the effectiveness of the Soviet counteroffensive that encircled Stalingrad in November 1942. And senior Red Army commanders held conferences before Stalingrad to ensure that their subordinates understood the new doctrine.

Red Army doctrine

The first problem was to penetrate the German defences in order to conduct a counteroffensive. The initial Soviet counterattacks of December 1941–January 7, 1942, had suffered from such dispersion that the German defenders often outnumbered their Soviet attackers. On January 10, 1942, Stavka Circular 3 directed the formation of a "shock group", concentrating combat power on a narrow frontage in order to break into the enemy defences. Division and larger units were instructed to mass on narrow frontages in this manner. Stalin's Order 306, dated October 8, 1942, supplemented this directive by explicitly forbidding the echelonment of infantry forces in the attack. Given the continuing shortages of equipment and firepower, the Soviets decided to maximize their available force by putting almost all the infantry into one echelon. Thus, in a typical rifle division, as many as 19 of the 27 rifle companies would be on line for an attack. The German defences in 1942 were stretched so thin that this forward Soviet massing of infantry was more important than echelonment to sustain the attack. Later in the war, when both sides defended in greater depth, the Soviets tended to echelon their attack accordingly. Even in 1945, however, shallow German defences prompted one-echelon Soviet attacks. Other orders in October 1942 governed the correct use of those tanks still assigned to assist the infantry assault. Because infantry commanders were still inexperienced, all such tank units were to be employed in mass under their own commanders.

Once the Soviets completed a penetration, their "mobile groups" would pass through for exploitation and encirclement operations, as described above. In effect, one such encirclement might include other, smaller encirclements within its pincers. Each field army attempted to use its own mobile group, composed of a tank, cavalry or mechanized corps, to exploit penetrations to a relatively shallow depth of 50km (31 miles) or less, defeating enemy reserves or

▲ *The Soviet Model 1942 anti-tank gun. Each Red Army rifle regiment in a rifle division had an anti-tank battery equipped with six of these guns.*

linking up with a similar group from a neighbouring army. Meanwhile, the tank armies acting as mobile groups for larger elements, such as a "front" (army group), penetrated even deeper into the German rear areas. This, at least, was the theory. The first of these large operational-level Soviet encirclements was in November 1942, when the German Sixth Army was surrounded at Stalingrad. In fact, the Soviet use of separate tank and mechanized corps in this battle may have been a test for the new tank army structure adopted two months later.

Red Army infantry

Mention must be made of the Russian soldier, the ordinary "Ivan" who was the backbone of the Soviet war effort throughout World War II. During the war on the Eastern Front the frugality of the Russian soldier was beyond German comprehension. The average rifleman was able to hold out for days without hot food, prepared rations, bread or tobacco. At such times he subsisted on wild berries or the bark of trees. His personal equipment consisted of a small field bag, an overcoat and occasionally one blanket, which had to suffice even in severe winter weather. Since he travelled so light, he was extremely mobile and did not depend on the arrival of rations and personal equipment during the course of operations.

Opposing Forces

From the outset of the Russian campaign German tactical superiority was partly compensated for by the greater physical fitness of Russian officers and men. During the first winter on the Eastern Front, for example, the German Army High Command noticed to its grave concern that the Russians had no intention of digging in and allowing operations to stagnate along fixed fronts. The lack of shelter failed to deter the Russians from besieging German strongpoints by day and night, even though the temperature had dropped to minus 40 degrees. Officers, commissars and men were exposed to subzero temperatures for many days without relief.

The essentially healthy Russian soldier with his high standard of physical fitness was also capable of superior physical courage in combat, which was another nasty surprise to the Germans, who believed the average Slav soldier to be racially inferior to them, and certainly incapable of matching them with regard to courage or intelligence. And whereas the Germans believed they could learn nothing from the enemy, the Russians observed their opponents closely.

During the course of the war the Russians patterned their tactics more and more on those of the Germans. By the time they started their major

counteroffensives in late 1941 and early 1942, their methods of executing meticulously planned attacks, organizing strong fire support, and establishing defensive systems showed definite traces of German influence. The one feature distinguishing their operations throughout the war was their willingness to suffer heavy casualties. Two other characteristics peculiar to the combat methods of the Russians were their refusal to abandon territorial gains and their ability to improvise in any situation.

Infantry, frequently mounted on tanks and in trucks, at times even without weapons, was driven forward wave upon wave regardless of the casualties involved. Far from having no purpose, these tactics of mass assault played havoc with the nerves of the German defence forces and were reflected in their expenditure of ammunition. The Russians were not satisfied at merely being able to dominate an area with heavy weapons or tanks; it had to be occupied by infantry. Even when as many as 80 men out of 100 became casualties, the remaining 20 would hold the ground they had finally gained whenever the Germans failed to mop up the area immediately. In such situations the speed with which the Russian infantry dug in and the skill with which their commanders reinforced such decimated units and moved up heavy weapons were exemplary.

A quick grasp of the situation and instantaneous reaction to it were needed to exploit any moment of weakness that was bound to develop even after a Russian attack had met with initial success. This was equally true in the case of a successful German attack. Under the impression that they had thoroughly beaten and shattered their Russian opponents during an all-day battle, the Germans occasionally relaxed and left the follow-up operation or pursuit for the next morning. On every such occasion they paid dearly for underestimating their adversary.

Soviet deception techniques

The conduct of Red Army troops in the interim periods between major engagements provided clues to what had to be expected during the initial phase of the coming battle. The gathering of information was complicated by the fact that Soviet commanders put so much stress on concealing their plans during the build-up phase for an attack and during the preparation of a defensive system. The overall effectiveness of secrecy and adaptation to terrain was forcefully demonstrated in the shifting and regrouping of forces. While the speed with which Russian commanders effected an improvised regrouping of large-scale formations was in itself a remarkable achievement, the skill with which individual soldiers moved within a zone of attack or from one zone to another occasionally seemed unbelievable. To see a few soldiers moving about in the

◀ ***A Red Army T-34 burns after being knocked out. Among the T-34 production centres was the Stalingrad Tractor Factor, where 3700 T-34s were produced in total.***

▲ *Two of the major factors that contributed to the Soviet victory at Stalingrad: the ordinary Red Army soldier and the superb PPSh submachine gun.*

snow at great distance often meant little to a careless and superficial observer. However, constant observation and accurate head counts often revealed surprisingly quick changes in the enemy situation.

In view of the alertness of the Russian infantryman and the heavily mined outpost area of his positions, a hastily prepared reconnaissance in force by the Germans usually failed to produce the desired results. Under favourable circumstances the patrol returned with a single prisoner who either belonged to some service unit or was altogether uninformed. The Russian command maintained tight security, and the individual soldier rarely knew his unit's intentions. The resulting lack of information with regard to Russian offensive plans gave no assurance, however, that strong Soviet forces would not launch an attack at the same point the next day.

To celebrate major Soviet holidays, Red Army sharpshooters usually tried to break the standing marksmanship scores, and on those occasions German soldiers had to be particularly on the alert. In general, however, Russian attacks were likely to take place on any day, at any time, over any terrain, and under any weather conditions. These attacks derived their effectiveness mainly from the achievement and exploitation of surprise, towards which end the Russians employed infiltration tactics along stationary fronts as well as during mobile operations. The Russians were masters at penetrating German lines without visible preparation or major artillery fire support, and at airlanding or infiltrating individual squads, platoons or companies without arousing suspicion.

A tenacious foe

By taking advantage of the hours of darkness or the noon rest period, the weather conditions and terrain, or a feint attack at another point, Russian soldiers could infiltrate a German position or outflank it. They swam rivers, stalked through forests, scaled cliffs, wore civilian clothing or enemy uniforms, infiltrated German march columns; in short, suddenly they were everywhere. Only through immediate counterattacks could they be repelled or annihilated. Whenever the Germans were unable to organize a successful counterthrust, the infiltrating Russians entrenched themselves firmly and received reinforcements within a few hours. It was like a small flame that rapidly turned into a conflagration. Despite complete encirclement, Russian units that had infiltrated German positions could hold out for days, even though they suffered many privations. By holding out, they could tie down strong German forces and form a jump-off base for future operations.

Combat orders

In contrast to the steady stream of propaganda poured out by the political commissars, whose language abounded in flowery phrases and picturesque expressions designed to stimulate the Russian soldier's morale and patriotism, the combat orders of lower-echelon commanders were very simple. A few lines drawn on a sketch or on one of their excellent 1:50,000 maps indicated the friendly and hostile positions, and an arrow or an underscored place name spelled out the mission. As a rule such details as coordination with heavy weapons, tanks, artillery, tactical air support or service units were missing from orders, because more often than not the mission had to be accomplished without such assistance.

On the other hand, it would be unjust not to mention that these details were considered with utmost care by the intermediate and particularly by the higher-echelon command staffs. Whereas in the early stages of the 1942 campaign captured Russian divisional and regimental orders often showed a tendency towards stereotyped thinking and excessive attention to detail, during the later phases Russian staff work improved considerably in this respect.

The Battle of Stalingrad exemplified the Russian culture of mass. The excessive use of force plus acceptance of casualties and the resulting collateral damage are clearly linked and tied to the Russian way of conducting urban operations. No sacrifice was too great in pursuit of the mission. Whatever resource was at hand was willingly used. The vast casualties the Russians were willing to sustain further evidenced their total commitment. It is clear that the Red Army leveraged an extensive reserve of manpower to offset its lack of equipment, training and sophisticated tactics. Likewise, destruction of the city's infrastructure must have seemed the smaller price to pay for ultimate victory. In fact the collateral damage was not of concern; rather, it was used to their advantage.

The excessively high Russian losses at Stalingrad are attributable to the level of soldier motivation, readiness and the command's insistence on offensive operations. Two other factors also undoubtedly contributed to the Russian poor performance at Stalingrad, and ultimately the extreme number of casualties sustained there.

▼ ***The 7.62mm Degtaryev machine gun, nicknamed the "record player" due to its top-mounted circular magazine, was the standard Red Army infantry support weapon.***

The first factor was the purges carried out by Stalin in the 1930s. Like most dictators, Stalin was continually fearful of coups, and was particularly suspicious of ambitious generals because they commanded large numbers of troops. Stalin's paranoia manifested itself in the Great Terror that began in 1937 and ended only in June 1941, on the eve of the German invasion. During this time, he purged old guard Bolsheviks, Communist Party bosses, military leaders, industrial managers and government officials. The first commander to be removed was Marshal Mikhail Tukhachevsky in June 1937, ostensibly on charges of conspiracy with Germany, but probably because he and Stalin had been "debating" for years which of them had been responsible for the Red Army's defeat before Moscow in 1920 (Stalin had been a party emissary, Tukhachevsky a front commander). The purge then took on a life of its own, with most of the military commanders arrested and shot unknown to Stalin. These included three deputies of the people's commissar of defence, the people's commissar of the navy, sixteen military district commanders, five fleet commanders, eight directors of military academies, thirty-three corps commanders, seventy-six division commanders, forty brigade commanders, and two hundred and ninety-one regimental commanders. In total, 35,000 officers of the armed forces were either dismissed, imprisoned or executed (hundreds of scientists and weapons designers were also arrested). Tens of thousands signed "confessions" to being party to non-existent conspiracies (as the arrested and subsequently executed Marshal Bliukher stated: "When they start twisting your arms and legs, you will sign anything").

▼ The famous Katyusha rocket launcher – "Stalin's Organ" – comprised a rack of rails on which 16 or more rockets were mounted.

The purges were to cause incalculable damage to the ability of the Red Army to resist the German invasion in June 1941. First, they removed experienced and bold commanders and replaced them with those who lacked experience and were noted for a distinct lack of initiative (which, in the Red Army, could shorten life quicker than the German invaders). Second, the command vacuum meant incompetent leaders were over-promoted, resulting in disaster on the battlefield.

Perversely, the purges were also advantageous for Stalin and his regime. The removal of potential opponents meant there was no popular revolt against him during the disasters that took place during Operation Barbarossa (in this way the Soviet system survived for another 50 years instead of collapsing in the summer of 1941). In addition, the purges led Hitler and his planners to underestimate Soviet military potential. Mesmerized by the spectre of emasculated armed forces, they failed to take account of Soviet industrial capacity and ignored the geography of the areas in which the German Army would be operating.

Losses in Barbarossa

The Russians sustained another loss of valued leaders and resources during Barbarossa's initial phase in June and July 1941. Stalin, paranoid about losing any ground to the advancing German armies, had stationed many of his best units in forward positions. As a result, the Germans quickly encircled large static formations and captured over 320,000 of Russia's best soldiers.

Subsequently, in meeting the personnel demands after the debacle of 1941 the Red Army haphazardly drew upon Russian manpower reserves. This led to the use of hastily assembled and untrained divisions in the 1942 campaign. The Germans not only knew this but also knew the Russians would accept high casualties. On August 11, 1942, Halder commented: "the Russian divisions are admittedly not armed and

▲ ***Armoured trains were a feature of the war on the Eastern Front. They were used by the Red Army to provide mobile artillery support.***

equipped in our sense, and tactically they are badly led. But they exist; and when we destroy a dozen the Russians simply establish another dozen."

Amazingly, at a distinct disadvantage in training and heavy equipment, the Russians won at Stalingrad. Not because of superior tactics, but because they accepted massive casualties. The officers who had survived Stalin's purge and the first German assault believed in the sacrifice of the patriot to the motherland regardless of the numbers. This fervent commitment led to the belief that the ends justified the means regardless of cost. What the Russians lacked in leadership, training and equipment they made up for with a fanatical resistance to defeat

As well as its excellent soldiers, the Red Army had two other aces for use against the Germans: the T-34 tank and the PPSh-41 submachine gun. The T-34 with its 76.2mm main gun was one of the greatest tanks of World War II and certainly one of the most influential. One of the most innovative designs was its sloped armour, which not only saved weight compared with rolled plate, but was also more difficult for anti-tank rounds to penetrate. In addition, its Christie-type suspension, combined with a diesel power plant, gave it an excellent power-to-weight ratio and good cross-country mobility.

Designed by George Shpagin, the PPSh-41 entered service shortly before the German invasion of the USSR in June 1941. The PPSh-41 was designed to be as simple as possible. It used a minimum number of parts, a simple blow-back action and fired from the open bolt position. It soon proved itself to be effective as a weapon as well as easy to manufacture, and became one of the most famous small arms of World War II. Factories and workshops throughout the Soviet Union began turning out this reliable weapon, and more than five million were produced by 1945.

The Germans were also impressed with the weapon, particularly the large ammunition supply. This was either a 71-round drum or a 35-round box. Large numbers of captured PPSh-41s were issued to German troops on the Eastern Front.

▼ *Stukas fly over a column of panzers during the early phases of Operation Blue. The Red Army fell back before the Germans, trading space for time. There was to be no repeat of the great cauldron battles of 1941.*

Phase II: The German Assault

In the summer of 1942, following the defeat of Red Army offensives around Kharkov, Adolf Hitler launched Operation Blue. At first the panzers carried all before them, crossing the River Don and striking south into the Caucasus. The city of Stalingrad could have been taken easily, but Hitler began changing his mind about the operation's priorities. This resulted in a dispersal of his forces as German units were pushed deeper into the Caucasus and the Fourth Panzer Army was diverted away from Stalingrad. The Germans could have taken the city at the end of July without a fight, but they missed the opportunity and then faced a hard fight to take the city named after the Soviet dictator.

April 1

SOUTHERN USSR, *LAND WAR*
The Red Army musters its units for an offensive near Izyum. For this operation the Southwestern Front has the Twenty-First, Sixth, Thirty-Eighth, Fifty-Seventh, Ninth and Twenty-Eighth Armies. The Southern Front deploys the Thirty-Seventh, Twelfth, Eighteenth and Fifty-Sixth Armies. Facing these formations are the German Sixth, Seventeenth and First Panzer Armies.

April 5

GERMANY, *STRATEGY*
Hitler issues Directive No 41 outlining the aims of the forthcoming summer offensive on the Eastern Front. "In pursuit of the original plan for the Eastern campaign, the armies of the Central sector will stand fast, those in the North will capture Leningrad and link up with the Finns, while those on the southern flank will break through into the Caucasus."

The Wehrmacht is tasked with "destroying the enemy before the Don, in order to secure the Caucasian oil fields and the passes through the Caucasus mountains". To create favourable conditions, Hitler orders "mopping up and consolidation on the whole Eastern front and in the rear areas so that the greatest possible forces may be released for the main operation". Also, the Kerch Peninsula is to be cleared and Sevastopol captured.

▲ ***German troops of Army Group Centre take cover during a Red Army artillery barrage. By late April, the Soviet offensives in central Russia were petering out.***

April 9

SOUTHERN USSR, *LAND WAR*
Another Red Army attack on the Kerch Peninsula achieves little.

APRIL 14

CENTRAL USSR, *AIR WAR*
The Luftwaffe stops an attack by the Soviet Fiftieth Army aimed at relieving the encircled Thirty-Third Army. The Fiftieth is forced to retire with loss.

APRIL 19

CENTRAL USSR, *LAND WAR*
The Soviet Thirty-Third Army is wiped out and its commander, General Efremov, is killed in the fighting.

APRIL 20

NORTHERN USSR, *LAND WAR*
The Demyansk relief force links up with the 3rd SS *Totenkopf* Division on the River Lovat, though the rescue corridor is very fragile.

CENTRAL USSR, *LAND WAR*
Bryansk Front losses thus far in 1942 amount to 21,319 killed and missing and 39,807 wounded.

YUGOSLAVIA, *PARTISAN WAR*
A combined German-Italian-Croatian operation to clear eastern Bosnia, led by General Bader and under the operational control of the Italian Second Army, begins. The force consists of three Italian divisions: the German 718th Infantry Division, German units from Serbia, and Croatian national troops. It will last until May 3, by which time the partisans will have suffered 168 dead, 1309 prisoners taken and stocks of weapons, ammunition and other equipment captured. Unfortunately for the Germans, large numbers of guerrillas escape through Italian lines and make their way to Croatia.

APRIL 24

FINLAND, *LAND WAR*
The Finnish III Corps defeats a major assault by three rifle divisions of the Soviet Twenty-Sixth Army in the Kastenga area. Combat will continue for the next six days.

APRIL 30

NORTHERN USSR, *LAND WAR*
The Lyuban Offensive conducted by the Volkhov and Leningrad Fronts comes to an ignominious end. It has cost the Red Army 95,064 killed and missing and 213,303 wounded. The Second Shock Army has also been annihilated.

CENTRAL USSR, *LAND WAR*
Red Army losses in the central sector of the front since the beginning of the year have been massive, with the Kalinin Front having lost 123,400 killed and missing and another 217,800 wounded. The Western Front has lost 149,000 killed and missing and 286,000 wounded.

GERMANY, *ARMED FORCES*
The Fourth Panzer Army has relocated to the south to be deployed on the northern flank of Army Group South.

USSR, *ATROCITIES*
An Einsatzgruppen report states with satisfaction that there are no longer any Jews in the Crimea. The Jewish population in the area had numbered up to 60,000 men, women and children, but they have all been liquidated by SS squads assisted by local militias.

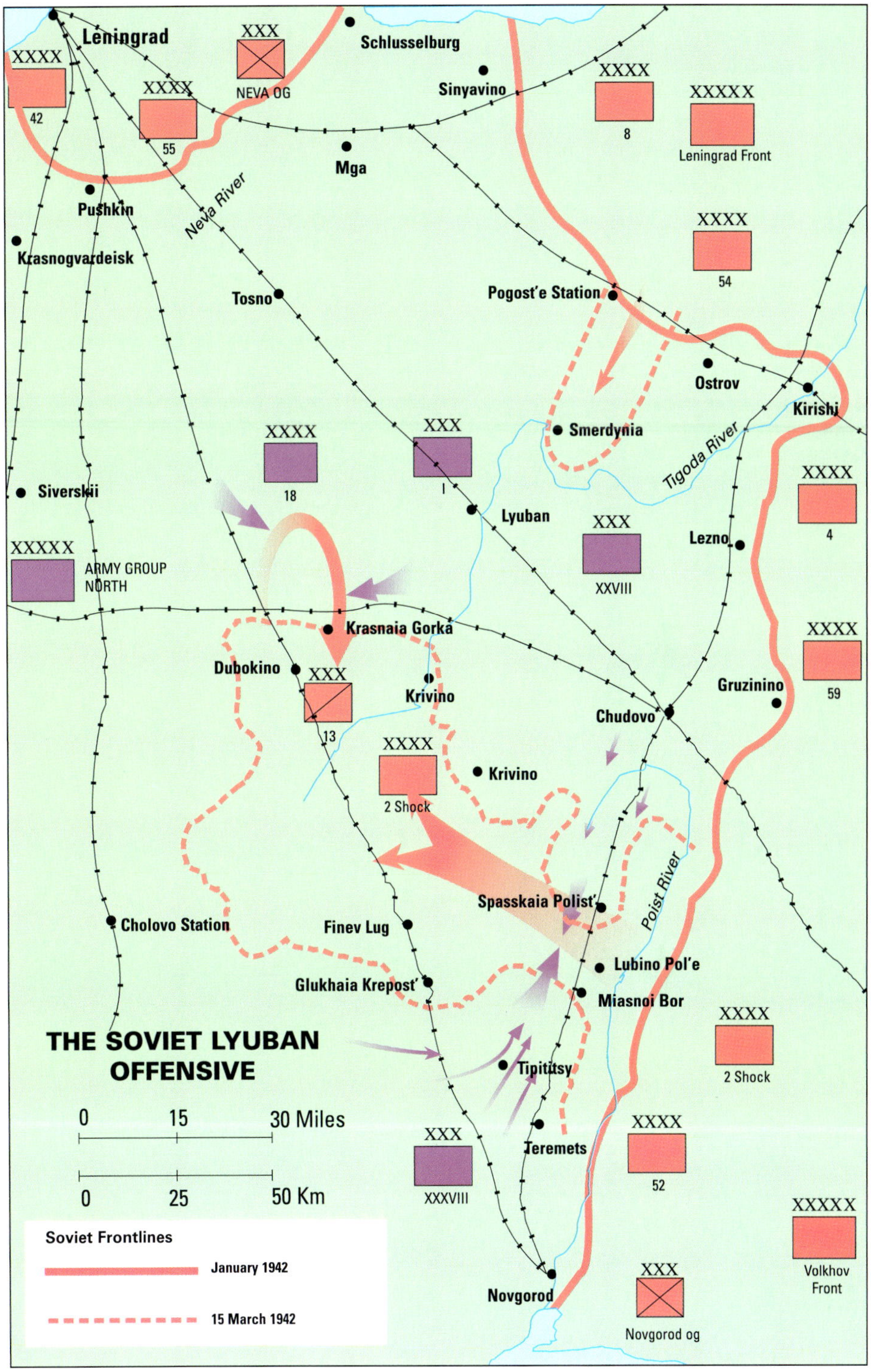

◀ *German troops in the siege lines before Leningrad. Hitler had told his propaganda minister, Goebbels, that the city should "disappear completely". In any case, the Führer remarked, it would be impossible to feed its population of five million. Once taken, the cradle of Bolshevism was to be razed to the ground – a "hard but justifiable nemesis of history", wrote Goebbels.*

▲ ***Troops of the Soviet Southwestern Front attack during the Kharkov Offensive. Designed to weaken any German attack against Moscow, it was a total disaster.***

MAY 5

NORTHERN USSR, *LAND WAR*
XXXIX Panzer Corps relieves the garrison of Cholm after fighting off the Soviet Third Shock Army, thus bringing to an end the 103-day siege. The defenders have lost 1500 troops killed and 2200 wounded. In addition, in its effort to keep the garrison supplied the Luftwaffe has lost 252 Ju 52 transport aircraft.

MAY 8

SOUTHERN USSR, *LAND WAR*
The German Eleventh Army launches Operation Bustard to destroy enemy forces in the Kerch Peninsula. For this task it deploys XXXII, VII Romanian and XXX Corps (LIV Corps covers Sevastopol). The attack makes a good start with XXX Corps attacking the Forty-Fourth Army in its front, whose southern flank soon collapses.

MAY 9

SOUTHERN USSR, *LAND WAR*
XXX Corps continues to cut through the Forty-Fourth Army's flank as the 22nd Panzer Division throws back the Soviet Fifty-First Army farther north. Though heavy rain allows some Red Army units to escape, the bulk of the two Soviet armies are surrounded by the 10th.

MAY 10

USSR, *ATROCITIES*
The Germans open a new death camp at Maly Trostenets, a small village outside the Belorussian city of Minsk. Some 250,000 Jews will be deported from Western Europe to the camp, where they will be killed in gas vans similar to those used at Chelmno and Riga.

MAY 11

The 22nd Panzer Division arrives at the northern coast of the Kerch Peninsula, thus achieving the encirclement of the Soviet Fifty-First Army. The Soviet Forty-Fourth Army has by this time been almost destroyed in the fighting.

MAY 12

The Soviet Southwestern Front launches the Kharkov Offensive designed to push German forces back to the River Dnieper from the Barvenkovo salient. To achieve this it has Group Bobkin and the Sixth, Twenty-First, Twenty-Eighth and Thirty-Eighth Armies. In addition, the Southern Front (Ninth and Fifty-Seventh Armies) will attack from the south. Total Red Army forces for the offensive are 765,000 troops, 1200 tanks, 13,000 artillery pieces

► ***Soviet cavalry in action during the Kharkov Offensive. This is probably a propaganda shot, for mounted cavalry charges were rare on the Eastern Front. The Red Army used horses for mobility, with troopers conducting combat dismounted.***

and 900 aircraft. Following lengthy artillery barrages the Twenty-First, Twenty-Eighth and Thirty-Eighth Armies attack, to achieve advances of only 9.6km (6 miles).

Despite taking heavy casualties, the German XVII and LI Corps hold their positions. To the south the Soviet Group Bobkin and the Sixth Army make better progress, advancing up to 16km (10 miles) on a 40km (25-mile) front.

MAY 14

SOUTHERN USSR, *LAND WAR*
The Kharkov Offensive is already running out of steam, with the Twenty-Eighth and Thirty-Eighth Armies grinding to a halt. Indeed, counterattacks by the 3rd and 23rd Panzer Divisions against the junction of the two armies push back the Soviet frontline. South of Kharkov the Sixth Army and Group Bobkin are having more success, pushing on towards Krasnograd. In the Crimea the Soviet Forty-Fourth and Fifty-First Armies have been annihilated. The German 170th Infantry Division enters Kerch.

MAY 15

FINLAND, *LAND WAR*
The German XXXVI Corps and Finnish III Corps attack the Soviet Twenty-Sixth Army at Kastenga. However, the attacks are beaten off.

SOUTHERN USSR, *LAND WAR*
North of Kharkov the German 3rd and 23rd Panzer Divisions continue their attacks, forcing the Soviet Twenty-Eighth and Thirty-Eighth Armies on to the defensive. However, Soviet success to the south of the city means Timoshenko can think about committing his mobile units to exploit the advance. If Krasnograd falls, the German Sixth and Seventeenth Armies will be endangered. In the Crimea the German Eleventh Army mops up after its victory. The Soviet Crimean Front has lost 162,282 dead or captured, 14,284 wounded and 1100 artillery pieces, 260 tanks and 3800 vehicles either destroyed or captured. In addition, the Soviets have lost more than 300 aircraft shot down.

GERMANY, *STRATEGY*
The High Command determines to counterattack the Southwestern Front and destroy it, thus increasing the chances of success for its own offensive in the area.

MAY 17

SOUTHERN USSR, *LAND WAR*
Under German pressure the Soviet Twenty-First, Twenty-Eighth and Thirty-Eighth Armies north of Kharkov are falling back. To the south of the city the German Group Kleist (III Panzer, XXXXIV and LII Corps) begins its counterattack between Barvenkovo and Slavyansk, hitting the Soviet Ninth Army head on. By the evening the Germans have captured Barvenkovo and created a 14.4km (9-mile) hole between the Ninth and Fifty-Seventh Armies and pushed 32km (20 miles) into the Soviet rear. To the west, meanwhile, Red Army units continue to attack, the 21st and 23rd Tank Corps advancing through the Soviet Sixth Army's positions.

KEY WEAPONS

T-34

The T-34 was one of the greatest tanks of World War II and certainly one of the most influential. One of the most innovative designs was its sloped armour, which not only saved weight compared with rolled plate, but was also more difficult for anti-tank rounds to penetrate. In addition, its Christie-type suspension, combined with a diesel powerplant, gave it an excellent power-to-weight ratio and good cross-country mobility.

It did have its drawbacks, such as no turret floor to revolve with the turret, which meant crewmen had to walk around on the top of ammunition boxes as the turret turned. This became difficult in battle when the turret floor was littered with empty shell cases. In addition, its 76.2mm main gun was outclassed by the 75mm models mounted on the Panzer IV and Panther tanks in the German Army in mid-1943. Indeed, by Kursk, 88 percent of T-34s hit by German guns were penetrated, compared with 46 percent in 1942. Nevertheless, the T-34 was an all-round excellent armoured fighting vehicle and could be produced in thousands. By Kursk, the T-34/76C had appeared, which had a commander's cupola. In an effort to make the T-34 more potent, its armour protection was increased and it was armed with an 85mm gun. The new vehicle was designated the T-34/85 and it entered service in February 1944 – the first units to receive it being 2nd, 6th, 10th and 11th Guards Tank Corps. In total, 49,000 T-34s were built during World War II.

Weight: 30,900kg (67,980lb)
Crew: 4
Speed: 55kmh (34.3mph)
Range: 250km (156 miles)
Dimensions: length: 6.1m (20ft); width: 3m (9.84ft); height: 2.4m (7.87ft)
Armament: 1 x 76mm cannon, 2 x 7.62mm machine guns
Ammunition: 100 x 76mm, 3150 x 7.62mm
Armour: front (maximum): 52mm (2in); side (maximum): 52mm (2in)

▲ *A German soldier, photographs of his family pinned to a tree, awaits the enemy during the Soviet Kharkov Offensive. Note the stick grenades on the lip of his trench – essential for close-quarter fighting.*

MAY 19

SOUTHERN USSR, *LAND WAR*
The Soviet Twenty-Eighth and Thirty-Eighth Armies try yet again to resume their attacks but are stopped in their tracks by German artillery. As the German XXXXIV Corps approaches Izyum, Red Army units inside the Barvenkovo salient are in danger of being encircled, particularly the Fifty-Seventh Army. In response the Soviets attempt to form defensive positions, the 21st and 23rd Tanks Corps having been ordered east. To the north, the Soviet Sixth Army continues its attacks, although with few gains. Timoshenko asks Stalin for permission for the Southwestern Front to go on to the defensive, but it is too late. Hitler orders Kleist to drive for Balakleya to complete the encirclement of all Soviet forces in the pocket.

▲ ***Some of the prisoners taken by the Germans after the failure of the Kharkov Offensive. Once again the Germans had displayed a mastery of mobile warfare.***

MAY 22

SOUTHERN USSR, *LAND WAR*
German forces seal the Barvenkovo Pocket by the day's end. Timoshenko orders the Thirty-Eighth Army to the north to attack to link up with the trapped units, but this formation is unable to move in time. He also orders the trapped Sixth and Fifty-Seventh Armies to break out.

MAY 23

FINLAND, *LAND WAR*
Finnish attacks in the Kastenga area come to an end; the Soviet Twenty-Sixth Army has beaten off all attacks and inflicted heavy losses on the Finns.

SOUTHERN USSR, *LAND WAR*
The Germans widen their corridor between Barvenkovo and Balakleya in the face of feeble attempts by the Soviet Ninth and Thirty-Eighth Armies to re-establish contact with the pocket.

MAY 26

BRITAIN, *DIPLOMACY*
The USSR and Britain sign a 20-year Mutual Assistance Agreement in London. In June, Molotov, Soviet foreign minister, will say of the agreement: "The treaty consolidates the friendly relations which have been established between the Soviet Union and Great Britain and their mutual military assistance in the struggle against Hitlerite Germany. It transforms these relations into a stable alliance. The treaty also defines the general line of our joint action with Great Britain in the post-war period." Stalin will actually renege on any agreements reached with Britain regarding the map of post-war Europe.

MAY 29

SOUTHERN USSR, *LAND WAR*
The fighting in the Barvenkovo Pocket comes to an end. It is another major disaster for the Red Army, with 170,958 killed or taken prisoner, 106,232 wounded and 1250 tanks and 2000 artillery pieces either destroyed or

captured. For its part the German Sixth Army has suffered 20,000 casualties.

UNITED STATES, *DIPLOMACY*
Molotov, Soviet foreign minister, is at the White House. President Roosevelt promises him that the Western Allies will open a second front in 1942. Molotov rejects a suggestion by Roosevelt that the USSR agrees a treaty with Germany on the prisoners of war issue. Soviet troops in German hands do not have any international protection as the USSR has not signed the Geneva Convention of 1929, which specifies humane treatment for prisoners of war. This official posture stems from the Soviet concept of battlefield behaviour. The Red Army field manual states that a loyal soldier is either fighting or is dead; surrender is considered to be treason. The wartime edition of the standard Soviet encyclopedia states that "the penalty for premeditated surrender into captivity not necessitated by combat conditions is death by shooting".

▲ ***German panzergrenadiers during the Kharkov battles. The Wehrmacht had shown its superior tactics by turning a potential defeat into a stunning victory.***

MAY 30

NORTHERN USSR, *LAND WAR*
A German counterattack along the River Volkhov cuts off the Soviet Second Shock Army, which is desperately short of food and ammunition. The efforts by the Fifty-Second and Fifty-Ninth Armies to reach the Second Shock Army come to nothing.

USSR, *ARMED FORCES*
The Central Staff of the USSR Partisan Movement is set up in Moscow to direct partisan operations behind German lines.

▲ ***Red Army troops during the Kharkov Offensive. The soldier in the foreground is armed with a 7.62mm Degtaryev machine gun, the standard section support weapon.***

◀ ***A Fieseler Fi 156 Storch observation aircraft flies over a Wehrmacht column after the reduction of the Barvenkovo Pocket. The ground was very dry at this time – it was 90 degrees in the shade.***

▶ *A hauptmann (captain), an Iron Cross pinned to his breast, of the German Eleventh Army during the assault on Sevastopol. On his left hip is a holster that contains his 9mm P38 handgun.*

JUNE 2

SOUTHERN USSR, *LAND WAR*
Manstein's Eleventh Army commences the air and artillery bombardment of the heavily defended port fortress of Sevastopol. This is no easy task as some of the fortress's defences date back to the days before the Crimean War, and have been reinforced with modern, concrete strongpoints. It also has numerous defence lines belted around the city, heavily entrenched in favourable mountainous terrain. Finally, there are heavy coastal artillery batteries on the shores. Most of the troops available to the Eleventh Army will be used for this operation. The German forces are supplemented by the Romanian VII Corps (10th and 19th Infantry Divisions), 4th Mountain Division and 8th Cavalry Brigade. The bombardment involves 1300 artillery pieces and Luftwaffe attacks.

JUNE 4

GERMANY, *DIPLOMACY*
Hitler visits Marshal Mannerheim in Finland to offer congratulations on the Finn's 75th birthday, and to strengthen the mutual relationships between Germany and Finland. The two men meet near the quiet Finnish border town of Imatra. The meeting is not a success: at one point Hitler demands that Finnish Jews be deported; Mannerheim answers, "over my dead body".

JUNE 5

USSR, *PARTISAN WAR*
The Germans launch Operation Birdsong between Roslavl and Bryansk with 5000 troops. Their target is 2500 partisans that are operating in the area. Over the next four weeks 1198 partisans will be killed for the loss of 58 dead. But the partisan attacks continue. One German officer states: "The partisans continued their old tactic of evading, withdrawing into the forests, or moving in larger groups into the areas south and southwest of the Roslavl–Bryansk highway and into the Kletnya area."

▲ *German forces on the eve of Operation Blue. Because of manpower shortages, German infantry divisions now comprised seven battalions instead of nine, with the strength of companies fixed at 80 men, not 180.*

JUNE 7

SOUTHERN USSR, *LAND WAR*
Following artillery and aerial bombardments, the Germans assault Sevastopol. The main thrust of the attack is launched from the north/northeast by LIV Corps (22nd, 24th, 50th and 132nd Infantry Divisions). The attack in the south is carried out by XXX Corps (72nd and 170th Infantry Divisions and 28th Light Division). In the centre the Romanians pin down the enemy and cover the German flanks. Soviet fire is accurate and deadly, resulting in many casualties.

JUNE 10

NORTHERN USSR, *LAND WAR*
The Soviet Fifty-Second Army, trying to punch a way through to the encircled Second Shock Army, is forced to retreat by the Luftwaffe.

CENTRAL USSR, *LAND WAR*
The Second Panzer Army holds an attack by the Soviet Western Front.

SOUTHERN USSR, *LAND WAR*
The German Sixth Army launches Operation Wilhelm, aimed at destroying the Soviet Twenty-Eighth Army near Volchansk to facilitate the smooth running of the forthcoming German offensive into the Caucasus.

JUNE 11

GERMANY, *ARMED FORCES*
The court martial of 26-year-old army captain Michael Kitzelmann ends in Orel. Kitzelmann, who holds an Iron Cross Second Class for bravery, has spoken out against atrocities being committed on the Eastern Front. He told his follow officers: "If these criminals should win I would have no wish to live any longer." A devout Catholic, he had written in a letter: "At home they banish the crucifixes from the schools, while here they tell us we're fighting

KEY PERSONALITIES

EWALD VON KLEIST

Born in 1885, Kleist saw service in World War I with the hussars. A corps commander during the invasion of Poland in 1939, he led a panzer group during the fall of France in May–June 1940. Although initially inexperienced in the proper use of armoured forces, he learnt quickly and had able subordinates such as Guderian and Zeitzler. Thus, by the spring of 1941 he was equipped to command mobile forces, and his First Panzer Group achieved rapid success in the Balkans campaign. During Barbarossa, his panzer group was attached to Army Group South, taking part in the great Uman and Kiev encirclements, before being ordered north to close the southern part of the Vyazma encirclement. On October 6, 1941, his panzer group became the First Panzer Army; it had taken Rostov by November, but was then forced to withdraw from the city and spend the winter of 1941–42 on the defensive.

During Operation Blue, Kleist and his army advanced into the Caucasus, but long supply lines and Red Army counterattacks forced him to retire once more at the end of 1942. By this time he was commander of Army Group A and had been promoted to field marshal. His army group by this time consisted of the Seventeenth Army, which was ordered to hold the Crimea at all costs. As commander of Army Group A he could not halt the Red Army during the spring of 1944, and was relieved of his command. After the war he was first arrested by the Yugoslavs as a war criminal and sentenced to 15 years in prison in 1948, before being handed over to the Soviets in 1949. He died in a Russian prison in November 1954.

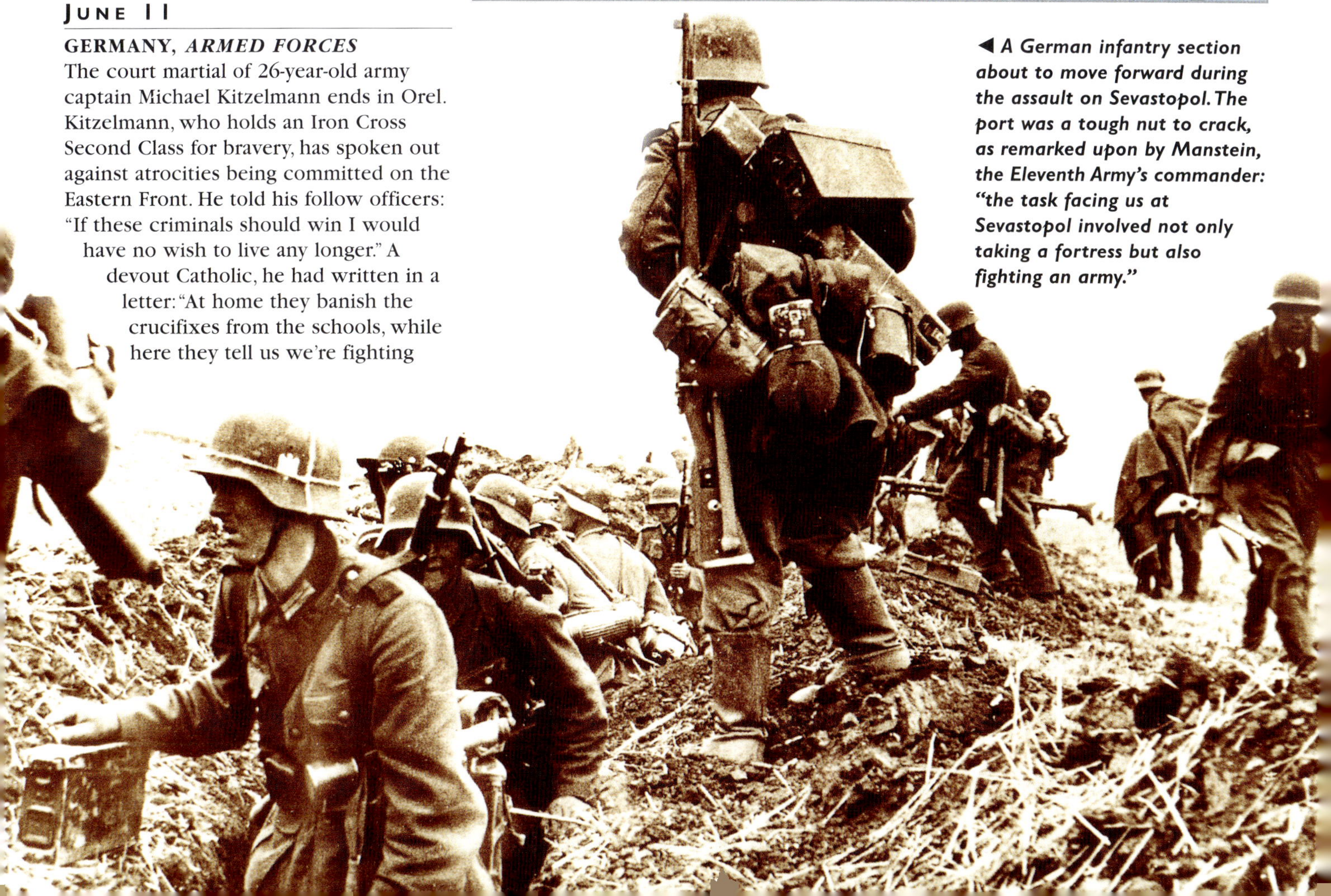

◀ *A German infantry section about to move forward during the assault on Sevastopol. The port was a tough nut to crack, as remarked upon by Manstein, the Eleventh Army's commander: "the task facing us at Sevastopol involved not only taking a fortress but also fighting an army."*

against godless communism." Before his execution he forgave the sergeant who had denounced him. His farewell letter stated: "God has granted me the grace of a holy death. I go ahead of you to our heavenly homeland. Divine Redeemer, grant me a merciful judgement when I come to you. Praised be Jesus Christ!" Kitzelmann is shot later in the day.

JUNE 15

SOUTHERN USSR, *LAND WAR*
The German Sixth Army completes the defeat of the Twenty-Eighth Army and pushes it back over the River Donets.

JUNE 17

NORTHERN USSR, *LAND WAR*
The Soviet 29th Tank Brigade creates a small corridor through to the trapped Second Shock Army. The troops of the latter make a dash for freedom, but are massacred by German fire.

SOUTHERN USSR, *LAND WAR*
In the Crimea, at Sevastopol, LIV Corps captures Fort Siberia after intense fighting; XXX Corps' 72nd Infantry Division takes the North Nose, Chapel Mount and Ruin Hill strongpoints; and

▲ ***The Red Army occupants of a bunker on the outskirts of Sevastopol surrender on June 28. The final German assault against the inner fortress area began the next day.***

the 170th Infantry Division storms Kamary. The supply efforts of the Soviet Black Sea Fleet to land troops and ammunition are proving inadequate.

JUNE 19

SOUTHERN USSR, *GERMAN STRATEGY*
Plans for the German offensive into the Caucasus, codenamed Blue, are captured by the Soviets when an aircraft carrying a staff officer of the 23rd Panzer Division, Major Reichel, is forced down. Reichel has in his possession a complete set of plans for the part XXXX Panzer Corps will play in Operation Blue. The plans are forwarded to the Stavka in Moscow, but Stalin comes to the conclusion that they are phoney and a German ploy: the Nazis want the Soviets to find them in order to throw them off the trail of the impending Moscow attack. This is truly a stroke of luck for Hitler.

JUNE 22

SOUTHERN USSR, *LAND WAR*
The German Sixth and First Panzer Armies commence a limited offensive to destroy the Soviet Ninth and Thirty-Eighth Armies in the Kupyansk area.

GERMANY, *ARMED FORCES*
Army Group South is now ready to launch Operation Blue. Its order of battle is as follows: Sixth Army (330,000 troops and 300 tanks and assault guns); Second Army (95,000 troops); Seventeenth Army (150,000 troops and 180 tanks and assault guns); First Panzer Army (220,000 troops and 480 tanks and assault guns); and Fourth Panzer Army (200,000 troops

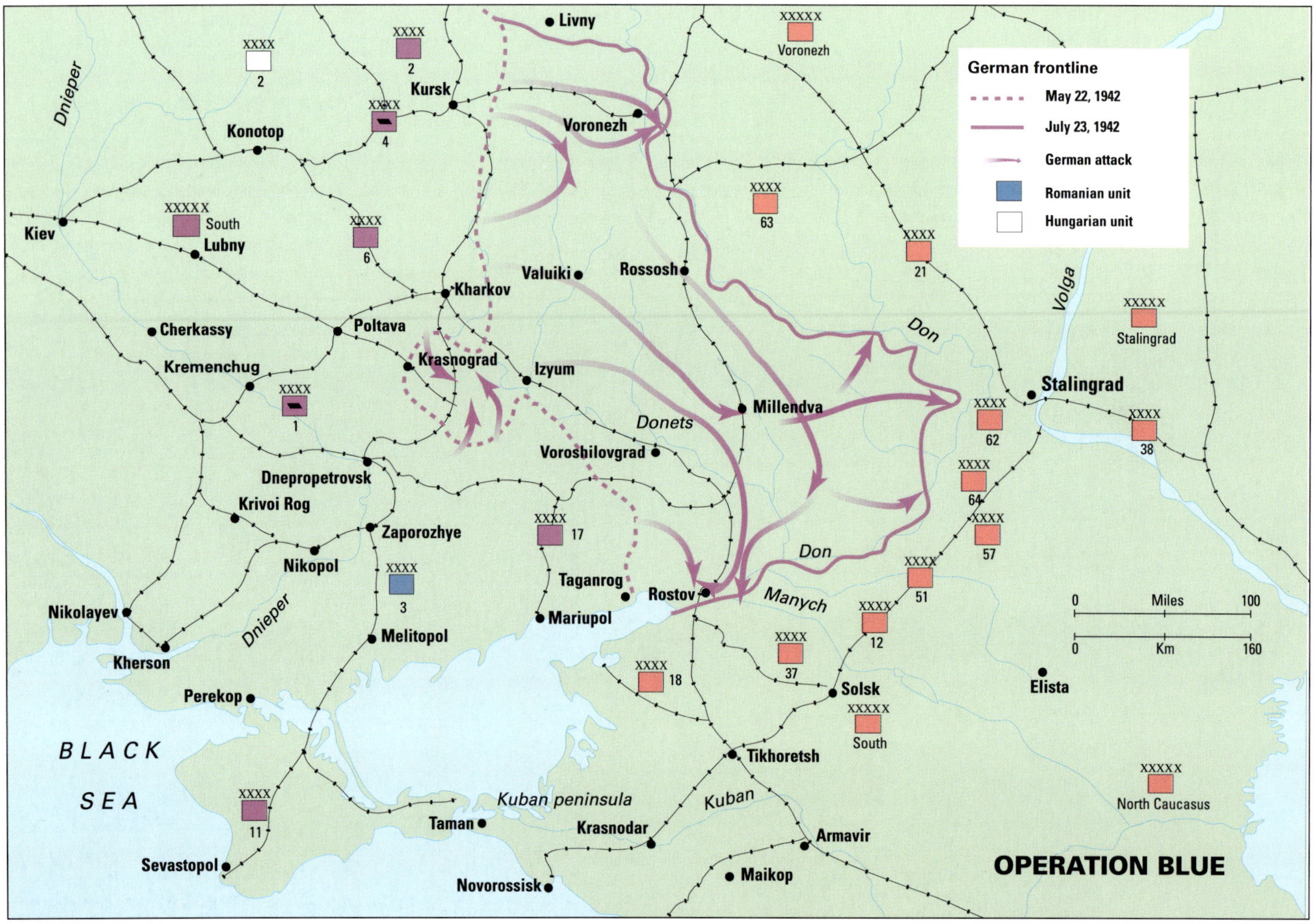

▶ ***Troops of the German Eleventh Army attacking at Sevastopol. Fortunately for the Germans, the Red Army withdrew from the port rather than fight to the last man.***

and 480 tanks). The Hungarian Second and Italian Eighth Armies, at present in transit, will also support the offensive. Luftwaffe support totals 2690 aircraft.

JUNE 25

NORTHERN USSR, *LAND WAR*
The Soviet Second Shock Army is annihilated by the Germans. Its commander, General Vlassov, has fallen into German hands. The disaster on the Volkhov has cost the Red Army 54,774 killed and missing and 39,977 wounded.

JUNE 26

SOUTHERN USSR, *LAND WAR*
The Sixth Army completes its operations against the Soviet Ninth and Thirty-Eighth Armies, who have suffered more than 40,000 troops captured. At Sevastopol the German Eleventh Army continues to grind its way into the city. The last Soviet supply ships leave the port loaded with wounded troops – there will be more. The Stavka has written off the garrison.

JUNE 27

USSR, *ARMED FORCES*
On the eve of Operation Blue, Soviet forces facing Army Group South are as follows: Bryansk Front (169,000 troops), Southwestern Front (610,000 troops) and Southern Front (522,500 troops). These fronts have a combined tank total of 3470, including 2300 T-34s and KVs.

JUNE 28

SOUTHERN USSR, *LAND WAR*
Operation Blue opens as the Fourth Panzer Army, supported by the Second Army, smashes into the junction of the Soviet Thirteenth and Fortieth Armies. By the evening XXXX Panzer Corps has reached the headquarters of the Fortieth Army, which becomes disorganized. In the Crimea the German 50th Infantry Division takes Inkerman.

GERMANY, *ATROCITIES*
OKW chief Keitel sends a telegraph to his commanders in the East: "Fleeing prisoners of war are to be shot without preliminary warning to stop. All resistance of POWs, even passive, must be entirely eliminated immediately by the use of arms."

◀ ***German officers observe the crossing of the Donets during Operation Blue. Units taking part had been brought up to strength by stripping other parts of the front.***

JULY 2

SOUTHERN USSR, *LAND WAR*
The Red Army retreats before the German advance, with the Fourth, Seventeenth, Twenty-Fourth and Fortieth Armies pulling back towards Voronezh. This means that the Fourth Panzer and Sixth Armies, as they link up at Stary Oskol, fail to trap any Red Army units.

JULY 4

ARCTIC, *SEA WAR*
The Allied convoy PQ-17 (35 merchant ships plus escort) is attacked by U-boats and aircraft, prompting the issuing of the order for the convoy to scatter. The convoy had left Iceland on June 27. Heavy ice floes were encountered by June 30, and a German aircraft sighted the ships the next day. From July 1 to July 10 a large part of the convoy was wiped out. On July 2 the Germans made several attacks.

On July 4 there are attacks in which two American ships, the *Christopher Newport* and the *William Hooper*, are sunk by torpedoes. About an hour and a half before midnight, the convoy receives orders to disperse. The British Admiralty receives intelligence that German capital ships, including *Tirpitz* and *Prinz Eugen*, have left Trondheim to intercept the convoy. This proves to be untrue. However, the convoy's orders leave the slow and heavily loaded merchant ships virtually defenceless.

Only 11 of the 35 merchantmen who left Iceland finally made it to the Soviet Union, either Archangel or Murmansk. Fourteen of the ships sunk were American. More than two-thirds of the convoy had gone to the bottom, along with 210 combat planes, 430 Sherman tanks, 3350 vehicles and nearly 105,000 tonnes (100,000 tons) of other cargo. More than 120 seamen were killed and countless others were crippled and maimed. To compound the disaster, the suspicious Soviets refused to believe that 24 ships from one convoy had been sunk. They openly accused their Western allies of lying about the disaster.

SOUTHERN USSR, *LAND WAR*
In response to XXXXVIII Panzer Corps crossing the River Don west of Voronezh, the Stavka commits the Fifth Tank Army to seal the gap between the Bryansk and Southwestern Fronts. Unfortunately, its 600 tanks are committed piecemeal, thus reducing their effectiveness. Luftwaffe attacks degrade their fighting capability further. In the Crimea Sevastopol has fallen to the Eleventh Army. The Red Army has lost 156,880 killed and missing and 43,601 wounded around the port since October 1941. Manstein takes 90,000 prisoners, together with 460 artillery pieces, 760 mortars and 155 anti-tank guns.

GERMANY, *ARMED FORCES*
Army Group South is reorganized, being divided into Army Groups A and B. Army Group B (Second, Fourth Panzer and Sixth Armies and the Hungarian Second Army) is ordered to destroy Soviet forces between the upper Donets and middle Don and secure a crossing of the Don near Voronezh. The Fourth Panzer and Sixth Armies will then race east to Stalingrad, from whence they will sweep south to support Army Group A in the Caucasus. The army group is supported by VIII Air Corps.

Army Group A (First Panzer, Seventeenth and Eleventh Armies) is to destroy enemy forces on the River Mius and then drive into the Caucasus. The army group is supported by IV Air Corps.

JULY 5

CENTRAL USSR, *LAND WAR*
The Western Front again attacks the Second Panzer Army to tie it down.

SOUTHERN USSR, *LAND WAR*
The Fourth Panzer Army enters Voronezh; the Second Army is covering its left flank.

USSR, ARMED FORCES
Stalin creates the Voronezh Front made up of the Third, Sixth and Fortieth Armies.

JULY 7

SOUTHERN USSR, *LAND WAR*
Voronezh is cleared of defenders as the German Fourth Panzer and Sixth Armies link up at Vayluki. However, the haul of prisoners is low – the Southwestern Front is trading space for time.

▶ A destroyer of the Soviet Black Sea Fleet lies crippled in Sevastopol harbour after being hit by Luftwaffe bombs. The Germans enjoyed overwhelming air power during the battle for the city.

◀ *A cargo ship of convoy PQ17 sinks after being torpedoed. The British decision to scatter the convoy, following reports that Kriegsmarine capital ships were approaching, doomed the merchantmen.*

JULY 10

SOUTHERN USSR, *LAND WAR*
Having run out of fuel, the Fourth Panzer Army is on the move again along the Don after receiving fresh supplies. Together with the Sixth Army it is mopping up on the river's west bank. Meanwhile, the German First Panzer and Seventeenth Armies are advancing towards the River Don and Rostov against little resistance.

JULY 11

SOUTHERN USSR, *LAND WAR*
Hitler orders the First and Fourth Panzer Armies to converge at Kamensk and Millerovo prior to a thrust into the Caucasus; the Sixth Army alone will advance on Stalingrad. Hitler believes that the Red Army has been defeated west of the Don and will not now secure the Volga before an attack south.

Hitler also issues Directive No 43 on the conduct of the war in the Crimea: "After clearing the Kerch Peninsula and capturing Sevastopol, the first task of the Eleventh Army will be ... to make all preparations for the main body of the army to cross the Kerch strait by the middle of August at the latest. The aim of this operation will be to thrust forward on either side of the western foothills of the Caucasus in a southeasterly and easterly direction. The operation will be known by the codename Blücher."

JULY 12

SOUTHERN USSR, *LAND WAR*
The Stavka creates the new Stalingrad Front (led by Timoshenko) to combat a German advance to the Volga. It includes the Sixty-Second, Sixty-Third and Sixty-Fourth Armies – 540,000 troops. The Southwestern Front retains the Twenty-First, Twenty-Eighth, Thirty-Eighth and Fifty-Seventh Armies, although the Twenty-Eighth and Thirty-Eighth will soon be taken out of the line and converted into the First and Fourth Tank Armies.

JULY 13

SOUTHERN USSR, *LAND WAR*
The Fourth Panzer Army and XXXX Panzer Corps link up at Boguchar, trapping just 14,000 prisoners. Hitler thinks this signals the end of Red Army resistance. All supplies are thus directed to the two panzer armies, leaving the Sixth Army stranded in the Don Elbow, thus allowing the Soviets to build up their strength at Stalingrad.

JULY 18

GERMANY, *STRATEGY*
Having dismissed Bock on the 15th for supposed lack of vigour in pursuing objectives, Hitler again changes priorities. Army Group B will now resume the advance on Stalingrad.

JULY 19

SOUTHERN USSR, *LAND WAR*
The Sixth Army is reinforced to enable it to fulfil Hitler's wishes. Again, Hitler changes his mind: the First and Fourth Panzer Armies will now advance on a broad front into the Caucasus.

USSR, *ATROCITIES*
Heinrich Himmler, SS chief, orders the start of Operation Reinhard. Its objectives are: to kill Polish Jews; to exploit the skilled or manual labour of some Polish Jews before killing them; to secure the personal property of the Jews (clothing, currency, jewellery); and to identify and secure immovable assets such as factories, apartments and land. The camps used for the extermination will be Belzec (opened March 1942), Sobibor (opened May 1942) and Treblinka (opened July 1942). In total 1.7 million Jews will be killed during Reinhard, plus an unknown number of Poles, gypsies and Soviet prisoners of war.

JULY 20

NORTHERN USSR, *LAND WAR*
Heavy fighting rages south of Leningrad as the Soviet Forty-Second Army tries to wear down the Eighteenth Army.

SOUTHERN USSR, *LAND WAR*
Re-supplied, the German Sixth Army attacks the Soviet Sixty-Second and Sixty-Fourth Armies (combined strength 160,000 troops), inflicting heavy losses.

JULY 23

SOUTHERN USSR, *LAND WAR*
The Sixth Army's attacks are causing the Soviet Sixty-Second and Sixty-Fourth Armies to break apart. At Rostov the 13th Panzer and 5th SS *Wiking* Divisions tighten their grip around the city. Buoyed by these successes, Hitler issues Directive No 45. It states: "The next task of Army Group A is to encircle enemy forces which have escaped across the Don in

▶ *A Soviet position explodes during the siege of Sevastopol. During the battle the Red Army turned the English Cemetery, containing the graves of soldiers killed in the Crimean War, into a strongpoint.*

the area south and southeast of Rostov, and to destroy them. Two armoured formations of Army Group A (including 24th Panzer Division) will come under command of Army Group B for further operations southeastwards.

"After the destruction of enemy forces south of the Don, the most important task of Army Group A will be to occupy the entire eastern coastline of the Black Sea, thereby eliminating the Black Sea ports and the enemy Black Sea Fleet. For this purpose the formations of Eleventh Army already designated (Romanian Mountain Corps) will be brought across the Kerch Straits as soon as the advance of the main body of Army Group A becomes effective, and will then push southeast along the Black Sea coast road.

"At the same time a force composed chiefly of fast-moving formations will give flank cover in the east and capture the Grozny area. Detachments will block the military road between Osetia and Grozny, if possible at the top of the passes. Thereafter the Baku area will be occupied by a thrust along the Caspian coast. These operations by Army Group A will be known by the cover name Edelweiss.

"The task of Army Group B is, as previously laid down, to develop the Don defences and, by a thrust forward to Stalingrad, to smash the enemy forces concentrated there, to occupy the town, and to block the land communications between the Don and the Volga, as well as the Don itself. Closely connected with this, fast-moving forces will advance along the Volga with the task of thrusting through to Astrakhan and blocking the main course of the Volga in the same way. These operations by Army Group B will be known by the cover name Heron."

▲ ***German forces in the rubble of Rostov. It took the Germans 50 hours of fierce fighting to clear the city, and the battle against NKVD machine-gunners on the Taganrog road was particularly brutal.***

JULY 24

SOUTHERN USSR, *LAND WAR*
Rostov falls to the Germans. Since the beginning of Operation Blue the Red Army has suffered the following losses: Bryansk Front, 37,000 killed and missing and 65,000 wounded; Voronezh Front, 43,000 killed and missing and 32,000 wounded; and Southern Front, 128,000 killed and missing and 65,000 wounded.

JULY 25

SOUTHERN USSR, *LAND WAR*
As German land and air attacks wear down the Soviet Sixty-Fourth Army, Army Group A begins its offensive from the River Don. The First Panzer Army pushes back the Soviet Twelfth and Thirty-Seventh Armies.

JULY 28

SOUTHERN USSR, *LAND WAR*
The German Sixth Army runs out of fuel and grinds to a halt, allowing the Soviet Sixty-Second and Sixty-Fourth Armies to fall back east. In the Caucasus the Southern Front is in a complete shambles (it has lost 15,000 killed and wounded in three days), prompting the Stavka to disband it and allocate its units to the North Caucasus Front. The latter has two main formations: Don Group (Twelfth, Thirty-Seventh and Fifty-First Armies) is to halt the First Panzer Army; and Coastal Group (Eighteenth, Forty-Seventh and Fifty-Sixth Armies and XVII

▶ ***German infantry on the way to the River Don. A German recorded in his diary: "On this steppe ... there were no forests to give protection from aircraft, and, above all, no water for the men and horses."***

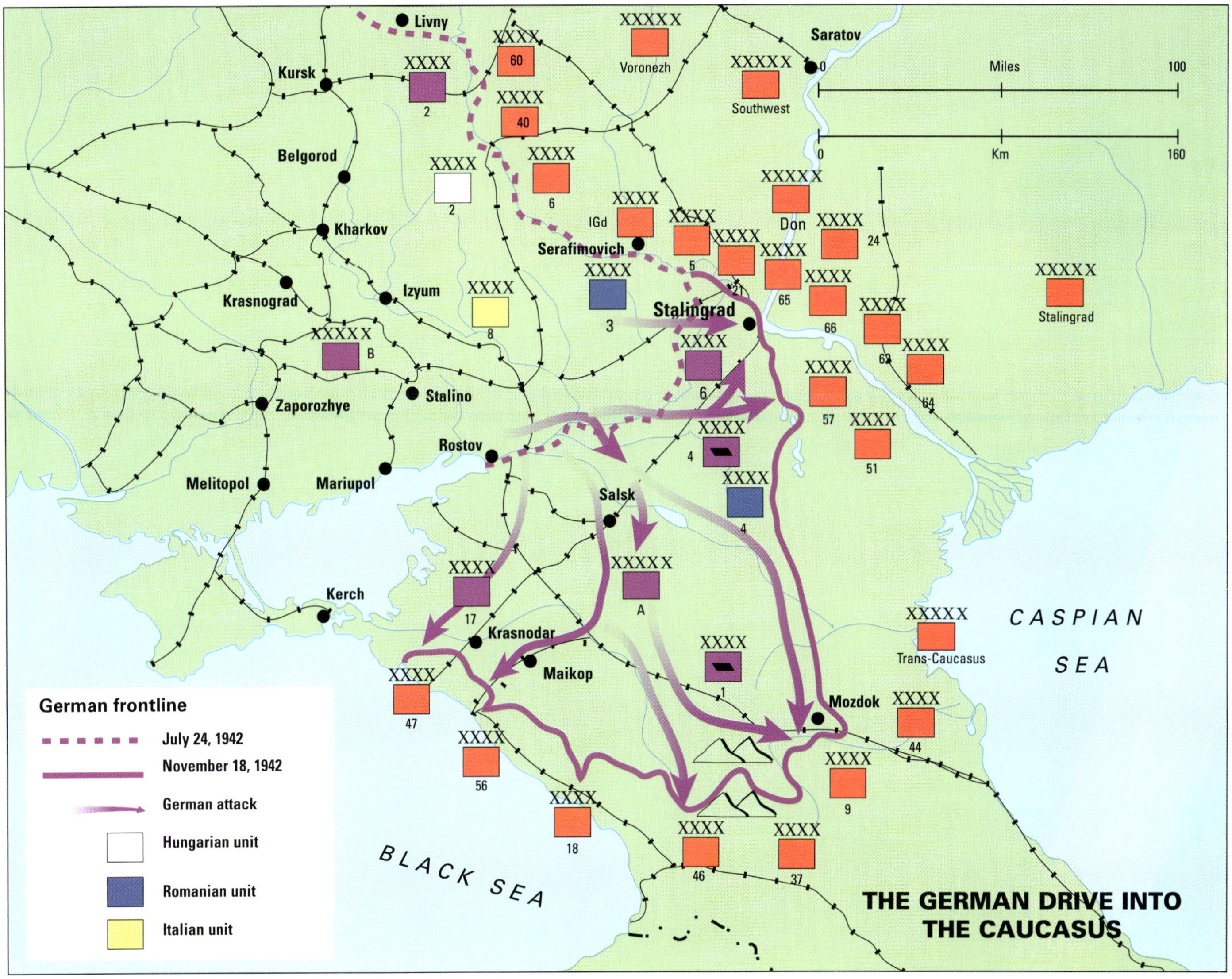

Cossack Cavalry Corps) is to stop the German Seventeenth Army and protect the Kuban and approaches to Krasnodar.

USSR, *STRATEGY*

Stalin issues Order No 227. In this he alludes to his concern about German gains: "The territory of the Soviet Union is not a wilderness, but people – workers, peasants, intelligentsia, our fathers and mothers, wives, brothers, children. Territory of USSR that has been captured by the enemy and which the enemy is longing to capture is bread and other resources for the army and the civilians, iron and fuel for the industries, factories and plants that supply the military with hardware and ammunition; this is also railroads. With the loss of Ukraine, Belorussia, the Baltics, Donets basin and other areas we have lost vast territories; that means that we have lost many people, bread, metals, factories and plants. We no longer have superiority over the enemy in human resources and in bread supply. Continuation of retreat means the destruction of our Motherland.

"The conclusion is that it is time to stop the retreat. Not a single step back! This should be our slogan from now on."

JULY 30

CENTRAL USSR, *LAND WAR*

The Kalinin Front (Twenty-Ninth, Thirtieth and Third Air Armies) and Western Front (Twentieth, Thirty-First and First Air Armies) launch the Rzhev-Sychevka Offensive.

SOUTHERN USSR, *LAND WAR*

The Stalingrad Front launches a counter-attack with the First and Fourth Tank Armies, resulting in a tank battle with XIV Panzer Corps. The Luftwaffe pummels the two Soviet armoured units. Meanwhile, the Soviet Sixty-Second and Sixty-Fourth Armies continue to suffer heavy losses.

▶ Destroyed Red Army vehicles west of Stalingrad. The diversion of the Fourth Panzer Army from the city to the lower Don meant the Germans lost the chance of taking Stalingrad without a fight in July.

JULY 31

SOUTHERN USSR, *LAND WAR*

The Soviet First and Fourth Tank Armies are stopped in their tracks; both have suffered massive losses. The Fourth Panzer Army fractures the Soviet Fifty-First Army and throws it back to Kotelnikovo. During July the Germans have lost 38,000 killed on the Eastern Front, insignificant compared to Red Army losses.

Operation Blue

Operation Blue represented Germany's last chance of defeating the Red Army on the Eastern Front. When it began at the end of June 1942, progress was initially excellent.

Though Stalingrad was not one of Operation Blue's strategic objectives, every attempt was to be made to seize Stalingrad or at least bring the city within reach of German artillery so that the Soviets would be deprived of its production and transportation facilities. Subsequent operations would be greatly facilitated if the bridges at Rostov could be seized intact and bridgeheads could be established south of the Don. The German attack force on the right, advancing eastwards from Taganrog, was to be reinforced with armoured and motorized divisions in order to prevent major Russian elements from escaping across the Don. Defensive positions would have to be built along the Don while the advance was in progress. These positions would have to be amply provided with anti-tank guns and so constructed that, if necessary, they could be of service during the winter. Allied forces, supported by German troops, would have to man these positions, and German divisions would have to serve as strategic reserves behind the Don Front.

Because of the advanced season, the movements across the Don towards the south would have to be so timed that the Caucasus could be reached without major halts. There is no doubt that Hitler's principal objective for the summer offensive of 1942 was the possession of the Caucasus and its oil resources. The shortage of combat troops and the precariousness of the transportation network made it necessary to place great emphasis on the preliminary operations, whereas the main drive towards the Caucasus was outlined only in its initial phase – the seizure of bridgeheads across the Don. More specific orders for a Caucasus operation were not issued until July 23, 1942, when the operation was in full swing and Hitler signed Directive No 45. At the time Directive No 41 was written, no basic conflict between the eastwards thrust towards Stalingrad and the southwards drive into the Caucasus was anticipated. Like Voronezh, for instance, Stalingrad was to be a stepping stone along the approach road towards the Caucasus. In the Führer's mind, however, the desire to conquer the city on the Volga by house-to-house fighting gradually became a fixation. This was all the more difficult to understand because in 1941 he had rejected any direct attack on Leningrad and Moscow. The diversion of more and more forces towards Stalingrad was made to the detriment of the principal drive into the Caucasus, and eventually both efforts were to bog down for lack of strength.

◀ Some of the 1.4 million Axis troops and 1495 armoured fighting vehicles that Hitler assembled for participation in Operation Blue in the summer of 1942.

Delay in preliminary operations

On April 16, General Erich von Manstein, commander of Eleventh Army in the Crimea, suggested to Hitler that the attack on the Kerch Peninsula be delayed until May 5 because he was still short of some essential supply items. Hitler approved Manstein's request, adding that the Luftwaffe would have to give strong support to the ground forces. As soon as Kerch was cleared, Army Group South was to pinch off and eliminate the Izyum salient, after which the siege of Sevastopol was to begin. The timing of these three preliminary operations was to be made contingent upon the availability of essential air support. Because of the delay in the start of the first attack, the Sevastopol operation would not begin before mid-June at the earliest.

The first phase of the summer offensive was to be conducted by Army Group South, composed of the Second and Sixth Armies, Fourth Panzer Army and the Hungarian First Army. During the second phase

First Panzer Army, the Italian Eighth Army, and probably also Eleventh Army were to intervene. The newly activated Army Group A was to assume control of the movements for the following phases, while Army Group South would become responsible for securing flank protection along the Don Front.

Preliminary moves

Three preliminary operations were to take place before the launching of Operation Blue. The first one, the seizure of the Kerch Peninsula, started on May 8. Under Manstein's leadership, Eleventh Army forces soon began to clear the peninsula against strong resistance. The second operation, directed against the Izyum salient, was codenamed Fredericus. According to the German plan, the ground forces needed for the elimination of the Russian salient were to be assembled by May 17. Five days earlier, however, the Red Army launched a strong spoiling attack south and east of Kharkov, against the right of Sixth Army. This Russian drive threatened the entire logistical buildup for Operation Blue because it was directed at the extensive depot and repair facilities in the Kharkov area, which were vital to the German supply system. The Russian manoeuvre also disrupted the rehabilitation of the spearhead units, since the threat to Kharkov led to a change in priorities and a diversion of tanks and self-propelled anti-tank guns to the danger area.

Operations around Kharkov

As soon as the fighting in the Kerch Peninsula had taken a favourable course, Hitler withdrew some of the air support units from the area and committed them for the defence of Kharkov. By May 13 the situation around that city had grown so serious that the Führer ordered the transfer of additional Luftwaffe contingents from the Crimea. He also decided to advance the date of the attack on the Izyum salient, originally scheduled for May 18. In Hitler's opinion this counterthrust would be the most effective and fastest method of assisting Sixth Army in the defence of Kharkov. One of the most disquieting facts about the Russian attack was that, for the first time since the start of the campaign, the Red Army committed its armour in mass formation, thus copying the hitherto successful German tactics.

On May 17 – a day earlier than scheduled – two corps of Seventeenth Army forming the southern arm of the Izyum pincers jumped off, while the forces that were to compose the northern arm were still being assembled. During the first three days the German countermove did little to relieve the defenders of Kharkov. It was not until May 20 that the acute danger at Kharkov seemed to have passed. The effect of the Russian spoiling attack was to be felt throughout the remaining weeks before the start of Operation Blue, mainly because of the changes in schedule that became necessary

Russian resistance on the Kerch Peninsula had collapsed by May 19. Five days later Hitler decided that the siege of Sevastopol, scheduled as the third and last preliminary operation, was to start on June 7 and the first phase of Operation Blue eight days later. Under these circumstances the air support

◀ Erich von Manstein, whose Eleventh Army captured the strategically important Black Sea port of Sevastopol at the end of June 1942.

▲ *The Soviet warship* Paris Commune. *Part of the Black Sea Fleet, it took part in the battle for Sevastopol in the summer of 1942.*

units would have to be withdrawn from the Izyum area by June 6 to assist the attack forces in the Crimea. After only three days in that part of the theatre, the Luftwaffe contingents would have to be redeployed in turn to the assembly area for Operation Blue, where they had to arrive by June 10 at the latest. Considerations of wear and tear on aircraft and crews apparently did not enter the calculations on which this tight schedule was based.

On May 28 Halder suggested a change in the timing and execution of the preliminary attacks. He wanted to continue the successful German counterattack northeast of Kharkov in the Volchansk area first, leaving the Izyum salient to be eliminated next. By applying this procedure, the Russian forces would be systematically destroyed and the preliminary operations would be more directly related to the offensive proper. Hitler approved Halder's ideas in principle, but decided to investigate the situation on the spot.

On June 1, the Führer and a small staff flew to Army Group South headquarters at Poltava. Field Marshal von Bock and the field commanders whose troops had been directly involved in the battle for Kharkov reported on the situation, whereupon Hitler explained his ideas on the continuation of operations. Advantage would have to be taken of the extremely favourable developments around Kharkov by destroying the Russian forces near Volchansk and Izyum as quickly as possible. The principle to be applied was that "whatever forces could be annihilated now, would not be there to interfere with Operation Blue," even if the practical application of this idea implied some change in plans.

On the basis of additional information provided by Bock, the Führer decided that the preliminary operations would be executed according to a revised schedule, even if Blue had to be delayed. The new schedule was as follows:

a. The attack on the Volchansk area was to take place on June 7.

b. The assault on Sevastopol was to begin on the same day.

c. The attack on the Izyum salient was to be launched on or after June 12.

d. Blue would begin on or before June 20.

► *German artillery under fire during the Soviet Kharkov Offensive in May 1942, which was defeated by Germany's Operation Fredericus in the same month.*

As it turned out, the Volchansk operation had to be delayed because of bad weather. The assaults on Sevastopol started on time, but made little progress despite intensive preparatory fire and air force bombardments lasting five days. Because of the strong resistance encountered at Sevastopol, Hitler reversed his previous decision and did not withdraw the air support units after only three days. By June 19, some of the outer defences of the fortress had been breached.

The Soviets learn of German plans

Approximately 10 days before the intended start of the summer offensive - June 19 - the operations officer of the 23d Panzer Division, which was to participate in the crucial breakthrough west of Voronezh, flew to the front, taking with him a number of highly classified documents in violation of security regulations. He crash-landed in Russian-held territory and the documents, which included a corps order outlining the entire attack plan for the first phase of Blue, had disappeared when a German patrol recovered his body three days later. Hitler relieved of command a number of officers whom he held responsible for this incident.

With this plan in Russian hands, the element of surprise was bound to have been lost during the crucial initial phase. Since a change in plans was no longer feasible because of the advanced season, Blue either had to be executed according to the plan or cancelled. Hitler decided to go ahead as planned.

▼ *Some of the 280,000 Soviet prisoners netted by the Germans during Fredericus. Once again the Germans had demonstrated their mastery of mechanized warfare.*

▲ ***Horsemen of the Red Army's 2nd Cavalry Corps, which was largely wiped out during the heavy fighting around Kharkov in May 1942.***

This decision may have been partly motivated by his low opinion of the Red Army in 1942. During the daily situation conference on June 25 he stated that approximately 80 Soviet divisions had been destroyed during the preliminary operations. Russian resistance was much weaker than during the preceding year. The various phases of Operation Blue would therefore be executed faster and easier than hitherto assumed by army planners. It might not even be necessary to commit all the armour earmarked for the second phase of the operation, and two of the panzer divisions could perhaps be diverted to cut off the Sukhinichi salient in the Army Group Centre area.

First phase (June 28–July 6, 1942)

By June 27 those German forces that were to participate in the first phase of the summer offensive had moved into their assembly areas according to schedule. On the next day Fourth Panzer Army and Second Army jumped off with forces consisting of three panzer, three motorized and nine infantry divisions. Four Hungarian divisions covered the southern flank; in addition two German and six Hungarian divisions, constituting the reserves, were still en route.

The mission of the spearhead divisions was to break through to Voronezh. The infantry divisions were then to build up strong flank protection along a line extending from Livny to Voronezh, while the motorized forces were to thrust southeastwards along the Don River. The forces available for this operation were none too strong. The protection of the Livny-Voronezh sector - about 160km (100 miles) wide - would divert most of the German infantry divisions, with the Hungarians taking over the defence of the Don south of Voronezh. From the very first day of the offensive the Russians launched counterattacks, committing numerous armoured brigades whose presence had not been discovered by German intelligence. Sizeable Russian forces were also detraining in the Yelets area.

By July 2 German spearheads were on the outskirts of Voronezh. The city fell after four days of furious

▲ ***German troops move through the ruined buildings of newly conquered Sevastopol. The Luftwaffe dropped 20,856 tonnes (20,528 tons) of bombs on the port.***

fighting, during which the divisions of the Fourth Panzer Army became more heavily engaged than Hitler had thought necessary. The first phase of the offensive was completed on that day, with flank protection being secured between Livny and Voronezh.

Second Phase (June 30–July 7, 1942)

During the second phase Sixth Army forces, consisting of two panzer, one motorized and 16 infantry divisions, jumped off from the area northeast of Kharkov, crossed the Oskol River and linked up with the armoured spearheads of Fourth Panzer Army on the upper course of the Valuy River. The manoeuvre was completed by July 7. To gain sufficient time for establishing defensive positions along the Don, the Russians had fought a series of delaying actions west of the river. In isolated instances, such as east of Kupyansk and opposite the first German bridgeheads across the Oskol, they seemed determined to make a temporary stand. Although some Soviet forces had been enveloped during the course of the German advance, in general the offensive had thus far proceeded according to expectation.

The German personnel shortage induced Halder to send a memorandum to Army Group South on July 2, requesting the latter to provide a new type of information. He first explained that current operations of Army Group South were conducted almost without reserves echeloned in depth. Because of the long distances to be covered to reach objectives, this shortage of forces could have grave consequences unless the Army High Command knew at all times the strength, condition and casualties of all units, particularly the armoured ones. Only with this information on hand could the Army High Command properly accomplish its functions.

German order of battle changes

The first two phases of the offensive had been directed by Field Marshal von Bock, whose command, Army Group South, was redesignated Army Group B on July 9. Four days later Bock was replaced by

General Maximilian von Weichs, the former commander of the Second Army, ostensibly because of Hitler's dissatisfaction with Bock's conduct of the Voronezh operation. In reality Hitler wanted to tighten his control over the conduct of the whole German summer offensive.

The first group of officers appointed to the staff of Army Group A arrived in Poltava at the end of May. When the new headquarters assumed control at the beginning of July, a forward echelon moved to Stalino, where the future headquarters of the army group was to be established. From the outset the command net broke down repeatedly because the signal troops were insufficiently trained.

Army Group A was to intervene during the third phase of Blue. Its forces were to jump off from the Taganrog–Artemovsk area, break through Russian lines, and drive eastwards across the Donets River as far as the Don bend, where they were to link up with the Sixth Army and Fourth Panzer Army spearheads driving down the Don. By this manoeuvre the Russians were to be trapped in the Don bend. Some allied forces were to provide flank protection – the Italians on both sides of Boguchar, the Romanians along the sector adjacent to the east. Other army group elements were to thrust southwards, envelop Rostov, and establish bridgeheads south of the Don.

Meanwhile, the Russian Southwest, South and Caucasus Fronts were commanded by Marshal Timoshenko, whose headquarters was in Stalingrad. German intelligence reports indicated that the defeats and losses suffered during the spring of 1942 seemed to have had little effect on the performance of the Russians. To explain the Russian soldier's attitude one had to see things from his point of view. Since he ate better rations, saw more and more comrades joining him in combat and noticed the relative stability of his sector, he probably felt that a definite change for the better had taken place since the last year's disastrous defeats.

Total German casualties for June had been slightly lower than those suffered in May, but higher by 10,000 than expected by the Army High Command. Approximately 157,000 reinforcements had arrived in the Russian theatre, exceeding the number of losses by about 31,000 men.

▼ German troops relax among the debris at Sevastopol following the capture of the port. This is one of the Red Army strongpoints, Maxim Gorky Fort.

Operation Blue

In calculating future manpower distribution quotas for August, it was estimated that 70,000 replacements would be available in August 1942. Of this total, 4000 men would be needed in northern Finland, 10,000 for activating a special desert unit and as replacements for Rommel's casualties in North Africa, and 9000 to make up for the July deficits of the First Panzer and Seventeenth Armies. Of the remaining 47,000 men, 15,000 would go to Army Group A, 10,000 to Army Group B, 14,000 to Army Group Centre and 8000 to Army Group North. In view of the scope of the summer offensive, the Army Groups A and B quotas were far from reassuring.

▼ A flight of Ju 87 Stuka dive-bombers, part of the Luftwaffe's Fourth Air Fleet that supported Operation Blue – 1550 aircraft in total.

On July 1, 1942, the total strength of the German Army on the Eastern Front, including civilians with assimilated ranks, was 3,948,200; the number of officers included in this figure was 150,100.

On July 7, Field Marshal List assumed command of Army Group A, composed of the First Panzer, Eleventh and Seventeenth Armies. Two days later his newly formed army group launched its attack, with First Panzer Army thrusting towards Voroshilovgrad. The advance proceeded according to schedule. On July 11 an order signed by Timoshenko was captured. In it Timoshenko instructed his unit commanders to halt the German offensive by using delaying tactics. Since the Germans considered the Russian lower command echelon incapable of executing such a complicated mission, Army Group A issued orders to hit the Russians wherever they bogged down

▲ ***German infantry hitch a ride on a Panzer III tank during the opening phase of Operation Blue, when the offensive was carrying all before it.***

during the retreat and to seize as much of their materiel as possible.

By July 13 Army Group A had made such good progress that Hitler wanted to initiate the southwards thrust towards the Caucasus. He therefore instructed List to advance southwards in the direction of Konstantinovskaya, seize the Don-crossing facilities in that city and at Tsymlyanskaya, envelop Russian forces west of the Donets and south of the Don by thrusting westwards to Rostov, and cut off the Salsk–Stalingrad rail line. To carry out these missions, Fourth Panzer Army and one infantry corps were transferred from Army Group B to Army Group A. The infantry divisions of Army Group A were to move up in forced marches so that they could assist the panzer spearheads in preventing a Russian withdrawal. Army Group B was to provide flank and rear protection for this manoeuvre by moving the Italian Eighth Army via Millerovo to the middle Don and covering the Chir River. On July 15, air reconnaissance information indicated that the Russians were speeding up the evacuation of the Donets Basin and were withdrawing south and southeastwards.

Even before mid-July, however, a shortage of petrol, oil and lubricants (POL) began to hamper the movements of the spearhead divisions of Army

Group B. Airlift operations were under consideration when, on July 15, Fourth Panzer Army reported that its further progress would be assured by the capture of sizeable quantities of gasoline. Soon after, however, the Germans discovered that the dump they had seized intact contained only about 203 tonnes (200 tons) of fuel, not even enough to fill the tanks of one weak panzer division.

By contrast, First Panzer Army still had sufficient fuel to continue its advance as scheduled. The Russian units opposing this army were disorganized; recently captured prisoners originated from as many as 30 different divisions and brigades. A tendency towards mass desertion became manifest at various points, such as at Millerovo, where an officer deserted with 500 enlisted men. Prisoner interrogation reports conveyed the impression that the Russian command had lost control in certain areas and that the confusion in the enemy ranks was spreading.

The Russian retreat was directed southwards behind the Don, with men and equipment crossing the river by ferries and across emergency bridges. At the same time trains out of Stalingrad were moving fresh troops westwards. To counter this manoeuvre, Fourth Panzer Army was ordered to drive straight towards Konstantinovskaya. The army was to protect its flank in the Millerovo area and east of the lower Donets River.

▲ German infantry pass a burning Russian village on July 20, 1942. Already the strain of marching great distances on foot in the heat of the Russian summer is starting to tell.

On July 11, Hitler issued Directive No 43, which dealt with the German flank attack from the Crimea across the Kerch Strait into the Caucasus. After mopping up the Kerch Peninsula and Sevastopol – the latter had fallen on July 1 after a surprise landing of German assault detachments north of the fortress – Eleventh Army was to make preparations for crossing the Kerch Strait by early August.

Strong units were to land in the rear of the enemy's coastal fortifications and capture the ports of Anapa and Novorossisk, thus depriving the Russians of these two naval bases. Most of the Eleventh

Army forces were then to advance along the northern slopes of the Caucasus and seize the Maikop oil fields. A secondary thrust along the coastal highway via Tuapse was also envisaged.

Five days after issuing this directive, Hitler moved to his newly established headquarters in the Ukraine, situated in small woods 16km (10 miles) northeast of Vinnitsa along the highway to Zhitomir. Hitler, his intimates and his military staff - the field echelon of the Armed Forces Operations Staff - were billeted in log cabins and prefabricated barracks. The Army High Command set up its field headquarters in Vinnitsa proper.

Operations continue

On July 16, a conference of Army Group A commanders, their chiefs of staff and the chief of staff of Fourth Air Force took place at Gorlovka. In his introductory remarks List stated that the advance had proceeded much faster than anticipated, since the army group forces had already reached the Don. He also revealed that First Panzer Army's tank losses were being replaced from new production. Each division of the First Panzer Army had one tank battalion. Whereas the German divisions of Seventeenth Army were considered good, the Italian ones - with the exception of one classified as "quite good" - had not yet been involved in any fighting. This army was particularly anxious to receive some self-propelled assault guns. Four of the Fourth Panzer Army's divisions were considered good, two very good. Their automotive equipment was very poor, however, and it was solely by expedients that the army kept rolling.

List then outlined his plan for future operations: the spearhead divisions of First Panzer Army were to cross the Donets near Kamensk and turn southwards to Shakhty; some of the infantry units were to follow the course of the Donets and advance in a southeastwards direction to protect the flank of the Fourth Panzer Army. The latter was to cross the Don near Konstantinovskaya and pivot west or southwestwards, according to the situation prevailing at that time. Infantry divisions were to follow with a minimum of delay to protect the army flank north of the Don, their deployment depending on developments in the Stalingrad area. On July 18, the Seventeenth Army was to launch an eastwards or southeastwards attack from the Kuybyshevo area. The purpose of this attack was to tie down the Russians and close in on Rostov as soon as possible.

By July 19 the Russians were withdrawing the bulk of their forces towards Rostov. They covered their retreat by leaving strong rearguards, particularly opposite the right of Seventeenth Army. List intended to throw an ever-tightening ring around Rostov while Fourth Panzer Army forces were to send two panzer corps across the Don and form bridgeheads as soon as possible. Their task was complicated by the fact that, when they finally reached the Don at the confluence of the Donets, the bridges had been blown and the Russians were entrenched on the south bank of the river. According to an intelligence estimate dated July 18, the Russians had been able to withdraw two-thirds of their infantry strength across the Don. No figures regarding the armoured brigades were available. By that date the number of prisoners taken by Army Group A was 54,000. Because of the disorganization and loss of materiel caused by the withdrawal, the

▶ During the opening phases of Operation Blue the Luftwaffe had total air superiority, allowing Soviet rolling stock to be attacked at will.

▶ ***Motorcyclists of the German Sixth Army heading west, towards the city of Stalingrad, in July 1942. Note the clouds of dust, which greatly increased engine wear.***

combat strength of the Russian units had dropped considerably.

By July 20 only the infantry divisions of Sixth Army and the units of one panzer corps of Army Group B continued to advance in the direction of Stalingrad. The bulk of the German forces in the south were engaged in the Rostov operation under the control of Army Group A. Flank protection along the Don up to the area east of Boguchar had been established. The Hungarian Second Army had taken over its designated sector south of Voronezh, while the Italian Eighth Army was marching northeastwards from the Voroshilovgrad area in order to relieve the German forces in the Boguchar sector. The German Second Army front between Voronezh and Livny had beat off a series of savage armoured assaults in the vicinity of Voronezh.

On July 21, a recently captured Russian General Staff officer stated during his interrogation that the Russians intended to defend Rostov to the bitter end. At Army Group A headquarters, however, the

▲ ***A German halftrack, part of the armoured forces of Field Marshal von List's Army Group A, on its way to the Caucasus at the end of July 1942.***

▲ *Soldiers of the Waffen-SS* **Wiking** *Division head into the Caucasus during Operation Blue in August 1942, an image that conveys the area's endless steppe terrain.*

impression prevailed that Russian resistance in the city would soon collapse because the garrison had lost much of its equipment and morale seemed to be low. This opinion was soon justified: Rostov fell on July 24.

At this decisive moment Hitler began to show increasing interest in Stalingrad, the Volga city that was still approximately 160km (100 miles) from the German spearheads. The old Russian dictum that the motherland could not be defeated unless the invader got across the Volga seemed to have gained new significance in Hitler's mind. Several of his requests to divert two panzer divisions from the Rostov operation had previously been ignored in the heat of battle. Now he issued a direct order transferring one panzer corps composed of two panzer divisions from Fourth Panzer to Sixth Army, and thus from the Caucasus to the Stalingrad operation. The concept of an orderly advance by consecutive phase lines, which had been followed since the beginning of the summer offensive, gave way to two simultaneous drives in divergent directions, one towards the oil fields, the other towards Stalingrad.

Directive No 45, dealing with the continuation of the summer offensive, was issued on July 23. In the preamble Hitler stated that during an offensive of little more than three weeks' duration, the long-range objectives set for the southern attack forces had been attained for all intents and purposes. Only a few small contingents of Timoshenko's armies had been able to escape and reach the other bank of the Don, where they would probably be reinforced from the Caucasus area. Another Russian force was being assembled in the Stalingrad area, where the Soviet command apparently intended to offer strong resistance.

As its next objective Army Group A was to encircle and annihilate those enemy forces south and southeast of Rostov which had escaped across the Don. Strong motorized units were to advance southwest and cut the rail line connecting Tikhoretsk with Stalingrad.

In addition to losing the panzer corps transferred to Army Group B for the continuation of the drive towards Stalingrad, Army Group A was to release the Motorized Infantry Division *Grossdeutschland*, which was to stop its advance as soon as it reached the Manych River and prepare its units for transfer to the West.

After accomplishing the mission of destroying the Russians south of the Don, Army Group A was to seize the Black Sea coast and thus paralyze the Black Sea Fleet. As soon as the movement of the main army group forces had progressed sufficiently, elements of Eleventh Army were to cross the Kerch Strait and advance along the Black Sea coastal road.

Another force, consisting of mountain and light divisions, was to cross the Kuban River and seize the elevated ground near Maikop and Armavir. The mountain divisions were to cross the western Caucasus passes and operate in conjunction with the forces advancing along the Black Sea coast. At the same time, an attack force consisting of motorized elements was to move into the Grozny area, block the passes of the Ossetin and Georgian military roads leading across the central Caucasus, and then thrust along the Caspian towards Baku.

Plans to cross the Don

In addition to building up a defence line along the Don, Army Group B was to advance towards Stalingrad, destroy the Russian forces assembling in that area, and block the corridor between the Don and the Volga. Motorized units were then to drive down the lower Volga towards Astrakhan and there block the principal branch of the river.

The Luftwaffe was to support the ground forces crossing the Don and advancing towards Tikhoretsk, and concentrate on destroying Timoshenko's forces and the city of Stalingrad. Occasional raids were to be conducted on Astrakhan, and shipping on the lower Volga was to be disrupted by the sowing of mines. During the further course of the operation the air force was to operate in conjunction with the ground forces advancing towards the Black Sea ports and protect them from Russian naval interference. Other Luftwaffe units were to support the thrust via Grozny to Baku.

Because of the crucial importance of Caucasus oil to the future German war effort, air attacks against oil wells or oil tanks were to be made only in cases of absolute necessity. The Russians, however, were to be deprived of Caucasus oil deliveries by German air attacks, which were to disrupt the rail and pipe lines and destroy the port installations.

The navy was to lend its support during the crossing of the Kerch Strait and prevent the Russian Black Sea Fleet from interfering. Moreover, the navy was to organize light forces for disrupting Russian communications across the Caspian Sea.

The local operations previously planned for Army Groups Centre and North were to be executed with a minimum of delay in order to produce the greatest

◀ *Red Army troops in the Caucasus in August 1942. Their stiffening resistance, plus German supply problems and manpower shortages, slowed Army Group A's advance.*

▲ ***By mid-August 1942, many of the infantry divisions of Army Group A were on average 4000 troops below their paper strength of 17,000 soldiers.***

possible effect on the opposing forces. Army Group North was to seize Leningrad by the beginning of September. For this purpose five divisions, as well as the non-organic medium and heavy artillery units of the Eleventh Army, were to be transferred from the Crimea to the north. Two German and two Romanian divisions were to be left in the Crimea.

Directive No 45 resulted in the diversion of one motorized infantry division of Army Group A and five divisions of Eleventh Army from the Caucasus operation. Hitler's absolute confidence in victory induced him to leave in the Caucasus only sufficient forces to carry out a pursuit. The breach in the Soviet front seemed so enormous that the shifting of a few divisions from Army Group A to Army Group B could not possibly affect the Caucasus drive. At the same time, he felt that such a move would guarantee a speedy advance to the lower Volga. The Russian forces assembling in the Stalingrad area would be overrun by the German spearhead divisions. After reaching the city, the latter would immediately turn southeast and continue their drive towards Astrakhan and the Caspian Sea.

Thus in a way Hitler reverted to the original concept on which the Operations Division of the Army High Command in October 1941 had based its plan

▲ *Vehicles of the First Panzer Army on their way south in August 1942. Ominously, by this date the army had already experienced fuel and ammunition shortages.*

for the Caucasus operation. According to this plan an offensive across the Caucasus Mountains could be envisaged only after the German flank along the lower Volga had been secured. The instructions issued in Directive No 45 constituted a belated attempt to secure the Volga flank while relatively weak forces simultaneously advanced into the Caucasus.

Shortages

On July 25, the number of tanks in serviceable condition in the Army Group A area totalled 435 for eight spearhead divisions, or an average of 54 tanks per division. The First Panzer Army's shortage of gasoline was so great that all motorized elements of XLIV Infantry Corps were immobilized and the infantry units were unable to move because of the breakdown of the supply system.

By late July the gasoline situation had grown more critical than ever. When General Halder inquired at Army Group A headquarters why gasoline supplies were so unsatisfactory, he was told that the shortage was caused by bad weather, the long distances covered during the offensive, and the priority given to the Sixth Army for its assault on Stalingrad. Airlifts had temporarily alleviated shortages, but the bulk of the essential POL requirements could not be moved by this mode of transportation. Since the available truck transportation had proved insufficient, an improvement could be expected only after the Stalino–Shakhty railroad had been repaired. Both panzer armies were temporarily immobilized by lack of gasoline.

Stalingrad takes priority

On July 29, the last rail line connecting the Caucasus with central Russia was blown up at several points by German armoured elements. The Caucasus was isolated and Hitler seemed to believe that it was his for the taking. On the next day Army Group A was warned that the heavy fighting near Stalingrad would force OKH to transfer one additional German corps and two Romanian ones with a number of divisions to Army Group B in order to assist Sixth Army in its struggle. The Fourth Panzer Army headquarters might also be pulled out to take charge of this support thrust, in which case only one of its corps would continue to participate in the drive towards Maikop under First Panzer Army control. The definite decision would depend on developments in the Stalingrad situation.

That same evening List told Halder that the transfer of three corps, which apparently was under consideration, would endanger the eastern flank of the southwards thrust into the Caucasus. Halder replied that the transfer would take place after the corps had reached the south bank of the Don and that their diversion in the direction of Stalingrad would actually constitute an alternative flank protection. List thereupon insisted that at least the *Grossdeutschland* Division remain with Army Group A to protect its flank against a Russian surprise thrust. Halder reassured him that the division would not be transferred to the West before mid-August.

The Caucasus gamble

Halder continued by saying that Hitler did not believe the Army Group A flank would be in danger. List did not share this opinion. He wanted at least the *Grossdeutschland* Division in reserve. The army group commander then reminded Halder that the success of the Caucasus operation would depend primarily on the ready availability of POL. Hitler's plan struck him as a great gamble, since driving into the Caucasus with relatively weak forces, whose flank was not sufficiently protected, meant taking extraordinary risks. While these conversations were taking place, Russian troops were retreating into the Caucasus with no sign of a new front being built up farther to the south. Stalin's order, that every officer and enlisted man would have to fight to the end without giving way, showed that Stavka was aware of the seriousness of the situation.

On July 31 Halder sent an order to Army Groups A and B in which he confirmed the transfer of Fourth Panzer Army. In the introductory remarks he stated that, with the severing of the rail communications between the Caucasus and Stalingrad, the Russian front south of the Don was split wide open. The Red Army in front of Army Group A would attempt to stop the German advance into the Caucasus but it seemed doubtful whether they would have the necessary forces to do so. At Stalingrad they would throw all their resources into the battle to maintain control over their lifeline, the Volga. Army Group A's immediate mission was to seize the Black Sea coast and thus paralyze the Russian fleet, which in turn would guarantee the security of the German lines of communications across that body of water.

On August 1 the Fourth Panzer Army with two German and one Romanian corps, a total of eight divisions plus corps and army troops, would be transferred from the Caucasus to the Stalingrad operation. Army Group A was to assemble its remaining motorized units under First Panzer Army for a drive in the direction of Maikop. From there some army elements were to cut off the withdrawing Russian forces, while others were to drive via Tuapse towards Batum. Some motorized units would have to protect the eastern flank of the army. Mountain divisions were to be employed for the thrusts across the passes in the Caucasus. The *Grossdeutschland* Division would be available for eight more days. The mission of Army Group B was to remain unchanged.

▶ A German artillery detachment in the Caucasus. By the beginning of August 1942 Army Group A was poised to strike towards Maikop and Baku.

▼ *Soldiers and vehicles of the 16th Panzer Division, part of the German Sixth Army, on the approach to Stalingrad in August 1942.*

Phase III: Target Stalingrad

At the end of July 1942 Hitler had decreed that Stalingrad, initially given scant regard by the Führer, was now an objective of Operation Blue. It was to be captured by General Paulus' Sixth Army, and Hitler believed that it would fall with ease. But Stalingrad's civilian population had been mobilized to strengthen the city's defences and the Soviet Sixty-Second Army was moved into the city to fight the Germans. By September the Sixth Army was fighting in Stalingrad itself, but hopes of an easy victory evaporated as both sides became locked in a vicious close-quarters battle of attrition that sucked in more and more troops and reduced the city to rubble.

Timeline: August 3–September 14, 1942

August 3

SOUTHERN USSR, *LAND WAR*

The right flank of the Soviet Sixty-Second Army is broken by the German Sixth Army, which reaches the River Don. As the Fourth Panzer Army continues to push back the Soviet Fifty-First Army, in the Caucasus the Don and Coastal Groups are forced apart by the Germans.

August 5

SOUTHERN USSR, *LAND WAR*

The Fourth Panzer Army attacks the Soviet Fifty-Seventh and Sixty-Fourth Armies southwest of Stalingrad, but becomes bogged down in enemy defences and is then stopped by a counterattack. However, farther north the German Sixth Army ploughs into the Soviet Sixty-Fourth Army. To the south the First Panzer Army crosses the River Kuban as the Red Army retreats before it. In an effort to catch and destroy the Soviet units, Army Group A is divided: Group Ruoff (Seventeenth Army) will destroy the Coastal Group and secure the Black Sea coast; Group Kleist (First Panzer Army) will capture Baku and the oil fields.

August 6

NORTHERN USSR, *LAND WAR*

The Soviet Eleventh Army attacks the Demyansk salient, aimed at isolating the German units therein.

CENTRAL USSR, *LAND WAR*

Heavy armoured engagements rage around Rzhev as the Soviets commit the 8th Tank Corps and 2nd Guards Cavalry Corps as reinforcements for the Twentieth and Thirty-First Armies.

SOUTHERN USSR, *LAND WAR*

The First Panzer Army crosses the Kuban after having taken Armavir. Group Kleist continues its southern advance, the Soviet Twelfth and Eighteenth Armies retreating before it.

August 9

SOUTHERN USSR, *LAND WAR*

The Soviet Sixty-Second Army and parts of the First Tank Army are encircled by

▼ Troops of the First Panzer Army on the open steppe southeast of Rostov. Führer Directive No 45 gave the army the task of advancing to Baku – 1120km (700 miles).

▲ *German infantry attacking a Soviet position east of Rostov. The hot weather meant that the infantry were very quickly caked with a layer of dust.*

◀ *The German Sixth Army on the way to Stalingrad. The steppe between the Don and Volga, bone dry in August, was good tank country.*

the 16th and 24th Panzer Divisions. Kleist's panzers enter Maikop. The Germans had planned to start pumping oil right away but they find the oil fields burning - sabotaged by the retreating Red Army.

AUGUST 11

SOUTHERN USSR, *LAND WAR*
The units of the Soviet Sixty-Second Army in the Don bend are destroyed, some 35,000 troops being killed or captured. The German Sixth Army rolls into Kalach as Red Army units fall back towards Stalingrad.

AUGUST 12

USSR, *DIPLOMACY*
As the fighting rages around Stalingrad and in the Caucasus, the First Moscow Conference begins. It is attended by British Prime Minister Winston Churchill and US Ambassador W Averell Harriman, representing President Roosevelt. The main purpose is to discuss a common war strategy. Churchill, with the support of Ambassador Harriman, informs Stalin that it will be impossible for the British and Americans to open a second front in Europe in 1942.

NORTHERN USSR, *LAND WAR*
Heavy rain halts Red Army attacks against the neck of the Demyansk salient.

SOUTHERN USSR, *LAND WAR*
The German Seventeenth Army captures Slavyansk as the Coastal Group fights desperately to prevent the Germans from capturing the Black Sea coast.

GERMANY, *ARMED FORCES*
The Eleventh Army is broken up, the headquarters being ordered to the Leningrad area, four divisions remaining in the Crimea and the rest scattered along the Eastern Front.

AUGUST 15

SOUTHERN USSR, *LAND WAR*
A new offensive by the German Sixth Army shatters the Soviet First Guards and Fourth Tank Army in the Don Elbow and also hits the flank of the Sixty-Second Army at Perepolnyi. Red Army units continue to stream back across the Don. The city of Stalingrad is becoming the focus of the campaign as each side reinforces its armies in the battle for the city. On the Soviet side the Stalingrad

Front has the First Guards, Fourth Tank, Twenty-First, Twenty-Fourth, Sixty-Third and Sixty-Sixth Armies – 414,000 troops, 200 tanks and 200 artillery pieces. The Southeastern Front has the Fifty-First, Fifty-Seventh, Sixty-Second and Sixty-Fourth Armies – 160,000 troops, 70 tanks and 1400 artillery pieces. On the German side the Sixth Army under General Friedrich Paulus numbers 430,000 troops, 440 tanks and 5300 artillery pieces, and General Hermann "Papa" Hoth's Fourth Panzer Army musters 158,000 troops and 2100 artillery pieces.

AUGUST 16

CENTRAL USSR, *LAND WAR*

In the fighting around Rzhev the German Ninth Army has thus far suffered 20,000 casualties holding off attacks by the Soviet Twentieth, Twenty-Ninth, Thirtieth and Thirty-First Armies.

SOUTHERN USSR, *LAND WAR*

The German conquest of the Kuban is complete. Army Group A starts to regroup for the next phase of the campaign. The First Panzer Army will advance southeast towards Grozny and Baku in an effort to trap enemy forces against the Turkish border. The Seventeenth Army will advance down the Black Sea coast to the Turkish border.

AUGUST 19

NORTHERN USSR, *LAND WAR*

The Soviet Neva Group and Thirteenth Air Army of the Leningrad Front, plus the Volkhov Front's Second Shock, Eighth and Fourteenth Air Armies, launch the Sinyavino Offensive and capture small bridgeheads on the left bank of the Neva.

AUGUST 20

SOUTHERN USSR, *LAND WAR*

A Soviet attack against the Italian Eighth Army, which provides flank protection to the German Sixth Army, causes the Italians some discomfort but does not halt the Sixth's assault. To the south, the Fourth Panzer Army unleashes the 14th and 24th Panzer Divisions and 29th Panzergrenadier Division against the southwestern approaches to Stalingrad. The panzers are temporarily halted by minefields and Red Army resistance. Stalingrad, "the city of Stalin", will act as a magnet for German forces because, for Hitler, it will assume a massive psychological significance – he

▲ Ju 87 Stukas on their way to bomb Stalingrad, August 23. The air raid terrorized the city's inhabitants: at the hospital the staff abandoned their patients and fled.

▼ On the fringes of the Reich: a German machine-gunner in the Caucasus Mountains. Army Group A was stretched very thin in the Caucasus, as well as being at the end of a very long and vulnerable supply chain.

will become obsessed by it. Similarly, for Stalin the city will also become an obsession. It has been named after him as a result of his defence of the city during the Russian Civil War. He insists that it should be held at all costs. On a more practical level, he knows that if the Germans take the city Moscow will be vulnerable to an attack from the south.

AUGUST 23

SOUTHERN USSR, *LAND WAR*
XIV Panzer Corps crosses the River Don at Vertyachi and races east. By early evening the 16th Panzer Division has reached the River Volga and secured Spartakovka to the north of Stalingrad. Fierce Red Army resistance slows the advance of the rest of the corps, which does not reach the 16th Panzer. A platoon of the 1st Gebirgsjäger Division hoists the swastika on the summit of Mount Elbrus, the highest peak in the Caucasus.

SOUTHERN USSR, *AIR WAR*
The Luftwaffe launches a massive air raid against Stalingrad. In total 600 bombers conduct 4000 sorties over two days. Oil storage tanks along the River Volga burst into flame and fires break out in the city. The population numbers 600,000, and up to 40,000 are killed in the raids.

AUGUST 27

NORTHERN USSR, *LAND WAR*
The Soviet Volkhov Front begins an offensive designed to relieve Leningrad, the Second Shock Army hitting the German Eighteenth Army hard near Gaitolovo. Fortunately for the Germans, units of the Eleventh Army arrive on the scene to prevent the siege of the city being lifted.

SOUTHERN USSR, *LAND WAR*
The Red Army continues to put up fierce resistance on the approaches to Stalingrad, so much so that the 16th Panzer Division is in danger of being destroyed. The Sixth Army continues to grind its way forward, but the Stavka is concentrating the First Guards, Twenty-Fourth and Sixty-Sixth Armies to threaten XIV Panzer Corps.

AUGUST 28

SOUTHERN USSR, *LAND WAR*
Red Army pressure against XIV Panzer Corps prevents it from advancing into Stalingrad itself. The 3rd Panzergrenadier Division links up with the beleaguered 16th Panzer Division, which has successfully fought off assaults by the Soviet Sixty-Sixth Army (which is now in a state of exhaustion).

ARMED FORCES

PRISONERS OF WAR

It is often stated that the failure of the USSR to sign the Geneva Convention of 1929, which required that belligerents treat prisoners of war humanely, furnish information about them, and permit official visits to prison camps by representatives of neutral states, gave the Nazis licence to mistreat Soviet prisoners of war (POWs) during World War II. However, even if the Soviets had signed the convention, the Germans would not have treated Russian POWs any less brutally. Hitler's war in the East was one of ideological destruction, a conflict in which "sub-human" Slav prisoners could expect little mercy.

The Germans captured 5.7 million Red Army soldiers between June 1941 and the end of the war. Of these, 3.3 million died in captivity; almost 2 million were dead by February 1942. This high death rate was due to inhumane treatment, inadequate accommodation, the manner of their transportation, hunger and the murder of specific groups of prisoners (Jews and Communist Party members). By August 1941, on average only one-fifth of Soviet prisoners in a transport arrived at their destination alive, a consequence of inadequate nourishment. Prisoners were often forced to march for hundreds of kilometres to reach prison camps, which were often just empty fields with barbed wire fences and no buildings (prisoners had to exist in holes or mud huts that they built themselves). The death rate increased with the onset of winter: between October and December 1941, 46 percent of Soviet prisoners held in occupied Poland and in the Ukraine died.

Hundreds of thousands of prisoners died during the long marches to the camps, exhausted prisoners being shot on the spot. Others froze to death in the winter while being transported in open railway wagons: in December 1941, 25–70 percent of prisoners died during transportation to the camps. Even if prisoners survived the transportation, lack of nutrition and the Russian winter, the SS was constantly trawling the camps looking for Jews and communists, who were either shot on the spot or sent to concentration camps. Finally, the survivors were packed off to factories or farms to work as slave labourers to feed the German war effort, often being worked to death.

The Soviets captured 3,155,000 Wehrmacht personnel in the war. Of these, 1,185,000 died in captivity. German prisoners were forced to work in the camps of the Gulag, many until the 1950s. The Soviets did not embark on a conscious policy to work their captives to death, but they did keep them in conditions that were very similar to those in which Soviet POWs had existed during the war: inadequate rations, poor shelter, transportation in sub-zero conditions and brutal guards. As such, thousands died of malnutrition, exhaustion, disease and ill treatment.

AUGUST 30

SOUTHERN USSR, *LAND WAR*
The German LI and VIII Corps secure the Don-Volga land bridge as XXXXVIII Panzer Corps advances to within 48km (30 miles) of Stalingrad. The Soviet Sixty-Second and Sixty-Fourth Armies retreat into the city. In the Caucasus, meanwhile, the First Panzer Army approaches Grozny and crosses the Terek at Ishcherskaya. As at Stalingrad, the Red Army is battling fiercely and giving ground grudgingly.

AUGUST 31

SOUTHERN USSR, *LAND WAR*
The Soviet First Guards Army attacks XIV Panzer Corps north of Stalingrad, while to the south XXXXVIII Panzer Corps advances close to Pitomnik in the rear of the Sixty-Second and Sixty-Fourth Armies. In the Caucasus, the Soviets are unable to prevent the First Panzer Army from strengthening its bridgeheads on the Terek. Red Army losses in the region have been severe, North Caucasus Front losing 35,000 killed and missing since the end of July, and the Trans-Caucasus Front suffering 7300 killed and missing in the same period. However, Army Group A is experiencing fuel shortages, which are hampering panzer operations.

▲ German troops order Soviet prisoners to the rear. Operation Blue failed to trap large enemy formations, which meant the German haul of prisoners was low.

SEPTEMBER 3

▶ ***General Paulus directing his artillery at Stalingrad. The Sixth Army's commander was not in the best of health, suffering from recurrent dysentery and stress.***

SEPTEMBER 3

SOUTHERN USSR, *LAND WAR*

In an attempt to take the pressure off the Sixty-Second and Sixty-Fourth Armies, the Soviet First Guards Army, located north of Stalingrad, attacks XIV Panzer Corps. The operation is a shambles, with the Soviets suffering greatly at the hands of German artillery. The attack is called off. The Fourth Panzer and Sixth Armies continue to push the two aforementioned Soviet armies back into the city, but they have missed an opportunity to encircle them. In the Caucasus, both the Seventeenth and First Panzer Armies continue their advance, but both are having their strength reduced and are at the end of very long supply lines.

SOUTHERN USSR, *AIR WAR*

Air Fleet 4 continues to pound Stalingrad, but is merely turning the city into an environment that is aiding the defence and making panzer operations very difficult in the rubble.

SEPTEMBER 4

NORTHERN USSR, *LAND WAR*

The arrival of the German Eleventh Army on the Volkhov is paying dividends. Manstein deploys XXVI Corps on the northern wing and XXX Corps in the south to contain the Soviet threat.

SOUTHERN USSR, *LAND WAR*

Yet another futile Soviet attack by the First Guards, Twenty-Fourth and Sixty-Sixth Armies against XIV Panzer Corps suffers at the hands of German artillery and comes to nothing. Overhead, the Luftwaffe continues its round-the-clock attacks against the city.

SEPTEMBER 7

SOUTHERN USSR, *LAND WAR*

The German LI Corps of the Sixth Army attempts to reach Stalingrad city centre, specifically the Mamayev Kurgan hill, whose heights hold a commanding position over the whole city, the Volga and the area across the river. Both sides realize that he who holds the hill holds the city. As such, it will be the centre of

▶ ***Halftracks of XIV Panzer Corps on the approaches to Stalingrad. The vehicle on the right is an SdKfz 251/10 mounting a Pak 35/36 anti-tank gun.***

KEY WEAPONS

YAK-9

The Yak-9 was the mainstay of the Soviet Air Force in the middle and later years of World War II, and was produced in greater numbers than any other Soviet fighter. By the middle of 1944, for example, there were more Yak-9s in service than all other Soviet fighters combined. First flying in June 1942, it was powered by a liquid-cooled "V" engine, the VK-105PF, which generated 1260 horsepower. Armament comprised one 20mm cannon firing through the centre of the propeller boss, and two 12.7mm machine guns firing through the engine cowling. The Yak-9 could also carry up to six rockets or two 100kg (220lb) bombs.

The Yak-9T was a tank-busting, ground-attack version that entered service in early 1943. It was usually armed with a 32mm or 37mm cannon and had wing racks for anti-personnel bomblets in special containers. The long-range DD version escorted US bombers shuttling to the USSR. The excellent fighter could from the beginning out-fly the German Messerschmitt Bf 109, and later variants could out-perform the Focke-Wulf 190.

Type: single-seat fighter
Powerplant: 1 x 1260hp Klimov VK-105PF
Wingspan: 10m (32.8ft)
Length: 8.54m (28ft)
Height: 2.44m (8ft)
Maximum speed: 600kmh (375mph)
Service ceiling: 10,500m (34,500ft)
Maximum range: 890km (550 miles)
Armament: 1 x 20mm cannon, 2 x 12.7mm machine gun, 2 x 100kg (220lb) bombs

fierce battles during the coming weeks. In the Caucasus the Soviet Forty-Seventh Army tries to throw the German Seventeenth Army out of Novorossisk.

SEPTEMBER 9

SOUTHERN USSR, *LAND WAR*

The German LI Corps approaches Mamayev Kurgan in Stalingrad, as the Soviet Sixty-Second Army is hit in the centre by LI Corps, in the north by XIV Panzer Corps and in the south by XXXXVIII Panzer Corps. The Fourth Panzer Army is also closing on the city from the south, grinding into the Sixty-Fourth Army as it does so.

GERMANY, *ARMED FORCES*

Hitler relieves Field Marshal Wilhelm List from command of Army Group A for not achieving more (an indication of the Führer's continuing frustration with his senior army commanders, and his failure to understand military logistics), deciding that he will take personal command of the formation.

SEPTEMBER 11

SOUTHERN USSR, *LAND WAR*

The German Sixth and Fourth Panzer Armies continue to push their way into Stalingrad. In the north they secure a stretch of the Volga river bank, allowing them to range their artillery on Soviet river traffic. In the Caucasus, the fight for Novorossisk goes on.

◀ *German panzergrenadiers near Stalingrad. The lack of Soviet aircraft in the skies at this time meant German vehicles could move unimpeded outside the city.*

SEPTEMBER 12

SOUTHERN USSR, *LAND WAR*

General Vasily Chuikov assumes command of the Sixty-Second Army. The German Sixth and Fourth Panzer Armies have a combined total of 590,000 troops, 10,000 artillery pieces and 100 tanks. Facing them are the Stalingrad Front (First Guards, Twenty-Fourth, Twenty-First, Sixty-Sixth and Fourth Tank Armies) and Southeastern Front (Sixty-Second, Sixty-Fourth, Fifty-Seventh, Fifty-First Armies), with a combined total of 590,000 troops, 7000 artillery pieces and 600 tanks.

SEPTEMBER 13

SOUTHERN USSR, *LAND WAR*

A massive German assault begins at Stalingrad. The 71st, 76th and 295th Infantry Divisions attack from Gumrak against the centre of the Sixty-Second Army. Farther south, the 94th Infantry, 29th Panzergrenadier and 14th and 24th Panzer Divisions smash through the Yelshanka and Dar Gova suburbs and reach the Volga. The fighting rages throughout the night. Stalin orders the 13th Guards Rifle Division to cross the Volga into the city to reinforce the Sixty-Second Army.

SEPTEMBER 14

SOUTHERN USSR, *LAND WAR*

The German assaults, backed up by massive artillery fire and Luftwaffe aircraft, continue. XXXXVIII Panzer Corps takes the Tsaritsyn quarter while, south of Mamayev Kurgan, the 76th Infantry Division makes steady gains, taking the railway station (it changes hands four times during the day). Mamayev Kurgan falls to the 295th Infantry Division, cutting the Sixty-Second Army in two. During the night the 13th Guards Rifle Division crosses the river and establishes a small bridgehead in the face of fierce resistance.

SOUTHERN USSR, *AIR WAR*

The Luftwaffe drops mines in the River Volga at Stalingrad.

Attack on Stalingrad

Against a background of indecision at the highest levels and a continuing focus on the drive into the Caucasus, the German Sixth Army inched its way towards the River Volga and Stalingrad.

German hopes that Army Group A would be able to encircle the enemy forces in the region immediately south of the lower Don were unfulfilled. The Russians evaded destruction by withdrawing to the Caucasus, whereupon the Germans seized Krasnodar and Maikop against light resistance. Their divisions followed the retreating Russians closely and penetrated into the western Caucasus up to the mountain passes. Fully realizing the danger which threatened them, the Russians successfully blocked the only road leading over the mountains to Tuapse.

In the Crimea elements of the German Eleventh Army prepared for the crossing of the Kerch Strait. In the central Caucasus area the First Panzer Army moved in the direction of the Grozny oil fields, but very slowly, being greatly handicapped by fuel shortages at the very time when Russian resistance was stiffening.

The operations of Army Group A thus gave the impression of a dispersed effort, with 20 divisions advancing along a front of more than 800km (500 miles). The army group's two points of main effort – northeast of Tuapse and at Pyatigorsk – were 320km (200 miles) apart. Most of the air support units had been shifted to the Stalingrad area after the army group had crossed the Don. Because of the shortage of rolling stock, the only rail line leading from the Rostov area into the Caucasus could not satisfy more than the most elementary requirements, and insignificant shipments across the Sea of Azov failed to alleviate the shortages.

Army Group B's situation was also disappointing. The Soviets in the Don Bend took advantage of the slowness of the Sixth Army's advance – caused by the 10-day lack of gasoline and shortage of ammunition – and suddenly offered strong resistance. Although this manoeuvre led to the encirclement of some Russian forces, it also helped the Soviet command to gain time for the strengthening of the defences at Stalingrad. After some confusion, caused by an almost 180-degree turn of its forces, Fourth Panzer Army had moved into the area north of Kotelnikovski and was ready to push towards Stalingrad from the south. Flank protection along the Don was provided by the Italian Eighth and Hungarian Second Armies, which – supported by a few German divisions – occupied wide sectors. The Romanian Third Army, scheduled to take over the sector on both sides of Kletskaya, was unable to take its place because of rail transport difficulties. For the time being Sixth Army had to assign German divisions to this sector, which in turn reduced the striking power of the assault forces at Stalingrad. During the preparatory attacks the Luftwaffe gave close support and simultaneously carried out some strategic bombing missions against the lines of communications connecting Stalingrad with Moscow.

The German supply situation was alarmingly bad. The assault forces were dependent on a single, low-capacity railroad which ran eastwards from the Donets Basin. Available truck transportation was insufficient to bridge the long distances between the supply bases and the spearhead units.

The distribution of Luftwaffe units corresponded to that of the ground forces. Of some 1230 operational aircraft available in the Russian theatre in mid-August 1942, approximately 720 were supporting Army Groups A and B.

In a letter to Marshal Keitel, General Halder again drew the attention of OKW to the seriousness of the army's personnel situation. According to recent

◀ Troops of the German Sixth Army march east towards Stalingrad in September 1942. The infantry's lack of motor transport seriously impeded their rate of advance.

▲ *The long march to Stalingrad. On the way the German troops looted local farms of chickens, ducks and geese – anything that was easy to prepare for the pot.*

estimates, the Russian theatre would be short of at least 120,000 replacements by November 1,1942. The 400,000 men who would be inducted and trained in the interim period might compensate for current losses, but would not reduce this deficit, and the requirements of other theatres had not been taken into account. In any event, the estimated shortage of more than 700,000 replacements would create serious problems on the Eastern Front.

In addition to the vexing personnel shortages at the front, the partisan problem had assumed such importance that Hitler issued Directive No 46 on August 18 in order to standardize German operating procedures against the enemy in the rear areas. In this directive the Führer ordered every German in partisan-infested areas to participate in the anti-guerrilla struggle. However, though the new policy was well intended, its enforcement suffered from a chronic shortage of personnel and equipment, which permitted great numbers of partisans to escape from one well-set trap after another.

This same personnel shortage created another problem. Germany's allies, who had had to bear such heavy burdens during the summer offensive in order to supplement the Wehrmacht's strength, now stood along greatly exposed sectors of the Don Front. In this connection Hitler was apprehensive lest Stalin repeat his classic manoeuvre of 1920: an attack across the Don near Serafimovich in the direction of Rostov, similar to the one the Bolsheviks had launched against Wrangel's White Russian Army with such devastating results. The Führer felt that the Italian Eighth Army, which was responsible for the security of this Don sector, would be incapable of stopping such an attack. He therefore urged repeatedly that the 22nd Panzer Division be withdrawn from Stalingrad and rehabilitated behind the Italian Eighth Army sector.

The Romanians, who were providing the largest contingent among Germany's allies, were the subject of a memorandum Halder sent to Army Groups A and B on August 18. Those Romanian units assigned to Army Group A – with the exception of the four mountain divisions committed in the Crimea and Caucasus – were to secure the area west and southwest of Astrakhan after the Russian Black Sea coast had been cleared and the fleet eliminated. The plans, however, would be subject to approval by Marshal Antonescu, who was to assume command of a newly activated Romanian army group composed of the Romanian Third and Fourth and German Sixth Armies. The army group would secure the German flank along the lower Volga after the fall of Stalingrad.

On August 19, Army Group A headquarters estimated the situation in the Caucasus as follows: Russian resistance in the northwestern parts of the Caucasus Mountains was extremely stubborn. Around 20 Russian reserve divisions known to be in the Caucasus had not yet been committed for the defence of this area, perhaps because they were insufficiently trained and equipped (the fact that the Red Army considered Caucasian replacements as unreliable might have delayed their employment).

There was no indication of any assembly of Russian forces in the Astrakhan area. The Russians apparently did not intend to threaten the flank and rear of Army Groups A and B from that side. On the contrary, repeated air attacks on Elista – the German-held town in the gap between Army Groups A and B – seemed to indicate that the Russians were worried about a German thrust towards Astrakhan.

Situation in the Caucasus

In its conclusions the report stated that the Russians seemed to employ delaying tactics in the Caucasus. They were continuing the evacuation of industrial machinery and military forces. Because of the advanced season, however, it was not to be expected that they would completely evacuate the Transcaucasus. In carrying out their mission, the army group forces would have to face a hard and time-consuming struggle along the entire Caucasus front, even though sizeable Russian forces had been destroyed during the previous weeks. The steadily growing lines of communications, the vast territory to be kept under control, the scarcity of motor fuel, and the increasing terrain obstacles were the principal factors that would slow down the advance.

The acute shortage of gasoline was at this point the primary cause for the delay in the advance, because it prevented the heavy truck columns from moving up supplies from distant railheads. Instead, the Germans had to use short, undamaged or repaired sections of rail lines and establish truck shuttle services between detraining and entraining points. The delays incurred by trans-shipping bulky supplies were reflected in the unsatisfactory progress of the army group forces.

Growing Red Army resistance

By August 28, the Russian forces opposite Army Group A had set up their defences. By this date the Red Army had mostly regained control over its units, reorganized its forces and had also moved up reinforcements from Transcaucasia, Iran and also – via the Caspian – from central Russia itself. By the end of August strong Russian ground forces, having the advantage of local air superiority, blocked the access to Novorossisk along well-built, deeply echeloned defence lines and launched occasional counterattacks. The Russians also were on the offensive along the Tuapse road, where German motorized units were restricted to the few existing mountain roads.

▲ *"As far as the eye can see, armoured vehicles and halftracks are rolling forward over the steppe." (German observer with the Fourth Panzer Army, August 1942.)*

Attack on Stalingrad

The advance of the German mountain corps was delayed by smaller, but equally well-entrenched forces. The Italian Alpine Corps that was to participate in the thrust across the Caucasus failed to arrive, apparently because the Italian Eighth Army refused to transfer the corps to the respective German Army command. Along the Terek River bend the Russians had concentrated strong ground forces that had the advantage of local air superiority.

At the end of August there were 10–12 Soviet divisions along the Black Sea coast, 1–2 in the mountains and eight divisions along the Terek Front: a total of 19–22 divisions. Additional forces were arriving. The Soviets seemed to be determined to hold their Caucasus positions until the winter, but were continuing to evacuate industrial and agricultural supplies and machinery from the Caucasus area.

On August 31, Hitler, who was very dissatisfied with the situation at Army Group A, received Field Marshal List, its commander, at his headquarters. List explained that he intended to continue his thrusts into the western Caucasus at three points:

1. Near Anapa and Novorossisk and, after the seizure of these two cities, along the coastal road.

2. On both sides of the mountain road to Tuapse.

3. Along the Sukhumi road, where the mountain troops were to make their main effort.

In the central Caucasus, List suggested, the First Panzer Army should destroy the Russian forces in the Terek bend and seize the Grozny oil fields beyond that river. Hitler approved these plans. General Warlimont, Deputy Chief of the Operations Staff, visited Army Group A during the last days of August and reported that morale was high. Its commanders apparently felt confident that they would be capable of accomplishing their missions.

In the Stalingrad sector, early on August 23 one corps of General Paulus' Sixth Army crossed the Don in force and reached the Volga north of Stalingrad that same evening. The next day heavy Russian counterattacks endangered the German toehold

▼ ***German panzers engage Soviet tanks on the steppe. General Strecker, commander of XI Corps, described the steppe as "an ocean that might drown an invader".***

which, however, was strengthened by the arrival of additional units on the west bank of the Volga.

Fourth Panzer Army and Sixth Army had the mission of seizing Stalingrad and securing the lower Volga. The two armies totalled 25 divisions, some of which were greatly understrength. The Russian Sixty-Second Army, composed of some eight divisions under General Chuikov, was responsible for the defence of the city. The Germans had local air superiority, being supported by some 1000 aircraft of all types. During the last days of August, the Germans advanced with relative ease through the outer suburbs of Stalingrad.

While this advance was proceeding in a satisfactory manner, Hitler continued to be preoccupied with protecting both flanks of the forces driving across the Don towards Stalingrad. He ordered one of the few remaining motorized infantry divisions of Army Group A detached from the Caucasus drive and shifted to the Elista area, west of Astrakhan, to secure the gap between Army Groups A and B.

▲ ***As the Sixth Army approached Stalingrad, Luftflotte IV devoted most of its air assets against the city. The first big raid was launched on August 23.***

Axis frailties

On the other flank the Russians attempted to gain another bridgehead against the Italian Eighth Army deployed along the Don. Although the Russians attacked cautiously and with only relatively small forces, the Italian right withdrew, apparently without offering resistance. The Russians thereupon moved a guard cavalry corps into the area of penetration and two days of heavy counterattacks were required before the situation was restored on August 27. Two additional Soviet bridgeheads existed opposite the Hungarian Second Army, which held the Don sector adjacent to the Italian left. Farther to the north, the Germans observed that the Russians were gradually transferring forces from the Voronezh to the Stalingrad area.

On August 28, General Wolfram von Richthofen, commander of VIII Air Corps, made a personal reconnaissance of the region and consulted with the commanders of Fourth Panzer and Sixth Armies. The consensus was that no interference from strong enemy forces was to be expected in the Stalingrad area. Luftwaffe reconnaissance aircraft flying northwards were unable to discover any Russian forces in a terrain that offered little cover or concealment. Richthofen's general impression was that the Russian command was disorganized in this area.

Halder, however, contested the accuracy of this information. Hitler thereupon decided to move the forward echelon of Army Group B's headquarters far to the front and airlift infantry replacements to Sixth Army to speed up the conquest of Stalingrad.

German command crisis

Throughout the summer of 1942 General Halder (Chief of the Army General Staff) had noted in his diary that he was experiencing increasing difficulties in working with Hitler. The latter's tendency of underrating Russian capabilities had assumed grotesque proportions, finally developing into a positive danger. In fact, the situation had become more and more intolerable for the military. According to Halder, it was almost impossible to accomplish anything useful. Hitler's exercise of command was characterized by pathological reactions to impressions of the moment and by his complete lack of understanding of command procedures.

Under such circumstances, the military men in top-level positions were bound to be the first victims of any unfavourable turn of events. As early as August 30, for example, while German progress was

▲ ***Stalingrad did not command all the Luftwaffe's air assets. These are oil tanks ablaze following a German bomber attack on a Soviet target in the Caucasus.***

still quite satisfactory, Halder noted that the army leaders had once again been the target of the Führer's abuse. According to Hitler, they suffered from intellectual conceit, mental inflexibility and a complete incapacity to grasp essentials.

During the first days of September the military events continued to be favourable for the Germans. On the first day of the month German troops succeeded in crossing the Kerch Strait and landing on the Taman Peninsula. After seizing Anapa, they joined in the drive along the Black Sea coast towards Novorossisk. A few days later Marshal List suggested that the bulk of IL Mountain Corps, engaged in the central Caucasus, be pulled out after leaving some blocking units near the passes. This mountain corps could be more advantageously employed in the Maikop area to achieve a breakthrough towards the coast. Since he did not share List's opinion, Hitler sent General Jodl (Chief of the Armed Forces Operations Staff) to investigate on the spot and discuss the matter with List

Upon his return Jodl reported that List's plan seemed sound and he advocated its implementation. In the subsequent argument Hitler accused List of having not followed orders and of having dispersed his forces over much too wide an area. In his reply Jodl tried to prove that List had followed to the letter all orders he had been given. The Führer thereupon became extremely irritated and asked that his orders to List, including notes of verbal instructions, be submitted to him. In addition, he ordered that court stenographers be brought from Berlin to Vinnitsa to take down the minutes of all future military conversations and conferences.

On September 9, Hitler was informed by Halder that List intended to let the Soviets attack the German bridgeheads across the Terek until their strength had been exhausted, and that he would then resume the offensive. Hitler considered this idea as fundamentally wrong, since its execution would imperil the very existence of the German bridgeheads against which the Russians were moving a constant stream of reinforcements.

List is dismissed

This last misunderstanding, coming after so many similar conflicts, led Hitler to consider a number of changes in top-level positions. List was asked to hand in his resignation, which he did on the evening of September 9. For the time being Hitler decided to assume command of Army Group A in person, so that in addition to his civilian functions he now held the position of an army group commander in Russia, commander-in-chief of the German Army, and commander-in-chief of the German armed forces. Three top echelons of military command had thus been unified in a singular manner.

The chief of staff of Army Group A, General von Greiffenberg, remained at army group headquarters at Stalino. Halder was notified on the same day that Hitler intended to relieve him because he "was no longer equal to the psychic demands of his position". General Kurt Zeitzler replaced General Halder on September 24.

The conflict between Hitler and Jodl – brought to the surface by Jodl taking List's side – was so deep that Hitler considered the dismissal of his closest military adviser. He was to be replaced by Paulus, who a few months later was to play such a tragic role when he surrendered the remnants of the Sixth Army at Stalingrad. Keitel's position as Chief of Staff,

Armed Forces High Command, was also jeopardized, with Göring trying to replace him with one of his own protégés. General Warlimont, Jodl's immediate assistant, fell out of favour and was sent on extended leave from which he did not return to duty until his superior – who had survived the turmoil – recalled him after the Allied landings in North Africa in November 1942.

On September 9, the Eastern Intelligence Division submitted an estimate according to which the Soviets seemed to have no sizeable reserves along the entire front. On the contrary, in order to form points of main effort, they had to shift units over long distances. Because of insufficient training and a shortage of equipment, the troops still available and the units presently in the process of activation would probably not be ready for commitment for some time.

Such favourable information was always well received by Hitler who, on September 13, ordered Army Group B to launch a pursuit in the event of Russian resistance north of Stalingrad collapsing. At the same time the existing plans for a thrust towards Astrakhan were to be re-examined. Hitler then instructed the army group commander to launch local attacks at the boundary of Sixth Army and the Italian Eighth Army, correct some dents in the German lines in the Don bend, and construct a switch position behind the German front west of Voronezh.

Despite the estimates of German intelligence, it was clear that none of the objectives of the summer offensive were attained by the Germans. Although Army Group A made local gains in the direction of Tuapse and Grozny, these minor successes were not decisive. The army group had exhausted its strength. The only major oil fields that had fallen into German hands – those at Maikop – were almost completely destroyed. Only two storage tanks and a few stretches of pipeline were found intact.

Army Group B's assault on Stalingrad met with unexpected resistance. Beginning on September 14

▼ A Ju 87 Stuka flies over the Volga north of Stalingrad in late August 1942. The air defence of the city was the responsibility of the Soviet 102nd Air Division.

the Russian garrison received a steady flow of reinforcements, and on September 16 Sixth Army was given control of all German units that had entered the city, including some Fourth Panzer Army elements. As early as September 20 Halder noted that the attack forces were gradually succumbing to exhaustion. But for the next two months the battle raged within the city.

During these weeks of house-to-house fighting Stalingrad lost its initial significance as a flank protection anchor for the Caucasus offensive. Instead of a means to an end, Stalingrad had become an end in itself. More and more troops poured into the city from both sides. After the Romanian Third Army had finally arrived and taken up its positions along the Don between the Italian Eighth and the German Sixth Armies, Paulus was able to shift into the city those German divisions that had hitherto protected his flank.

The Romanians felt none too happy about the new assignment they had received. In an inquiry addressed to the Operations Division of OKH on September 24, they pointed out that their Third Army would have to defend a 168km (105-mile) sector with 69 battalions, or an average of 2.4km (1.5 miles) per battalion. Considering that the Romanians had no mobile forces for counterattacks and no self-propelled anti-tank guns, the Romanian line was very weak. If present plans were implemented, the situation of the Romanian Fourth Army would be even worse, since only 33 battalions would have to hold a frontage of 400km (250 miles). This army would be scarcely strong enough to keep its sector under observation.

The Germans did not attach too much importance to these alarming weaknesses; in their reply they pointed out to the Romanians that everything would depend on the outcome at Stalingrad. They also answered evasively other Romanian questions regarding German armoured support and the availability of motor transport.

Stalingrad had not originally been a major factor in German planning, and the Fourth Panzer Army could have reached it much earlier. But Hitler became increasingly fascinated with the city with his issuance of Directive No 45, a decision that still mystifies historians. It would now constitute the foundation for his conquest of the Caucasus. The

German Sixth Army was to seize Stalingrad from the west. Hitler changed his mind, however, and also directed the Fourth Panzer Army to assist Paulus by advancing on Stalingrad from the south. It moved forward against tough resistance, only reaching the suburbs south of the city on September 10. The previous fighting had already reduced its infantry divisions' strength by 40–50 percent.

The city was long and narrow, befitting its location: its population of 500,000 spread itself almost 48km (30 miles) along the western bank of the Volga, but edges of the city were rarely more than 4km (2.5 miles) wide and sometimes as narrow as 1.5km (.93 mile). Only three terrain features of any significance were noted on the tactical maps: the river bank, which was high enough in places to afford some protection for troops just landed; the River Tsaritsyn, which bisected the city; and the Mamayev Kurgan, an old Tartar burial mount some 102m (335ft) high. In the southern half of the city, only a massive concrete grain elevator stood out.

The city possessed other, special tactical attributes, not the sort usually noted on standard military maps. Strung out, one after another, for 8km (5 miles) north from Mamayev Kurgan were four massive factories and their surrounding complexes. The first of these was the Lazure Chemical Plant. Slightly north of that came the Red October metal works, which was followed in turn by the Barrikady weapons plant and the Stalingrad Tractor Factory, which had been converted to tank production.

▲ *By the end of August the Luftwaffe was pulverizing Stalingrad at will, and BF 109 fighters were shooting down Soviet Yak fighters with ease.*

By August, there were good reasons for the Russians to leave Stalingrad. Russia's Sixty-Second Army counted only 20,000 soldiers at the time. The army had retreated into the city, herded eastwards by the Sixth Army's advance across the Don River. Just as it took refuge inside Stalingrad, the Sixth Army was becoming the single largest formation of the entire Wehrmacht, with a strength approaching one-third of a million men. Its commander, General Friedrich Paulus, estimated that his army would need 10 days to take the city and then 14 days to regroup and cross the Volga to the steppes beyond.

Paulus issued his order for the attack on August 19. Sixth Army headquarters expected both difficult fighting in the city and Soviet counterattacks with armour from north of the city. XIV Panzer Corps would conduct the main thrust towards the northern

◀ *As the city's buildings were reduced to rubble, the authorities put up posters proclaiming: "We shall never surrender the city of our birth."*

suburbs of Stalingrad. LI Corps would cover the panzers' right flank, while VIII Corps covered the left or northern flank. Even farther north, Sixth Army's XXIV Panzer Corps maintained a bridgehead over the Don River near Kalach. The main effort north of Stalingrad planned to cut the city's main line of communications north along the Volga, though German planners knew this would not cut off all supplies. In the tradition of the German General Staff, the plan had no contingent scenarios; it provided no details on fighting in the city. Ironically, the previous year Hitler had prohibited the German Army from fighting in Leningrad and Moscow, while German doctrinal literature tended to downplay the subject of urban combat. Thus, the German Army had little if any training in or experience of city fighting.

On August 21, the Sixth Army seized a bridgehead over the Don River at Wertjatschij, and two days the XIV Panzer Corps began its dash eastwards. Breaking through scattered opposition, the 16th Panzer Division broke into Rynok on August 23, looking down on the broad Volga north of Stalingrad. It seized Rynok from Red Army anti-aircraft units, all-female units that had been deploying north and east of Stalingrad during August. Throughout the remaining hours of the day, the 16th Panzer Division observed as the Luftwaffe began bombing Stalingrad.

▲ ***In the German bombing raids many of Stalingrad's surviving citizens lost all their possessions, though families shared whatever they had left.***

Luftflotte IV, tasked with supporting the advance into southern Russia, fielded half the air assets on the Eastern Front. It, too, was drawn to Stalingrad – its VIII Air Corps supported the army with an average of 1000 sorties a day. Throughout August 23, Richthofen's flyers pounded the city, burning down the wooden houses in the southwest corner. The large petroleum facility burned for days. The walls of the white four- and five-story apartment buildings remained standing, but the bombs burned the interiors, collapsing the floors. The waterworks and communications centre were also knocked out. The aerial bombardment during the week killed an estimated 40,000 Russians, while the many Soviet anti-aircraft units only managed to bring down three aircraft, a consequence of insufficient training and very limited ammunition. Although the Luftwaffe created considerable destruction, historian Anthony Beevor observed: "Richthofen's massive bombing raids had not only failed to destroy the enemy's will,

◀ ***Gutted buildings in Stalingrad. Ironically, the Luftwaffe's bombing raids created vast piles of rubble that would seriously impede the progress of German troops.***

▲ ***A Russian soldier, sailor and a political officer (commissar) in Stalingrad on September 23. They are resting in a shelter dug into the Volga's bank.***

their very force of destruction had turned the city into a perfect killing ground for the Russians to use against them."

Richthofen's forces were able to maintain air superiority until late October, by which time combat and mechanical failures had considerably weakened them. Simultaneously, the Russian Air Force began to receive considerably more and better aircraft, while their anti-aircraft forces continued to improve. Thereafter both air forces limited themselves to ground support of the army, reconnaissance and short-range bombing.

An observer with an eye for tactics would have noticed how the steppes are cut up by innumerable steep-sloped gullies that, in Russian, are called *balka*. The Tsaritsyn gully was the major *balka*, which separated the southern third of Stalingrad from the northern two-thirds of the city. At the mouth of the *balka* was the old town centre, where the tsar's officials and businessmen maintained their two-story houses. South of the Tsaritsyn was a residential sector. Its train station was near the grain silos across from the large island in the Volga. North of the Tsaritsyn was the city centre, which had its own train station, several plazas, a post office and waterworks. This area housed the local Communist Party headquarters. To the north was the large petroleum complex along the Volga. West of the oil complex was Stalingrad's dominant feature, the Mamayev Kurgan (on German maps, Height 102), on the northern edge of the residential sector that overlooks the Volga River. To the west of the Mamayev Kurgan was the airport. The northern sector was the industrial region.

Despite seeing their city pulverized and continuing combat operations, 300,000–350,000 civilians were still in Stalingrad. Most of them lived in holes, cellars and homemade bunkers. Since even the

German Army was incapable of its own logistics support, many civilians faced eventual starvation. Most of those remaining were women, children and old men. German authorities knew the civilians required evacuation but were unable to move them. By mid-October, 25,000 civilians had fled the rubble, walking towards Kalatch. Some of the outskirts of the city still stood, mostly grimy houses occupied by workers. Other than several major streets, most of the roads were unpaved. Russian artillery units that deployed en masse east of the Volga could hit streets running east and west. Streets running north and south were under Russian small-arms fire.

Besides the enormous military problem of taking Stalingrad, Paulus also had to safeguard his northern flank along the Don River. He never solved this task because the Soviets held a number of bridgeheads, from which they launched numerous offensives. Three Soviet armies launched the first offensive on August 24. Although they suffered great casualties, they succeeded in slowing down the German divisions' arrival in Stalingrad.

Stalin and Stalingrad

Just as Hitler changed his mind concerning the conduct of Operation Blue, Stalin also failed to maintain a consistent approach to operations around Stalingrad. Three weeks into the German summer offensive, for example, he remained convinced that the main attack would be against Moscow. He responded clumsily in fits and starts, first splitting Stalingrad between two front headquarters. In mid-July, however, he corrected this error and created the Stalingrad Front under General A. I. Yeremenko, consisting of the Twenty-Eighth, Fifty-First, Fifty-Seventh, Sixty-Second and Sixty-Fourth Armies. Stavka also deployed the North Caucasus, South, Southwest and Bryansk Fronts in southern Russia. Most men of military age in Stalingrad had already been drafted, but local Communist Party officials mobilized an additional 200,000 men and women to serve in "Worker's Columns", while unneeded workers were placed in militia battalions. Stalin ordered that Stalingrad would not be given up and dispatched the dreaded

▼ ***A StuG assault gun of the Sixth Army moves into Stalingrad in September 1942. With its 75mm gun, the StuG was an excellent infantry support weapon.***

▲ *German troops in a foxhole covered by a wrecked T-34 tank, Stalingrad, September 23. By this time the city was full of shell craters which served as trenches for both sides.*

NKVD to enforce discipline. The latter soon controlled all the boats on the Volga and allowed no one out of the city.

The last major headquarters left in Stalingrad was General Vasily I. Chuikov's Sixty-Second Army. While the Sixth Army methodically attacked Stalingrad, Chuikov ferried over the Volga the equivalent of nine rifle divisions and two tank brigades. As the struggle wore on and he gained greater strength, he increasingly resorted to aggressive counterattacks with anywhere from 200–800 men, sometimes with tank support. This form of defence forced the Germans to shift repeatedly from offence to defence and made the battle of attrition ever more costly.

Stalin's advisers tried unsuccessfully to stop him from launching several major counteroffensives from bridgeheads north of Stalingrad. Three reserve armies filled with untrained conscripts attacked on September 5 but were checked with substantial losses. The USSR had already suffered millions of

▲ *A Stuka circles Stalingrad in September. By this date Luftwaffe pilots were flying up to five missions a day.*

▲ *As the Germans ground their way into Stalingrad, the fighting raged around strongpoints, such as the Mamayev Kurgan and the massive grain silo (above).*

losses, including most of its prewar military. The Germans also occupied most of its industrial and manpower centres. Despite this, the Soviets still possessed numerical superiority in men and weapon systems. Factories continued to produce enormous numbers of tanks and aircraft, and a new military élite had begun to emerge from the earlier disasters of the war: men who understood the Germans' weaknesses and were not afraid of the Germans or of taking casualties. Related to this development was the re-emergence of the Soviet General Staff, which had arduously compiled lessons learned from which their recipe for victory evolved. An action symptomatic of this emergence of a new Soviet military élite occurred on October 9, 1942, when the Red Army gave commanders relative autonomy, reducing the old co-responsibility of the political commissar. That said, in late 1942 the Soviet military was still recovering from its serious wounds.

Soon after the arrival of his infantry divisions on September 10, Paulus launched a concerted attack on the city. It progressed rapidly through the suburbs but slowed in the inner city. The Germans seized the Mamayev Kurgan on September 13, but it changed hands repeatedly throughout the following months. For both sides, casualties climbed precipitously. The Soviets threw in the 13th Guards Division, which sacrificed many of its 10,000 men in grinding down the German advance. This was the first of four German attacks in Stalingrad. It faltered on September 19 and 20 as a result of massive casualties and dwindling ammunition. This pattern recurred in the three subsequent attacks. The first, from September 22 to October 6, reached the Volga at the mouth of the Tsaritsyn. The attack from October 14 to early November from the north reduced the Soviet hold in Stalingrad to two small bridgeheads. The final assault from November 11 to 17 was against the two small bridgeheads.

On September 23, a German General Staff officer visited the 295th and 71st Infantry Divisions in the centre of the town. He noted that the Soviet troops

▶ *German artillery pounds Red Army positions in the northern suburbs of Stalingrad. Artillery fire created piles of rubble over which the infantry had to fight.*

remained as physically close to the Germans as possible to reduce the effectiveness of the Germans' firepower. The Soviet troops were ever alert, and whenever they thought they spotted a German weakness, they immediately counterattacked. They were particularly tough now that there was little room left to retreat. The officer observed that, after a heavy artillery bombardment, troops quickly emerged from their cellar holes ready to fire. Despite German countermeasures, the Soviets continued to move supplies across the Volga at night.

The two German divisions the staff officer visited were old, battle-tested formations that had been considerably weakened by infantry casualties. He observed that their combat power was dropping daily and that the average strength of an infantry company was 10–15 men. Losses were particularly high among officers and noncommissioned officers (NCOs). Although replacements had arrived, they were insufficient in number and lacked experience, training and soldierly bearing. When an officer fell, the men drifted back to their starting point. To get them moving forward again, a higher-ranking officer had to lead them. The soldiers depended on divisional StuG assault guns whose 75mm guns were designed to take out point targets for the infantry. The small bands of infantry did not want to attack without a StuG and viewed it as a failure in leadership if one was not provided to them. The German officer concluded that attacking through the ruins had exhausted the infantry and that they were too tired and dulled. With so few troops, there was no rest because every soldier had to be deployed. And there were no reserves.

It was especially hard to get necessary supplies forward to the combat infantry troops. Their diet

▼ To the north of Stalingrad the Germans had to hold off Red Army attempts to relieve the city. Here, a machine-gun team keeps watch for the Soviets.

▲ *The tanks of both sides were very vulnerable in Stalingrad. This T-34 was knocked out at close range.*

▲ *The swastika flies from a ruined building in Stalingrad, which acted as Friedrich Paulus' field headquarters in October 1942.*

suffered considerably. The troops expressed bitterness towards the Luftwaffe's perceived luxury. They had also become resentful towards the special food bonuses the armoured units received. The officers maintained that it was pointless to offer the infantry propaganda since none of the promises could be kept. Out in the steppes of southern Russia, all supplies had to be brought from Germany. Besides food, the infantry's major requirement was 80mm mortar shells, one of the few ways to get to the enemy holed up in cellars and gully cliffs.

German tactical problems

In the last week of September, Paulus launched his second attack on Stalingrad. He exchanged divisions with his northern flank and used the new units to renew the offensive. It pushed the Soviets back into the northern sector of Stalingrad, but casualties and ammunition expenditures were so high that Paulus called off the offensive. The Sixth Army did not begin its third offensive until October 14, when Paulus sent four divisions supported by armour to assist in taking the northern factory complexes. This created a crisis for the defenders, when on the second day the Germans captured the tractor factory and reached the Volga. Despite the heavy rain, snow and the mud, the attack made remarkable progress, capturing the ruins of several blocks of houses, the Red October Factory and some other burned-out hulks. But at the end of the month the attacks fizzled out from the high casualties and insufficient ammunition. Chuikov's garrison had been reduced to two small pockets and the block ice in the Volga had created a logistical nightmare, but the Germans were spent. Paulus launched the fourth and final attack on November 11, based on the arrival of five engineer battalions. The attack advanced very slowly against tough resistance. It, too, expired after several days, and on the 19th the Soviets launched Operation Uranus, which would destroy the Sixth Army.

German panzergrenadiers had never fought in a large city and had to rethink many of their methods. All German infantry loved the StuG because they could take cover behind the heavily armoured vehicle as it advanced and fired. It was a serious mistake, however, for the infantry to use tanks in the same manner as the StuG, because the Panzer III and IV tanks were too vulnerable to enemy fire. Instead, they were urged to advance with several tanks behind them, providing fire support.

Although tanks and panzergrenadiers had been working together in combat since 1939, they had hardly ever seen each other on the battlefield. Putting tanks and armoured infantry in a small urban space consequently required a different, more intimate level of cooperation. The combined-arms team in such a scenario required a small number of tanks, armoured infantry and engineers. Rubble, narrow streets and bomb craters restricted the number of tanks that could operate effectively in such an area. German commanders were urged to examine the terrain beforehand, noting obstacles, cover and the enemy situation. An attack plan had to come from this orientation, reaching an understanding of

who would do what. The tank commander, for example, had to enter the fight knowing how limited his vision would be and how dependent the tanks would be on the other branches.

Mines were the greatest danger for tanks. German after-action reports recommended that when a tank hit a mine, all tanks in the attack halt and engineers move forward to clear paths. Infantry had to deploy forward to thwart Russian infantry and to protect recovery teams, for it was critical to retrieve damaged vehicles as soon as possible. It was also necessary to withdraw the tanks before sunset, because support vehicles were unarmoured. A panzer division had less infantry and artillery than an infantry division, which made it more difficult to replace infantry losses and punish the enemy with artillery fire.

The Red Army also lost many tanks in the Stalingrad street fighting. In late September, VIII Corps counted 62 T-34 hulks in its sector, and XIV Panzer Corps reported that on September 30 it had destroyed 24 Russian and 100 non-Russian tanks. The latter consisted of eight American M3 Lee tanks, 47 American M3 Stuarts and 24 British Valentines.

Despite the massive firepower used against the defenders of Stalingrad in September and October 1942, Paulus had failed in his efforts to capture the city. Worse, his army was being sucked into a battle of attrition that seemingly had no end.

▼ As both sides fed more and more troops into the city during September, the city was blanketed by mass artillery barrages and aerial bombardment.

▼ *Red Army infantry moves through Stalingrad. Soviet troops were equipped with liberal quantities of grenades for use against the enemy, and Chuikov tried to ensure that all his men were armed with submachine guns.*

Phase IV: War of the Rats

The Battle of Stalingrad was fought in and over rubble. The Red Army used the bomb craters and shattered buildings as positions for platoons, squads, sections and snipers - hundreds of snipers. The fighting deteriorated into dozens of local actions against individual positions and buildings, all fought under the most savage conditions, with little quarter asked for or given. The German soldiers called it Rattenkrieg: the war of the rats. Their Blitzkrieg tactics that had conquered much of Europe were useless in Stalingrad, as the battle for the ruined city was reduced to hundreds of small-unit actions, often fought with knives, bayonets and entrenching tools.

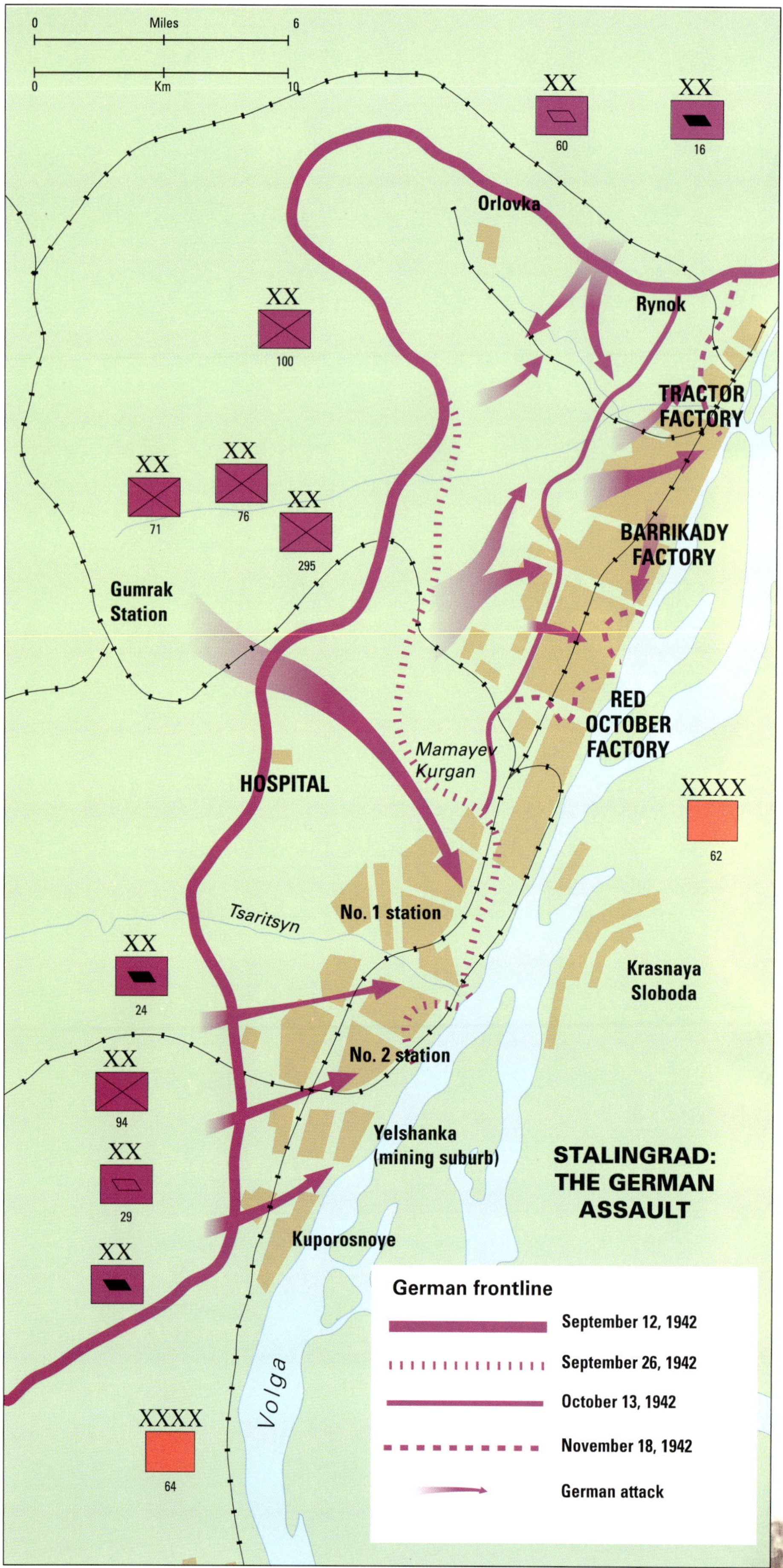

September 15

SOUTHERN USSR, *LAND WAR*

The railway station becomes the focus of the fighting at Stalingrad, while the 13th Guards Division attacks the Mamayev Kurgan. To the south the German 94th Infantry, 14th and 24th Panzer Divisions increase their efforts to prise apart the Soviet Sixty-Second and Sixty-Fourth Armies at Kuporosnoye.

September 16

SOUTHERN USSR, *LAND WAR*

The Soviet 13th Guards Division retakes the railway station and Mamayev Kurgan, the latter with the help of the 112th Rifle Division. It then doggedly defends the hill in the face of massive German firepower.

September 18

SOUTHERN USSR, *LAND WAR*

An attack by the Soviet First Guards Army north of Stalingrad is halted by German artillery and Luftwaffe attacks. A counterattack then throws the First Guards back to its start lines. The 92nd Rifle Brigade wards off all German efforts to dislodge it from the grain elevator. Similarly, LI Corps tries to retake Mamayev Kurgan, to no avail. The bombing and shelling results in a permanent pall of smoke hanging over the city.

September 20

SOUTHERN USSR, *LAND WAR*

The Soviet First Guards, Twenty-Fourth and Sixty-Sixth Armies launch assaults to break through to the beleaguered Sixty-Second Army, but all fail. Under ferocious artillery and Luftwaffe assaults, followed by infantry and panzers, the 13th Guards Division is forced out of the railway station into the nail factory.

▲ ***Germans on the western edge of Stalingrad. The fighting was much harder than expected, an ill omen for the future.***

◄ *German troops near the tractor factory in Stalingrad. At the end of September the Germans squeezed the Orlovka salient, forcing the Soviets back towards the tractor and Barrikady factories.*

SEPTEMBER 21

NORTHERN USSR, *LAND WAR*
The German Eleventh Army counter-attacks at Gaitolovo and soon has the enemy surrounded in a pocket, which is then hammered by constant artillery bombardments and aerial attacks.

SOUTHERN USSR, *LAND WAR*
The German Sixth Army fends off attacks by the First Guards, Twenty-Fourth and Sixty-Sixth Armies. In Stalingrad the Soviets are forced out of the nail factory. XXXXVIII Panzer Corps clears the bed of the Tsaritsyn stream and thus isolates the 92nd and 42nd Rifle Brigades on the southern flank of the Sixty-Second Army. Fighting continues around Mamayev Kurgan and the grain elevator.

SEPTEMBER 23

SOUTHERN USSR, *LAND WAR*
The Soviet 284th Rifle Division crosses the Volga at Stalingrad and, together with the 95th Rifle Division, drives the Germans back from the southern slopes of Mamayev Kurgan to the railway station. Farther south, the 42nd and 92nd Rifle Brigades are worn down by German fire and are amalgamated. In the Caucasus, Group Ruoff begins Operation Attica designed to destroy Soviet defences in the Caucasus Mountains. Employing two corps of the Seventeenth Army, they strike the Eighteenth and Fifty-Sixth Armies but make little headway.

SEPTEMBER 24

SOUTHERN USSR, *LAND WAR*
The German Sixth Army regroups for a fresh attack at Stalingrad. Paulus will direct his attacks against the factory district and Orlovka salient on the Sixth Army's left flank. Fresh attacks will be made against Mamayev Kurgan and the Red October factory.

GERMANY, *ARMED FORCES*
Halder is dismissed as Chief of the General Staff and replaced by Kurt Zeitzler. Hitler states: "I dismissed General Halder because he could not understand the spirit of my plans."

SEPTEMBER 27

SOUTHERN USSR, *LAND WAR*
Chuikov launches a spoiling attack inside Stalingrad with the Sixty-Second Army and 36th Guards Rifle Division of the Sixty-Fourth Army, which is stopped by Luftwaffe attacks. The Germans then assault the Mamayev Kurgan and the Red October factory, taking the summit of the hill. The Germans reach the Volga on an 8km (5 mile) front in the south. The Soviet 193rd Rifle Division crosses the river and deploys in the Red October coke house. In the Caucasus, the German 13th Panzer, 370th Infantry and 5th SS *Wiking* Divisions storm Elchetvo.

SEPTEMBER 28

USSR, *ARMED FORCES*
The Stavka reorganizes its Stalingrad formations. The Southeastern Front becomes the Stalingrad Front, and the old Stalingrad Front becomes the Don Front under General Konstantin Rokossovsky.

SEPTEMBER 29

SOUTHERN USSR, *LAND WAR*
The Orlovka salient is attacked by the German 16th Panzer, 60th Panzer-grenadier and 389th and 100th Infantry Divisions, forcing the defending units back into Orlovka itself. In Stalingrad, fighting continues on the Mamayev Kurgan and at the Red October factory.

SEPTEMBER 30

SOUTHERN USSR, *LAND WAR*
More Red Army units are fed into Stalingrad: the reformed 42nd Rifle Brigade, the 92nd Rifle Brigade to relieve the 23rd Tank Corps and the 4000-strong 39th Guards Division to support the 193rd Rifle Division west of the Red October factory. The Stavka also plans to send the Third and Fifth Tank and the Forty-Third Armies from the reserve to Stalingrad.

▼ *Stalingrad under attack on September 28, when heavy Luftwaffe attacks against the Volga ferries resulted in substantial Soviet losses. On the west bank of the river, the Germans attacked the Red October and Silikat factories.*

OCTOBER 1

SOUTHERN USSR, *LAND WAR*

German attacks in the Orlovka sector continue. In the factory district the Germans pound the 193rd Rifle Division in front of the Red October factory, and also strike the 284th Rifle and 13th Guards Divisions. However, the latter units defeat all German efforts to break through to the Volga. But the Soviets are hard pressed, prompting Chuikov to deploy the 39th Guards Division to the Red October workshops. The Sixth Army has suffered 40,000 casualties since September 13; the Soviet Sixty-Second Army, 78,000.

OCTOBER 2

NORTHERN USSR, *LAND WAR*

What is left of the Soviet Second Shock Army in the Gaitolovo Pocket is wiped out, with 24,000 troops captured and killed, plus 300 artillery pieces, 500 mortars and 240 tanks lost.

SOUTHERN USSR, *LAND WAR*

The Soviet 13th Guards Division defeats an assault by the 295th Division as German forces penetrate into the Barrikady, tractor and Red October installations at Stalingrad. An attack in the south by the Sixty-Fourth Army is defeated. During the night the Soviet 308th Rifle and 37th Guards Divisions cross the Volga to reinforce the Sixty-Second Army.

▼ A German soldier takes aim in Stalingrad. In mid-October the Germans launched a fresh offensive in the city involving 90,000 troops and 300 tanks.

OCTOBER 5

SOUTHERN USSR, *LAND WAR*

The Soviets unleash a 300-gun barrage against German units in the factory area of Stalingrad, inflicting heavy casualties. But the Soviets are forced out of the Silikat factory and the 42nd and 92nd Rifle Brigades and 6th Guards Tank Brigade are isolated.

OCTOBER 7

SOUTHERN USSR, *LAND WAR*

The Germans finally clear the Orlovka sector at Stalingrad, as the 37th Guards Division struggles to hold the tractor factory against intensive attacks. German units also battle the 193rd Rifle Division in the city's sports stadium.

OCTOBER 9

SOUTHERN USSR, *LAND WAR*

The fighting temporarily halts in Stalingrad as the Germans are exhausted.

USSR, *ARMED FORCES*

The Red Army ends its system of dual leadership by abolishing the position of communist political commissar in favour of a single military commander in each unit. Party representatives will continue to serve in the army, but will no longer direct military operations.

OCTOBER 14

SOUTHERN USSR, *LAND WAR*

The German offensive in Stalingrad resumes, with the 94th and 389th Infantry, 100th Jäger and 14th and 24th Panzer Divisions attacking the factory districts. By the afternoon the Germans have surrounded the 112th and 37th Guards Divisions and annihilated the right flank of the 308th Rifle Division. During the night the Germans reach the tractor factory and break through to the Volga. The 37th Guards Division has been all but destroyed. Chuikov ferries the 138th Rifle Division across the river during the night. In the Caucasus, Group Ruoff again fails to breach Red Army defences to reach the Black Sea.

OCTOBER 15

SOUTHERN USSR, *LAND WAR*

German firepower halts all daytime traffic across the Volga as the Germans isolate enemy forces in the tractor factory. In an effort to relieve the Sixty-Second Army, the Stavka launches attacks in the north with the Twenty-Fourth and Sixty-Sixth Armies, and in the south with the Fifty-First and Fifty-Seventh Armies.

OCTOBER 18

SOUTHERN USSR, *LAND WAR*

The Germans have taken the tractor factory and wiped out the 37th Guards Division. They break through the 84th Tank Brigade and attack the Barrikady factory, fighting every inch of the way.

OCTOBER 21

SOUTHERN USSR, *LAND WAR*

The German 79th Infantry Division is repulsed from the Red October and Barrikady factories. The Germans make minor gains in the Red October area.

OCTOBER 22

SOUTHERN USSR, *LAND WAR*

The first snows fall at Stalingrad. The Soviet Sixty-Fourth Army launches an attack from the Beketovka salient designed to link up with the Sixty-Second. It is stopped by intensive German artillery fire, which inflicts heavy casualties.

USSR, *ARMED FORCES*

Plans for the Soviet counteroffensive around Stalingrad, codenamed Uranus, are gathering pace. The Southwestern Front under General Nikolay Vatutin is activated, comprising the Fifth Tank, Twenty-First and Sixty-Third Armies and the Second and Seventeenth Air Armies. The Don Front comprises the Twenty-Fourth, Sixty-Fifth and Sixty-Sixth Armies. The Stavka also has the Second Guards Army that it

◀ ***German artillery at Stalingrad, with the grain elevator in the background. Despite their massive firepower, the Germans had to reduce enemy pockets one by one.***

intends to use against the Romanian Fourth Army.

OCTOBER 25

SOUTHERN USSR, *LAND WAR*

As the Germans continue to blast their way into the Red October and Barrikady factory complexes, the Soviet Sixty-Fourth Army launches a fresh attack towards Stalingrad, meeting fierce German resistance. In the Caucasus, an assault by III Panzer Corps towards Nalchik forces the Soviet Thirty-Seventh Army to retreat.

USSR, *STRATEGY*

For Operation Uranus the Stavka will deploy the Southwestern Front (340,000 troops), Don Front (292,000 troops) and Stalingrad Front (383,000 troops).

OCTOBER 27

SOUTHERN USSR, *LAND WAR*

The Germans can now fire on Red Army landing areas on the west bank of the Volga, causing heavy casualties among Soviet units before they even enter the battle. However, the Sixth Army is all but exhausted, having used up its reserves.

OCTOBER 28

SOUTHERN USSR, *LAND WAR*

XIV Panzer and LI Corps can make no impression upon the Red October and Barrikady factories at Stalingrad.

OCTOBER 30

USSR, *STRATEGY*

The Stavka finalizes its Uranus plans. The Southwestern Front will attack the Chir and Kalach lines while the Stalingrad Front will strike for Sovetski and Kalach. The battered Sixty-Second Army will pin the Sixth Army in Stalingrad and the Sixty-Fourth Army will attack from the Beketovka salient.

OCTOBER 31

GERMANY, *ATROCITIES*

In a secret memorandum, Keitel confirms Hitler's orders for the use of Soviet prisoners in German industry: "The lack of workers is becoming an increasingly dangerous hindrance for the future German war and armaments industry. The expected relief through discharges from the armed forces is uncertain as to the extent and date; however, its possible extent will by no means correspond to expectations and requirements in view of the great demand.

"The Führer has now ordered that the working power of the Russian prisoners of war should be utilized to a large extent by large-scale assignment for the requirements of the war industry. The prerequisite for production is adequate nourishment."

KEY WEAPONS

TIGER

Following encounters with Soviet T-34 and KV-1 tanks in 1941, German tank designers were instructed to produce a heavy tank that would restore mastery of the battlefield to the Germans. The result was the Panzer VI Ausf E – the Tiger I – which entered service in August 1942. It was armed with the powerful 88mm gun (originally developed from the 88mm Flak 36 L/56 gun), which meant it could knock out any Allied tank then in service. Its thick (but not shot-deflecting) armour made it virtually indestructible (the US Sherman, armed with a 76mm gun, and Russian T-34/85, armed with an 85mm gun, only stood a chance against a Tiger at close range, and only with a shot against its side or rear).

The Tiger had a five-man crew: commander, gunner, loader, radio operator and driver. The tank's suspension was composed of driving sprocket, rear idler and inter-leaved road wheels (36 in total). This arrangement gave a very smooth ride cross-country, but in cold weather caused mud, ice and rocks to jam the track mechanism and immobilize the tank. To overcome this problem, the running gear needed constant attention.

In the right hands the Tiger could be very effective: on July 7, 1943, at Kursk, a single Tiger commanded by *SS-Oberscharführer* Franz Staudegger of the 1st SS Panzer Division *Leibstandarte*, engaged 50 T-34s. Staudegger used up his entire ammunition after destroying some 22 enemy tanks, while the rest retreated. For his achievement Staudegger was awarded the Knight's Cross.

Weight: 57,000kg (125,400lb)
Crew: 5
Engine: 1 x Maybach HL 230 P45
Speed: 45.4kmph (28mph)
Range: 125km (78 miles)
Length: 8.45m (27.7ft)
Width: 3.7m (12ft)
Height: 2.93m (9.61ft)
Armament: 1 x 88mm cannon, 2 x 7.92mm machine gun
Ammunition: 92 x 88mm, 5700 x 7.92mm
Armour: front (maximum): 110mm (4.33in); side (maximum) 80mm (3.14in)

Rattenkrieg

The battle for the shell-blasted city sucked tens of thousands of men into a nightmare of house-to-house fighting where there were no fronts, just unrelenting combat and death at every turn.

At Stalingrad, military operations absorbed more and more troop units. This probably resulted from the infinitely greater compartmentalization that limited not only vision but also the range of direct-fire weapons. As a result, more combatants were required to fill or watch those compartments. For the more important compartments, heavy or specialized weapons were required. Combat in urban areas also magnified the dimension of vertical warfare. The massive destruction of Stalingrad limited vertical combat, although any remaining "high ground" remained critical for observation. Some soldiers described the conflict as "the war of rats" because so much of it concentrated on controlling holes and cellars. It was no accident that the German Army sent specially trained engineer battalions to Stalingrad. Their job was to blow up buildings with explosives. Paulus used this method to create "channels" throughout the city. But this required even more combatants to guard the long flanks of the channel and to reduce pockets of resistance that had survived the demolitions. All those additional troops required more ammunition.

The Soviets and the Germans expended an extraordinary amount of ammunition. Between January 10 and February 2, 1943, the Don Front fired some 24 million rifle and machine-gun rounds; 911,000 artillery shells and 990,000 mortar shells. In September 1942, the Sixth Army expended 23,035,863 rifle and machine-gun rounds, 575,828 anti-tank shells, 116,932 infantry cannon shells, and 752,747 mortar shells. It deployed 14,932 mines and its soldiers used 178,066 hand grenades. Apologists writing for one side or the other use such figures to assert that the enemy was cowardly or incompetent for such profligate expenditures. Despite the strain on the armies and the lack of training in many units, such high ammunition expenditures for both sides would suggest that other factors were involved.

Those larger numbers of troops fighting on urban terrain and firing greater amounts of munitions produced very high casualties. There remains a lack of clarity regarding Soviet losses, but General Chuikov observed that his divisions had already been considerably weakened before they reached Stalingrad. He noted that by September 14 one armoured brigade had only one tank left, and two other brigades without any tanks had to be sent across the Volga to refit. One division had two infantry brigades that were full, but the composite regiment of another division only fielded 100 infantrymen. Chuikov stated that another division had a total of 1500 men, "the motorized infantry brigade had 666 men, including no more than 200 infantrymen; the Guards Division of Colonel Dubyanski on the left flank had no more than 250 infantrymen".

Later, Chuikov went on to explain the effect of the high casualties on his units: "It means that our soldiers (even small units) crawled out from under German tanks, more often than not wounded, to another position, where they were received, incorporated into another unit, provided with equipment, usually ammunition, and then they went back into battle." Early in the battle some 10,000 men of the 13th Guards Rifle Division crossed the Volga without their heavy weapons. Chuikov threw them into a counterattack against the brick mill and the main train station. The division lost 30 percent of its men in the first 24 hours. By the time the battle ended, only 320 of the original soldiers were left.

Records of the Sixth Army indicate that the intensity of combat was high, both before reaching

◀ A German infantry squad, the majority armed with Mauser K98 bolt-action rifles, near the Barrikady Factory in October 1942. The NCO is armed with an MP40.

Stalingrad and later, during the city fighting. It crossed the Don River on August 21, 1942. From then until 16 October, it recorded the following losses:

	Officers	NCOs and Men
Killed	239	7456
Wounded	821	30,360
Missing	8	1127

During this period, Sixth Army recorded capturing 57,800 prisoners of war (POWs) and capturing or destroying 1950 tanks, 805 guns and 1969 aircraft. From September 13 to October 16, it suffered the following losses:

	Officers	NCOs and Men
Killed	69	2438
Wounded	271	10,107
Missing	3	298

Paulus's army not only fought in the city but also held a defensive front north of the city. On this northern front, Sixth Army captured 5625 POWs and captured or destroyed 616 tanks and 87 guns. In the city itself, Paulus's army captured 17,917 POWs and captured or destroyed 233 tanks and 302 guns.

For those fighting in Stalingrad, the time was one of unending horror and confusion. Joachim Stempel was a company commander in the German 103rd Panzergrenadier Regiment, attempting to force a way through to the banks of the Volga.

"OCTOBER 25 Early in the morning, I am ordered to the brigade commander, Colonel Freiherr von Falkenstein. He gives me a new mission: 'Report to Panzergrenadier Regiment 103. There you are to take over the remains of the panzergrenadiers as company commander. The commander of the 2nd Battalion is Captain Erich Domaschk. Afterwards you are to return to brigade. All the best, Hals-und-Beinbruch (literally 'Break your neck and leg!'; meaning, 'The best of luck').' I report my departure.

Another day in hell

"At the brigade command post my things are quickly packed. Then I am taken in a Kübel (German jeep) to the command post of Panzergrenadier Regiment 103. It is very difficult to get through the artillery shelling and a labyrinth of obstacles. Finally we arrive. In the ruins of the buildings I descend into a cellar, where the regimental staff has established itself. Then I am standing in front of the commander of Panzergrenadier Regiment 103, Lieutenant-Colonel Seydel. I report to him and am greeted with joy – at the front there is no officer to lead the 'regiment', now reduced to company strength.

"My briefing is short: the last hundred metres to the River Volga are at stake; they have to be taken! Everywhere bullets and shells strike the walls still standing. Onward, onward! Over shattered rails, through hollows with loose stones and iron beams that have come down, and again through factory halls, where parts of machines, work benches and materials of all sorts lie around, toppled, destroyed. From the iron girders that are still standing hang wavy metal plates and wiring.

"And then it is time. In front of us is the administration building of the 'Bread Factory'. We're attacking! Metre by metre we crawl forward, following the bombs that the Stukas are dropping in front of us. We are deafened by the howling of sirens and explosions. Fountains of mud caused by the exploding bombs erupt all around us, forcing us to take cover. More howls overhead – our own artillery! But also over from the other side! A whole series of salvoes by Soviet artillery makes the earth shake. With an exploding sound the shells impact against the factory walls that still are standing. The noise is like that of

◀ ***Bullet-ridden buildings and structures in the centre of Stalingrad. Ammunition expenditure was prodigious: the Germans fired 25 million rounds in September alone.***

▲ ***The Dzherzhinsky Tractor Factory, which on October 5 was hit by 700 Stuka sorties. The attack wiped out several Soviet infantry regiments in and around the factory.***

an underground train entering a station. Unbelievable, one cannot understand anything anymore. We continue to jump from shell crater to shell crater, from earth pile to the remains of a wall. Now quickly to the remains of a house, to the next cover. And once again they come down on us – Soviet shells. Onward. We have to seize the last hundred metres to the Volga!

"But the Russians are hanging on and bitterly contesting every hole in the earth and every pile of rubble. Enemy snipers hit us in the flank and inflict bloody losses. They are hiding all around, but we cannot see them.

"When it slowly gets dark, and the view is too unclear to make out anything, we stop the attack and take up defensive positions to safeguard us from any nightly surprises. There is no rest. We have to recover the killed and prepare the wounded for transport to the rear. I make an evening report with sketches and send it to battalion HQ. No one has any rest, we are all wide awake and ready for anything. And in the back of our minds is the question, what will tomorrow bring? Throughout the entire night 'the devil is loose' with us. Our food carriers have been taken out by the Russians behind us, to our rear! The Russians rise up out of tunnels, which lead behind our frontline and then in the dark wait for runners, ammunition and food carriers, and overwhelm and kill them.

"OCTOBER 26 The Soviets are still lurking in some buildings of the Bread Factory in front of us and to our right, so we attack again today. We prepare ourselves, look at each other once more and check watches. Metre by metre we advance slowly. We take hours to reach the next objective! We set up covering fire and work our way forward, pressing close to the earth and using even the smallest bit of cover. And we continuously look around us; where are the Russians lurking? And then we again see them, directly in front of us, only 50 metres way, the heads of Red Army men! Their gunfire flies round our ears. Again we suffer dead and wounded! My God, how many today will have to be recovered and dragged back tonight in the darkness? To the right of us the motorcycle riflemen attack again. We hear them, their cries and their firing. And over us all hangs the black smoke from burning buildings, burning oil tanks and the glowing remains of the factory halls.

"And then suddenly, again our Stukas are coming. We fire off white flares so they are able to recognize our forward lines and drop their bombs on the enemy as close as possible to us. Everywhere white and yellowish-white flares rise to the sky. How can the planes possibly recognize where the German outposts are? They circle and then suddenly go into a dive. With a deafening howl of sirens they come diving down. Far in front of us, directly in front of us and, my God, also behind us! Giant craters are made as fountains of earth darken the sky. Visibility is nil. Then machine-gun fire. Cries, shouts – engine noises!

"A Soviet counterattack. I can make them out, 30 or 40 meters in front of us - bent over, sprinting - without steel helmets, all wearing caps. We open up on them with all our weapons. We need an artillery barrage. Red flares! Quickly, quickly! It comes in howling, followed by mortar projectiles that whir and whistle. Taking cover is no use for the Soviets as the shells land among them. The attack is stopped.

"OCTOBER 27 We assemble again. Though tired to the point of exhaustion, we still have the will to force a decision. Immediately after breaking cover we suffer dead and wounded in the first few meters! Take cover! Where are the guys that are firing on us? Where is the damned fire coming from? There they are, in front of us. Straight in front of us and behind dark piles of earth, behind the remains of walls the group has taken up positions. 'Go! Flank them on the right and left, we will fire on them from the front.' We attack and take them out. They're surren-

▼ ***German StuG III assault guns in Stalingrad in September 1942. During that month one StuG III Ausf F destroyed nine Soviet tanks in 20 minutes in the city.***

▲ ***The administration buildings at the Bread Factory, located south of the Tractor Factory. Most of the factory had been captured by the Germans by October 23.***

dering! We wave at them to come closer, and in the crossfire some manage to reach our positions. They are ordered to lie down.

"By the evening we have finally taken possession of the administration building of the Bread Factory. We wait for a Russian counterattack, it will undoubtedly come. But for the moment all is quiet. Therefore the platoons and groups are organized differently for the night. We set up flanking fire positions among the terrain the Russians will have to use to get close to us. And when they come up, we'll shower them with concentrated fire. We will be safe from surprises out of the housing block halfway to the right of us and from the labyrinthine settlement area. I establish the company command post (CP) directly behind the groups in a potato cellar.

"I am ordered to the battalion CP. I make my way there, moving through a lunar landscape, until I reach the CP in the cellars of the Gun Foundry. I first report the situation of the company to the battalion commander, and then explain about the events of the day's combat. Subsequently I am briefed for tomorrow's attack.

"The battalion commander, Captain Domaschk, will be with the company in person, with all men of the battalion staff. We shake hands and I leave. How long can this man-to-man fighting, this bloodshed at close quarters, be kept up? I do not know. But it surely cannot last much longer, not with these casualties and losses! But perhaps we'll manage the few hundred meters remaining tomorrow, always tomorrow. The Soviets are holding in the steeply falling slopes to the Volga, and no fire can reach them there. And prisoners have indicated that Russian commanders have their bunkers there, too. They are sitting in their rocky slopes and each evening send new men into battle. We are living in holes in the earth. Stalingrad is nearly completely in our hands. Only the bit in front of us remains: a small Soviet bridgehead, which is of paramount importance to the Bolsheviks for the continuation of the defence of this horrid city.

"OCTOBER 28 The morning comes, the sun rises, it will again be a warm day for the time of year. Today, we are to reach and take the banks of the River Volga. Even the battalion commander has a steel helmet and machine pistol, with several staff soldiers following him. Once more we discuss the way the attack is to unfold, and then we assemble, supported by our artillery and all heavy weapons.

We leave our positions and work our way forward metre by metre. But almost at once our attack is spotted by the enemy. Rifle and machine-gun fire slams into us, forcing us to take cover. And then the 'big lumps' arrive: Soviet artillery and heavy mortars. Shells explode and howl in from all sides. I'm hit in the left hand. No time to see if it is serious.

"Onward, onward in any way possible. Don't stop! The men give it everything, all they have in their power, from the experienced sergeant-major by my side, the young corporals and old privates, to the boys that have arrived from our depot unit. In the last building of the housing complex that still belongs to the Bread Factory there is no more resistance. So, as ordered, 'left turn'. On to the collapsed houses in front of us. From there we should be able to see the Volga itself. But we see nothing, we just hear Russian shouts and commands. Then we spot them, 30 metres in front of us, in their positions, well camouflaged. Murderous small-arms fire meets us and forces us to go really low. We crawl into the earth, using any hollow and every pile of earth or rubble. In a bomb crater behind us we collect our wounded and pull the dead out of the hail of Russian bullets. Now we are lying here, so close before the objective, so close to the Volga. It's only 50 metres away. But we cannot advance any further, it is simply impossible. The battalion commander goes back to the rear and promises me that we are to get replacements during the night. But we'll have to hold our position.

▲ ***Soviet infantry in the ruins of Stalingrad armed with PPSh submachine guns, one of the key infantry weapons during the fighting in the city.***

▲ ***The German equivalent of the PPSh was the MP40, but they were usually only issued to squad and platoon commanders, the others having bolt-action rifles.***

"OCTOBER 29 Early in the morning, after a surprise barrage by our artillery, we go in again. But we are immediately forced to take cover in the face of a raging torrent of all sorts of infantry fire. We cannot advance and won't succeed in reaching the steeply descending banks of the Volga and throwing the Bolsheviks back over the river. They offer bitter resistance and do not retreat a metre. From our present positions we can see the bank of the Volga – the ridge before the steeply descending slope – and cover it with our fire. But because we are out in front, we once again suffer terrible losses. We can't even lift our heads to have a look around. The Russians are lying 30 metres opposite us. And behind them their commanders and commissars, and behind them the wide stream, the Volga. And so now, in the warming afternoon sun, we are stuck in our holes and wait for renewed support from the heavy artillery. And then all hell breaks loose. With a cry of 'Hurrah' the Russian infantry storm forth from their positions and try to overrun us. Everybody immediately opens fire. We stop them and force them back. The Soviets are also not capable of forcing us down on our knees. But our losses are heavy. How shall we deal with the next attack? Once again we lie opposite one another and wait for the rapidly falling dusk. Only then can we move freely again and control the open field. As all field telephone lines are either jammed or broken, it is only by radio that contact with battalion can be maintained. I end my 'sitrep' [situation report] with an urgent demand: 'We can only hold here if we get reinforcements.' And immediately battalion replies: 'Hold at all costs! Replacements will be led forward during the early hours of the night.' As we jot down this radio message our machine guns rattle again. Cries, shouts: the Russians are attacking again. As it is not completely dark yet, I can make out the Russians that are storming our positions. Machine pistols bark, 'full auto' is the setting, 'quick-firing rifles' crack, bright tracer rounds are flashing and snaking around us. Hand grenades, machine guns, continuous fire and hand grenades again! But what's going on out there? On the right flank our own people are walking? No, they are Russians. A few men around me jump up to attack them. We jump over our own men and attack into the flank of the advancing Russian infantrymen, firing all the time with our weapons. We throw them out of their trenches and shell holes which beforehand had been in our possession. The Russians flee.

▲ *A German machine gunner searches for targets in Stalingrad. Many German troops found fighting in an urban environment psychologically disorientating.*

"Once again the enemy assault has been repelled; the main line of resistance is in our hands as it was

▼ *One German lieutenant wrote: "There is only a burnt-out wasteland, a wilderness of rubble." Ironically, it had been the Germans who had created such a wasteland.*

before. How often can we do this? I could weep. Who is killed today, lying wounded and unattended in holes in the earth and cover, waiting for the protective cover of the night to be transported away? And there are noises again. Behind us! It is 23:00 hours – rattling, whispering, are those the food carriers already? No, it's the replacements. They are 80 young soldiers from the Field Replacement Battalion led by a young officer, First Lieutenant Ferch. All of them are 18 or 19 years old and haven't fired a round in anger. Added to that are more men from the rear area: convalescents and soldiers returned from leave. Group leaders are also present. My God, how strong we are again all of a sudden. The subordination has been prepared by battalion; we just have to divide them between platoons and groups. This is done quickly. The first lieutenant is older than me, and has come from home to this hell. He is wearing a clean jacket, clearly visible badges of rank, bright uniform collar and officer's cap. The entire night we sit squatting on a few covered stacks

◀ ***German infantry dug in near the grain silo. The machine gun is an MG34, which had a cyclic rate of fire of 900 rounds a minute. Note the ammunition boxes.***

▲ ***One Red Army weapon ill suited to the fighting in Stalingrad was the PTRD 1941 anti-tank rifle, being cumbersome and having poor penetrative capabilities.***

of coals and potatoes. In the fading light of a few candles I brief the lieutenant: the situation, orders for the morning, describe the area in front of us, and inform him of the events of the past few days. We continuously hear the monotonous flood of words from the observer, who is standing on the stairs of the cellar and reports what can be seen and observed outside. 'White flare, 200 metres to our right, muzzle blasts on the east bank of Volga. Rifle fire against the 2nd group!' And so the reports and observations continue throughout the night.

"OCTOBER 30 In the dawn light a Russian artillery bombardment begins. It lasts for 40 minutes. Then, suddenly, the shells land far behind us – the Russians have shifted their fire to the rear. And then they attack. They're jumping from cover to cover. Our position is then subjected to heavy 120mm mortar fire. We return fire with machine guns and hand grenades. We suffer frightful losses, especially among the 'new ones', as we have to come out from our cover to beat back the enemy.' They're coming!'

▲ *A posed shot of a Red Army sniper team in Stalingrad. When a Soviet sniper achieved 40 kills he would receive a "For Bravery" medal and the title "noble sniper".*

▲ *A female Red Army sniper. Just as deadly as their male counterparts, one German officer wrote: "The Russian woman has long been fully prepared for combat duties."*

Cries, shouts in Russian, medics are needed. The Russians break through. We launch an immediate counterattack. First Lieutenant Ferch leads it with two groups. He jumps out of the trench next to me and immediately falls back into it. A 20mm shell has shattered his skull. So the brave first sergeant leads the counterattack, cuts off the Russians that have penetrated our positions and destroys them. Again an enemy attack has been repulsed. Of the lads who arrived last night, many have been killed in their first firefight. They were killed as soon as the first bullets flew. Now we have to recover the dead and wounded. But we have to fight on amidst the many groaning and complaining wounded. In no-man's land there is movement that suggests that the Russians are preparing for a renewed attack. A few comforting words to the moaning wounded, 'wait till dark, then you'll be fetched, then you'll be cared for, then you'll get out of this hell.' But then the Russian artillery opens up again. The earth is quaking with the impacts, fountains of sand and mud pour down on us again and again, blinding us. And they attack again. We request artillery fire. Immediately flares go up 'Red! Enemy attacking!' Finally, after what seems like an eternity, the shells of our artillery scream overhead into the rear areas of the attacking enemy. With this the élan of their attack dies down and the Bolsheviks remain lying down in front of our positions. Slowly the firing dies down, we have control of no-man's land. Slowly it is getting dark; the time has come to prepare measures for later. And still the highest degree of alertness is called for, because between long intermissions the enemy artillery launches surprise bombardments against us. Now the wounded and dead are recovered and sent to the rear. Ammunition to the front, likewise the supplies. The 'evening report' must be compiled. Runners to the battalion command post.

"NOVEMBER 1 The new day begins quietly. We have to hold. There are no new attacks. The Russians also are behaving quietly for the moment, suspiciously quiet. In no-man's land nothing can be seen, which leads to the conclusion that a new attack is imminent. So we busy ourselves in our holes in the earth with improving our positions. We are finally able to clean our weapons and order our tools. All day it remains quiet. We await the coming night.

"We are lying here as if we had been nailed to the ground. At the moment we cannot lift our heads above ground. 'Human requirements' have to be taken care of in the trench. We use a steel helmet, which is then lifted over the edge of the trench with a plank and tipped over. Every time a steel helmet is lifted out of the cover and becomes visible to the enemy, fireworks erupt. And so it is not long before the damaged helmet is unusable even for this purpose. But there are many steel helmets lying around, damaged, torn by shell splinters, bent and twisted.

"Our losses are frightening. From October 28 to today, November 1, we have lost 17 killed and 33 wounded in the company. Then a young lieutenant comes into my hole in the ground, the company command post, and reports to me. Straight out of weapons school, via the replacement unit to the 103rd! For the briefing I order the platoon commanders to me, and so the 'new guy' gets to know them straight away. Now we again have a second officer. This gives me the opportunity to make my

▼ Vasily Zaitsev (extreme left) killed more than 300 Germans at Stalingrad. He died in 1991 and is buried on the Mamayev Kurgan mound in present-day Volgograd.

way to the battalion CP. Once there I report to the battalion commander, Captain Domaschk. I brief him on the situation and report to him in detail about how things are looking with the company. After that I learn something about the 'big picture'. At my father's division (371st Infantry Division) the Soviets are attacking night and day, also with their air force when our fighters are not in the skies. The Russians over there are trying with all their strength and energy to penetrate into the southern part of Stalingrad. But the 371st Infantry Division has repulsed all these attacks. If only I could talk to father once more, also about the situation here with us. He won't know that I am fighting as a company commander in Panzergrenadier Regiment 103 for the last few metres to the Volga!"

German tactics

At Stalingrad German commanders had to make thorough preparations, particularly in synchronizing fire support. It was better for all commanders to meet and, using an aerial photograph, quickly work out who would do what rather than relying on

▲ *Civilians in Stalingrad. Initially they were forbidden to leave the city as Stalin believed their presence would stiffen the resistance of the Red Army defenders.*

▶ ***Civilians were used to dig trenches and build fortifications, although at the end of September women and children were allowed to cross the Volga to safety.***

detailed written orders. Before the attack, it was counterproductive to withdraw to protect oneself from the artillery barrage and air strikes. The Germans discovered that, when they did that, the Russians moved forward onto the vacated ground. To gain surprise, it was better to attack early in the morning without preparatory fire and then call in adjusted fire as required. It was also preferable to halt and regroup upon attaining limited objectives because that was the best way to coordinate the various arms and weapon systems. Informing subordinates of what the daily objective was helped in this process. On occasion, it was necessary to organize an armoured assault group consisting of tanks, halftracks and other units as required. Nevertheless, the purpose of this was still to maximize the infantry combat power and provide one unified command. One constant was the engineers' active participation. To exploit success, reserves had to be kept close by at the ready and placed under some cover.

Severely restricted fields of fire and limited observation made defence in Stalingrad very difficult. It proved advisable to use a main line of resistance and to keep reserves at the ready. Heavy mortars used as batteries were very helpful, and the heavy and light infantry cannons were particularly valuable in the defence. Nightly harassment fire by artillery and heavy infantry weapons had to be coordinated in a division fire plan. These fires had the best results between dusk and about 22:30 hours, when the enemy carried out most of its logistics activities. It was important to continue to rapidly shift from the offence to the defence. This meant rapidly digging in, organizing a defence in depth, creating new reserves, deploying heavy weapons, planning defensive fires, and if possible, laying mines quickly and contacting flank units.

The fighting in Stalingrad required converting the German infantry squad into an assault squad. The latter required standard light machine guns and riflemen, but also needed sharpshooters, automatic weapons, various kinds of grenades and explosive charges. Those squads also required support from one or more StuG assault guns, several halftracks

armed with 20mm anti aircraft or 37mm anti-tank guns. An engineer squad also had to be available to remove mines and tank obstacles. In addition, after-action reports recommended that a flamethrower squad be available. The heavy infantry weapons required sufficient ammunition and rifle grenades proved very helpful. To counter enemy snipers or marksmen, the trench mirror was indispensable. And finally, assault squads required enough radios for efficient communications.

Massive destruction severely restricted movement through the city. Avoiding streets reduced casualties. Since all resistance "nests" had to be reduced, it was preferable to organize the advance in depth. It was important not to become imprisoned by linear conceptions of combat because units had to manoeuvre backwards, forwards or sideways to cover a flank. In Stalingrad, a good deal of effort was expended reducing resistance "nests" (mainly cellars). Particularly dangerous areas were street corners and flat, open spaces. Those areas without cover demanded smokescreens to facilitate crossing.

▲ ***Soviet troops in Stalingrad were ill-disposed to wearing helmets, believing them to be an indication of cowardice. They preferred the* pilotka *(side cap).***

A glimpse at the German 71st Infantry Division demonstrates the difficulties of such combat. On September 24, it advanced against heavy resistance towards the theatre and command post buildings. Soldiers had to fight through the remains of each house. POWs said that traditional concepts such as squads and platoons had generally lost their meaning by this time. Red Army soldiers were led by proven officers and commissars and were still receiving active assistance from civilians.

Neither side took many prisoners. Russian casualties were high. The 71st Division's artillery engaged Russian craft on the Volga and managed to silence two enemy batteries, destroying a large ammunition depot on the east bank of the river.

The 24th Panzer Division was satisfied with its artillery regiment but complained that it had limited supplies, particularly ammunition. In the attack, divisional artillery was not that helpful. To limit friendly fire casualties, only one gun was allowed to provide fire support for an assault squad. At division, the major problem was the inability to observe. At Stalingrad, the key artillery units were observation battalions that were army troops placed at the disposal of a corps headquarters. They set up their specialized equipment at the few quality observation spots. For example, on September 28, as LI Corps advanced against the Red October and Barrikady factories, its observation battalions identified 22 enemy batteries and engaged 14 with counter-battery fire.

It was still possible to coordinate fire, and the armoured artillery regiment's armoured observation vehicles proved ideal in supplementing the work of the observation battalions. It was too dangerous for the infantry divisions' observation sections to attempt to do this. At first the armoured artillery reconnaissance assets only had radios. They were, however, in Stalingrad long enough to supplement their signals with wire. Spotters had to be on the tallest surviving structure in the sector – it was much more efficient to run wire up to its "nest".

German weapons performance

The Germans had several types of tracked anti-tank guns. They were very useful in Stalingrad, where rubble and partially knocked-down walls provided them with cover up to their hulls. Deployed hull defilade behind infantry, they proved highly effective. Deploying them in the frontline, however, made these open-top vehicles too vulnerable to enemy artillery, hand grenades and sharpshooters. In the defence they had to be kept even farther back because of enemy observers. Ammunition resupply was difficult for the vehicles.

Regarding individual weapons and systems, the 50mm anti-tank vehicle gained notice not only for its insufficient firepower but also for its lack of manouevrability. In autumn 1942, German Army divisions still did not have telescopic rifles. The 24th Panzer Division concluded that there were numerous instances when marksmen with telescopic sights could have suppressed resistance nests and prevented casualties. The 80mm mortar proved very effective, as did the 75mm infantry cannon. The 150mm infantry cannon, however, was too difficult to manoeuvre in the rubble.

Red Army performance

The Red Army was equally tenacious in the fighting in the city. Stalin committed his soldiers, civilians and resources to a battle of attrition. Large numbers would be needed to offset the lack of training and poor leadership of the civilians and militia. He had to simply outlast his opponent. He used what he had, an abundance of civilians, with little regard of the cost. This ruthlessness was no doubt sewn into the fabric of the Red Army officer corps. In one instance a division commander at Stalingrad chose to deal with low morale, low because of the hopelessness of the situation, by calling a formation and shooting every tenth man until his magazine was empty. The individual soldiers merely stood by hoping they would not be chosen.

The manifestation of excess began early for the new recruits. The Russians, having committed the last of their available reserves, continued to piecemeal untrained militia into existing units. The replacements disembarked from trains near the city and boarded boats to cross the Volga. As the ferries crossed the nearly mile-wide river, German aircraft and artillery attacked them. Armed Russian escorts prevented mass desertion in the face of such carnage. In some instances when fear overpowered the new

▶ ***One of the hundreds of shattered buildings in Stalingrad. In such structures German and Red Army troops would occupy different floors at the same time.***

recruits they jumped into the water to escape the impending slaughter, only to have the armed escorts shoot them for desertion. Over a month long period, this method ferried nearly 100,000 replacements to the Sixty-Second Army.

Stalin's new willingness to fight often went to the extreme. Lieutenant Anton Dragan demonstrated the fanatical commitment and the depth to which it penetrated the officer corps. German attacks left his battalion decimated and leaderless. Dragan took charge of the remnants of the unit and established a strongpoint in a three-story complex referred to as the Nail Factory. After several days and countless attacks by the Germans, Dragan and his men ran out of ammunition. Still Dragan refused to leave. The Germans, growing impatient, fired a devastating barrage of artillery and tank rounds to collapse the building. To Dragan the significance of the building was simply that the Germans wanted it. The building was not tactically significant and he could have saved his battalion to fight another day, yet he chose to stay. The Germans, satisfied that the strongpoint was destroyed, continued on their mission, leaving Dragan for dead. Dragan and only six survivors of his battalion eventually got back to Russian lines.

The Russians were not just required to defend, they were also ordered to attack. While they had supported the elastic defence, Russians officers also believed in attrition warfare and were not averse to counterattacking, even when the situation warranted a more cautious approach. Chuikov believed that the active defence was essential to his success and coined the phrase, "constant, close and combined operation" to describe his tactic in the defence of Stalingrad. Chuikov's "hyperactive" defence was a constant series of attacks to prevent the Germans from consolidating gains. While successful, this method led to high casualties, as the Russians often did not have the requisite superiority in firepower to gain an advantage in an attack. And as most Red Army soldiers were newly arrived, their performance would certainly be questionable. Chuikov

▶ *German infantry in Stalingrad in October. By this date losses were mounting alarmingly. The 94th Infantry Division, for example, had only 535 frontline troops.*

▼ *A German squad rushes forward during an attack against a Red Army position. These assaults were usually preceded by aerial bombing, called "house warmings".*

▲ ***Russian troops fighting in the ruins of the Red October Factory in October. Note the PPSh-41 submachine guns and a soldier who had just been shot.***

proposed that by constantly attacking they could wear down the enemy and destroy him.

Rather than waning, Russian resistance continued to stiffen in the face of massive German firepower. By 17 October, the Sixty-Second Army had lost 13,000 troops, or nearly 25 percent of its combat power, defending Stalingrad. While the bravery of Red Army personnel was beyond reproach, heavy losses were incurred when assaults were made with little or no air or artillery support

A newly formed reserve division, the 284th, for example, held a line just east of the Mamayev Kurgan on September 23.This hill, now occupied by German forces, offered them a key panoramic view of the city and a majority of Soviet troop movements.The 284th Siberian Division's mission was to hold its line and if possible take the hill from the Germans.The division attacked several times up hill with at best parity in artillery but virtually no air support. In one day of fighting the 284th lost over 300 soldiers.The division's soldiers, like most of the defenders of Stalingrad, had little formalized training. A new recruit's primary means of training was during actual battle, and the losses should not have been surprising.The Russians seemed willing to accept massive loss of life itself to retain a city that was initially of little concern to either army.

◄ ***A Pak 38 anti-tank gun in action at Stalingrad. The high fragmentation of its high-explosive shell made it useful against groups of dug-in enemy troops.***

Fighting in Stalingrad was house-to-house and block-by-block. As the Germans entered houses or buildings from the lower floors, Russian defenders retained the floors above.The Russians used satchel charges, grenades and automatic weapons to retain rooms but were often short of supplies. Often, while under attack, desperate Russian defenders would risk picking up explosives thrown by the attacking German soldiers and throwing them back before the fuses detonated.

The exact number of Russian casualties at Stalingrad may never be known. Axis losses are estimated to be 250,000-300,000 troops, along with 1000 tanks and 1800 guns. Estimates for Soviet losses are four to eight times this number.

▲ ***A German machine-gun team near the River Don in early November 1942, just before the Red Army's offensive ripped the Axis front wide open.***

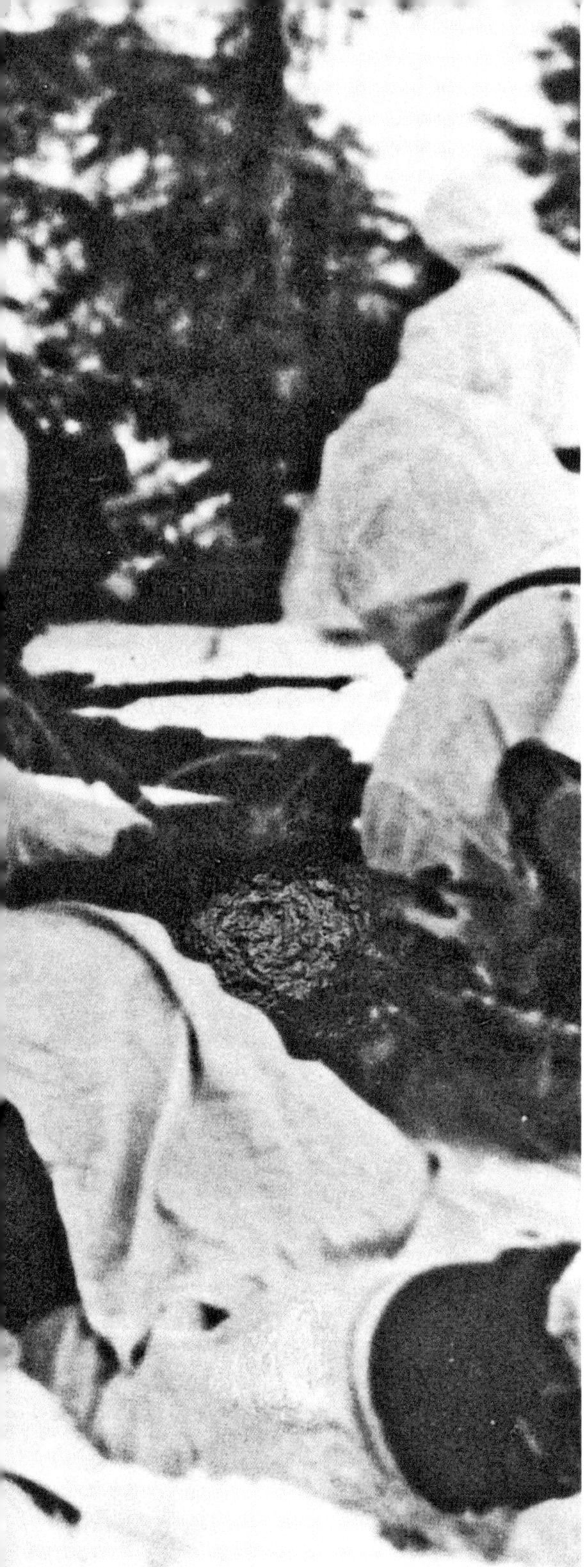

Phase V: Red Hammer

Following weeks of bloody urban combat in Stalingrad itself, early on November 19, 1942, Zhukov launched Operation Uranus. The attacking Soviet armies brushed aside all opposition, and then encircled the German Sixth Army in the Stalingrad Pocket. The Romanian armies holding the German flanks were shattered as hundreds of Soviet tanks drove deep into the Axis rear. Paulus requested permission to withdraw the Sixth Army from Stalingrad, but Hitler ordered him to stand fast. On November 23 the pocket had been sealed by the Soviets and the Sixth Army was trapped. The German besiegers had now become the besieged in the grandly titled "Fortress Stalingrad".

November 2

SOUTHERN USSR, *LAND WAR*
In the Caucasus, the 3rd Panzer Division nears Ordzhonikidze, the most south-easterly point reached by the Wehrmacht in World War II. The first snows begin to fall in this sector.

November 4

USSR, *STRATEGY*
The Stavka prepares Operation Saturn, the destruction of the Italian Eighth Army by the Southwestern and Voronezh Fronts, leading to the Red Army reaching the River Dnieper and cutting off Army Groups A and B. It will be spearheaded by the First Guards and Sixth Armies.

November 11

SOUTHERN USSR, *LAND WAR*
The German Sixth Army commences its final offensive at Stalingrad, preceded by artillery and air strikes. It succeeds in taking most of the Red October factory and isolating the Soviet 138th Division south of the Barrikady factory. By the evening, the Sixty-Second Army occupies three small pockets along the Volga: in the north 1000 troops at Rynok and Spartakovka; in the centre 500 troops near the Barrikady factory; and in the south 45,000 troops and 20 tanks.

November 17

SOUTHERN USSR, *LAND WAR*
In Stalingrad, the German assaults are annihilating the Sixty-Second Army. The group at Rynok and Spartakovka has been reduced to 300 troops at the hands of the 16th Panzer Division. Another problem now besets the Soviets: ice on the Volga.

▲ ***Paulus observes the Sixth Army's final assault at Stalingrad. It was a series of hammer blows designed to crush the Soviet Sixty-Second Army.***

Ice on the river stopped boat traffic three days ago, as the river was impassable. Efforts to air-drop supplies to the Sixty-Second Army have come to nothing, because the Red Army has such a slender strip of land and most of the material falls into German hands. Luftwaffe reconnaissance has detected Soviet build-ups to the northwest of the city, which worry Paulus.

▼ ***"I know about the difficulties of the battle for Stalingrad and about the loss of troops ... however, the difficulties are even greater for the Russians." Hitler to Paulus, November 17, 1942.***

November 18

SOUTHERN USSR, *LAND WAR*
The eve of Operation Uranus. The Stavka has amassed the following forces for the offensive: Southwestern Front (First Guards, Twenty-First and Fifth Tank Armies, 3rd Guards Cavalry and 4th Tanks Corps, and Seventeenth and Second Air Armies) – 398,000 troops, 6500 artillery pieces, 150 Katyushas, 730 tanks and 530 aircraft; Don Front (Twenty-Fourth, Sixty-Fifth and Sixty-Sixth Armies and Sixteenth Air Army) – 307,000 troops, 5300 artillery pieces, 150 Katyushas, 180 tanks and 260 aircraft; and Stalingrad Front (Fifty-First, Fifty-Seventh, Sixty-Second and Sixty-Fourth Armies, 4th and 13th Mechanized Corps, 4th Cavalry Corps and Eighth Air Army) – 429,000 troops, 5800 artillery pieces, 145 Katyushas and 650 tanks. Facing the Don and Southwestern Fronts is the Romanian Third Army (100,000 troops), while the Romanian Fourth Army (70,000 troops) faces the Soviet Fifty-First and Fifty-Seventh Armies. These are extremely weak formations to have as flank protection for the Fourth Panzer and Sixth Armies at Stalingrad.

November 19

SOUTHERN USSR, *LAND WAR*
Operation Uranus begins as the Southwestern and Don Fronts attack the Romanian Third Army. The Romanians defend stoutly and at first the Soviet Fifth Tank, Twenty-First and Sixty-Fifth Armies make slow progress. However, an assault by the 1st and 26th Tank Corps of the Fifth Tank Army eventually rips a hole in the Romanian front, through which the Soviets pour. By the end of the day the Romanians have suffered a staggering 55,000 casualties. The German XXXXVIII Panzer Corps is ordered to restore the situation, but attacks by the Romanian 1st Armoured Division north of Zhirkovski and 22nd Panzer Division from Peschany are costly failures. Paulus, ordered to restore his northern flank, decides to employ his three panzer divisions.

November 20

SOUTHERN USSR, *LAND WAR*
The Romanian 1st Armoured Division is destroyed by the Soviet Fifth Tank Army, which also mauls the 22nd Panzer Division as it falls back to the Chir. At Stalingrad a fuel shortage delays the advance of XIV Panzer Corps. To the south, the Romanian Fourth Army is hit by the Soviet Fifty-First, Fifty-Seventh and Sixty-Fourth Armies. As they retreat, only the German 29th Panzergrenadier and 297th Infantry Divisions hold up the attack.

GERMANY, ARMED FORCES
Hitler creates Army Group Don, led by Field Marshal Manstein, which is ordered to safeguard positions on the Chir and Don and restore the Sixth Army's flanks.

November 21

SOUTHERN USSR, *LAND WAR*
The German flanks behind Stalingrad are collapsing. The Fifth Tank Army brushes aside the 24th Panzer Division near the Don bridges.

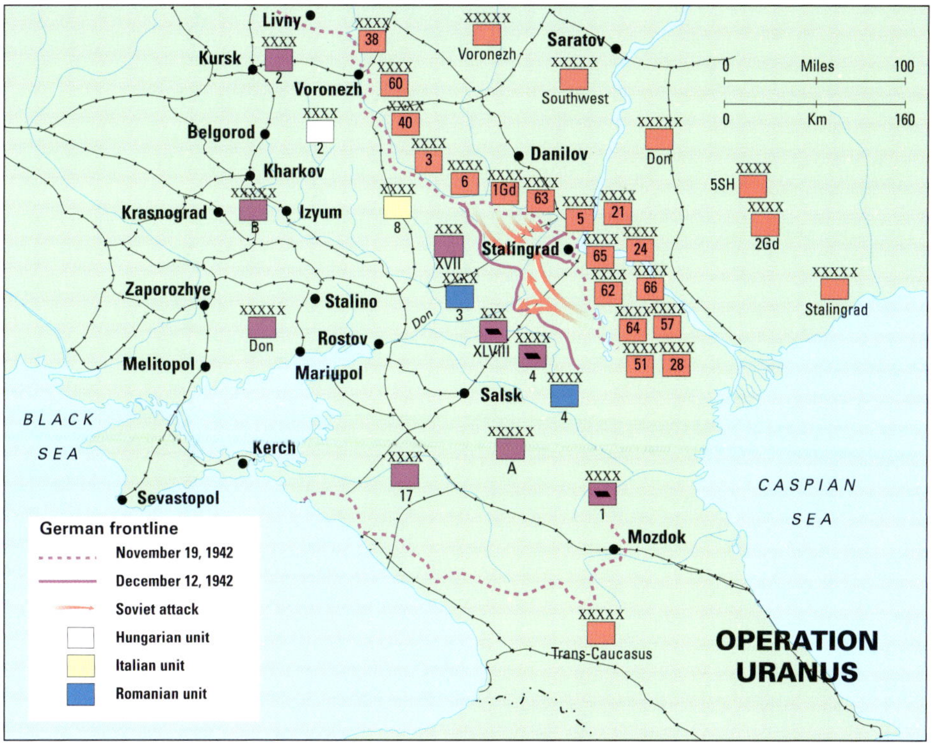

Army – he has just 298 transport aircraft for the task of landing 355 tonnes (350 tons) of supplies a day (he needs at least 500 transports).

NOVEMBER 23

SOUTHERN USSR, *LAND WAR*

Some 27,000 Romanian soldiers surrender, signalling the collapse of their Third Army, which has lost 90,000 casualties since the start of Uranus. Red Army units link up at Kalach, thus trapping the German Sixth, part of the Fourth Panzer and what is left of the Romanian Fourth Armies – 256,000 German troops, 11,000 Romanians, 100 tanks, 1800 artillery pieces, 10,000 motor vehicles and 23,000 horses.

General Paulus puts his forces into a giant hedgehog defensive posture as part of the grandly titled "Fortress Stalingrad". However, he has serious problems. First, establishing an effective defensive perimeter at Stalingrad is difficult due to a desperate shortage of infantry and the lack of prepared positions. Second, to the south and west lies almost completely treeless, shelter-free steppes. Third, a lack of fuel prevents the rapid deployment of his three panzer and three panzer-grenadier divisions as mobile reserves. Fourth, a general shortage of artillery ammunition also weakens the German defence.

NOVEMBER 24

CENTRAL USSR, *LAND WAR*

The eve of Operation Mars, Zhukov's plan to destroy enemy forces along the Moscow axis in the Rzhev salient (the German Ninth Army). This will be no easy task, as General Model's Ninth Army has built strong defences around the salient and fortified all cities and towns along the salient's edges, especially the key cities of Rzhev, Belyi and Sychevka.

SOUTHERN USSR, *AIR WAR*

Luftwaffe chief Hermann Göring assures Hitler that his aircraft can supply the Stalingrad Pocket. Zeitzler does not believe this boast. Wolfram von Richthofen, commander of the 4th Air Fleet, believes it will be impossible to supply the Sixth

NOVEMBER 25

CENTRAL USSR, *LAND WAR*

Operation Mars begins as the Soviet Twentieth, Thirty-First, Thirty-Ninth, Twenty-Second, Forty-First and Third Shock Armies smash into German positions. The Soviets make gains at Molodi Tud, Belyi and Velikiye Luki.

SOUTHERN USSR, *LAND WAR*

The Soviets have consolidated an inner ring around the German pocket at Stalingrad, consisting of the Twenty-First, Twenty-Fourth, Fifty-Seventh, Sixty-Second, Sixty-Fourth, Sixty-Fifth and Sixty-Sixth Armies – 490,000 troops.

NOVEMBER 27

CENTRAL USSR, *LAND WAR*

The Soviet 6th Tank Corps halts due to supply difficulties as the Twenty-Second and Thirty-Ninth Armies try to bludgeon their way forward. The result is heavy German and Soviet losses. Fierce battles continue around Belyi and Velikiye Luki.

NOVEMBER 30

CENTRAL USSR, *LAND WAR*

The Soviet 6th Tank Corps is destroyed near Osuga. At Belyi, the 1st and 20th Panzer Divisions force back the Forty-First Army.

SOUTHERN USSR, *LAND WAR*

Group Hollidt engages the Soviet Fifth Tank Army on the River Chir.

► *Troops of XXXV Corps, Italian Eighth Army, which held a sector of the River Don north-west of Stalingrad.*

26

Operation Uranus

On November 19, 1942, the Red Army launched Operation Uranus, a giant pincer movement whose jaws snapped shut at Kalach five days later, trapping the German Sixth Army in Stalingrad.

It was axiomatic that the Red Army preferred to carry out its major offensives in winter, because its troops were accustomed to that season, and were very well equipped and trained for it. Casualties from the cold were an exception in the Red Army (soldiers with frostbite were punished severely). Even in the harsh winter of 1941–42, the Russians were able to spend many days in the snow, protected only by simple windbreaks, without detriment to their health.

In the spring of 1942, Hitler prevailed on the Third Reich's allies to provide additional combat forces to augment the German armies. Romania, Hungary and Italy all reluctantly consented to deploy additional forces on the Eastern Front, though they each insisted that their contingents fight under their own army headquarters rather than as separate divisions in German corps and armies. By early August, 36 allied divisions were committed in the southern section of the front, roughly 40 percent of the total number of Axis divisions in that region. Even though German liaison staffs were assigned to these forces, the combat effectiveness of the allied armies was generally poor. By relegating friendly forces to purely defensive missions along the German flanks, the German High Command thought to minimize the demands placed on these forces while still conserving Wehrmacht divisions for crucial combat roles.

Throughout the early summer, the forces posted along Army Group B's northern flank had little difficulty in fending off Soviet assaults. A German Second Army after-action report on July 21, 1942, following the defeat of Soviet counterattacks near Voronezh, was particularly reassuring. Written at the request of the General Staff's Training Branch in Berlin, and circulated throughout the German Army's higher echelons, it allayed lingering fears caused by the Red Army's winter successes in 1941–42. "Russian infantry in the attack is even worse than before," the report began. "Much massing, greater vulnerability to artillery and mortar fire and to flanking manoeuvre. Scarcely any more night attacks." This report brightened the prospects for successful defence along Army Group B's northern flank.

◀ ***Russian T-34s on the eve of Uranus. When the offensive was launched, the tanks were followed by Soviet cavalrymen armed with submachine guns.***

Reasons for concern

Despite this reassurance, Army Group B's left wing remained vulnerable. Hitler's own interest in this potential weakness began in early spring, when he ordered that the Second Army be reinforced with several hundred anti-tank guns as an additional guarantee against the collapse of Blue's northern shield. In anticipation of its defensive operations, Second Army also had been assigned numerous engineer detachments, labour units and Organization Todt work parties for general construction and fortification. After its successful attack on Voronezh in early July, Second Army attempted to fortify its portion of the exposed flank using these assets throughout the remainder of the summer.

To the east beyond Second Army, however, the Don flank was held by troops of the Hungarian Second Army, the Italian Eighth Army and the Romanian Third Army. Other Romanian formations, temporarily under the command of Fourth Panzer Army, held the open flank south of Stalingrad. As expected, these forces proved to be mediocre in combat, leading German commanders to be even more uneasy about this long, exposed sector. By September 1942, General Maximilian von Weichs, the commander of Army Group B, regarded his northern flank to be so

◀ ***Axis formations that faced these T-34 tanks during Uranus were severely understrength. In the north the 22nd Panzer Division, for example, had only 30 tanks.***

endangered that he ordered special German "intervention units" (*Eingreifgruppen*) rotated into reserve behind the German- and allied-held portions of his left wing.

The use of intervention units was not new to German defensive doctrine. In fact, the elastic defence doctrine of 1917 and 1918 had required that intervention divisions be used to reinforce deliberate counterattacks against particularly stubborn enemy penetrations. In late 1942, however, the role of these units went beyond counterattack. They could also provide advance reinforcement to threatened sectors since, according to General Weichs' explanation, the Russians "seldom were able to conceal preparations for attack." Thus, the intervention units could support faltering allied contingents, hopefully steeling their resistance until additional help could arrive.

In October, General Zeitzler, the new Chief of the Army General Staff, began to echo Weichs' concerns. In a lengthy presentation to Hitler, Zeitzler argued that the allied lines between Voronezh and Stalingrad constituted "the most perilous sector of the Eastern Front", a situation that posed "an enormous danger which must be eliminated". Although Hitler made sympathetic noises, he refused to accept Zeitzler's conclusions and ordered no major changes to German deployments or missions.

Even though the Führer rejected Zeitzler's recommendation that German forces withdraw from Stalingrad, he did authorize minor actions to help shore up the allied armies. One of these measures was the interspersing of additional German units (primarily anti-tank battalions) among the allied divisions. In accordance with Hitler's defensive instructions, if the allied units were overrun these few German units were to "stand fast and limit the enemy's penetration or breakthrough. By holding out in this way, they should create more favourable conditions for our counterattack." Another protective measure was the repositioning of a combined German–Romanian panzer corps behind the Romanian Third Army. This unit, XLVIII Panzer Corps, consisted of only an untried Romanian armoured division and a battle-worn, poorly equipped German panzer division. Weak as it was, this corps was not placed under the control of the Romanians or even Weichs. Rather, it was designated as a special Führer Reserve under the personal direction of Hitler and

therefore could not be committed to combat without first obtaining his release. Finally, from October onwards, German signal teams were placed throughout the allied armies so the German High Command could monitor the day-to-day performance of those forces without having to rely on reports from the allies themselves. These and other measures were not executed without some friction, however: the Italians, for example, rejected German suggestions for improving their defensive positions.

The allied units were not the only soft spots on the defensive flank. By autumn, several newly raised German divisions, hastily consigned to Army Group B in June in order to flesh out its order of battle, were also causing some concern. For example, barely days before its preliminary June attack on Voronezh to secure the German flank, Second Army had received six brand-new German divisions. Although game enough in their initial attacks, these units quickly began to unravel due to poor training and inexperienced leadership. In one case, the 385th Infantry Division reportedly suffered "unnecessarily high losses," including half of its company commanders and five of six battalion commanders in just six weeks, due to deficient training. This fiery baptism ruined these divisions for later defensive use. The loss of so many personnel in such a short period of time left permanent scars, traumatizing the divisions before time and battle experience could produce new leaders and heal the units' psychological wounds. Second Army assessed the situation on October 1, 1942, and informed Army Group B that these once-new divisions were no longer fully reliable even for limited defensive purposes, and that heavy defensive fighting might well stampede them. Unless they could be pulled out of the line for rest and rehabilitation, these divisions, which accounted for nearly half of Second Army's total infantry strength, could only be trusted in the defence of small, quiet sectors.

▼ Throughout the autumn hundreds of T-34s had been ferried south to the Uranus staging areas, so that when the offensive began the Red Army had over 1500 tanks.

▲ *Red Army tank* **desant** *troops during Uranus. Well equipped for winter warfare, tank* **desant** *troops rode into battle clinging to the outside of tanks.*

The German southern offensive thus trusted its long northern flank to a conglomeration of listless allied and battle-weary German units. Like the forces farther north on the defensive front of Army Groups Centre and North, these armies were stretched taut, manning thin lines with few reserves beyond insubstantial local forces. Barely strong enough to hold small probing attacks at bay during the summer and early autumn, these armies lacked the strength to meet a major Russian offensive.

The storm clouds gather

As autumn wore on, the dire predictions began to become a reality as more and more Soviet units appeared in southern Russia. The Germans used all-source intelligence, but much of their success at the operational and tactical levels resulted from their ability to intercept Soviet radio traffic. They could pick up newly deployed units; however, the Germans did not know the scope of the deployment or where or when the Soviets would attack. Hitler thought the attack would be against Rostov. OKH still believed the major attack would be against Army Group Centre, even though more and more units appeared in the south. Finally, they detected a new Soviet Southwest Front headquarters and, on October 12 concluded that an attack in the near future against the Romanian Third Army could cut the railroad to Stalingrad. If that happened, it would threaten the German forces farther east, forcing them to withdraw from Stalingrad.

To summarize developments: Hitler had sent the strongest force available towards an objective that would not necessarily win the war. That force could not be logistically supported and had advanced into an ever-expanding space against an opponent that was gaining, not losing, strength. He had sent his most powerful army into Stalingrad, where it basically destroyed its combat power in costly attacks that played into the enemy's hands. And finally, although intelligence indicated the probability of a major Red Army counteroffensive, the Nazi military leadership resorted to conducting merely cosmetic measures to stiffen Sixth Army's flanks.

▲ ***German troops prepare barbed-wire defences on the Don before the Soviet attack. When it came, the broad tracks of the Soviet T-34s crushed the barbed wire.***

Stalin had dispatched two of the Stavka's most capable representatives, Generals Aleksandr Vasilevsky and Georgi Zhukov, to oversee operations in southern Russia. On October 4, they conducted a conference that began the planning process for what would be Operation Uranus, the counteroffensive against the German Sixth Army.

Despite the indifferent network of railroads available, the Stavka had succeeded in assembling the troops for the operation in utmost secrecy, mostly by night marches. The plan, which had been developed by General Zhukov and other officers at GHQ, was to be executed by General Rokossovsky's Don Front (three armies) and General Yeremenko's Stalingrad Front (five armies). Approximately one million men and 900 tanks were to conduct a classic double envelopment of the German Sixth Army by breaking through the hapless Romanian Third and Fourth Armies. The two Soviet front commanders had distinguished themselves in the defence of Moscow the year before.

The two fronts were to strike at the weak German flanks, northwest and south of Stalingrad, and envelop the German forces that were still battling in the city. Mobile units on Rokossovsky's right would launch the main penetration from the Serafimovich bridgehead. These troops were assigned the difficult mission of striking rapidly across the Don bend and then recrossing the river to attack Kalach from the west. Simultaneously, Rokossovsky's centre and left would launch holding attacks from other Don bridgeheads and frontal attacks between the Don and Volga. A mobile force from the Southwest Front (commanded by General Vatutin) would cover the right flank of the main penetration and strike to the south towards the Chir River. These troops would cut the Morozovski-Stalingrad railroad, the principal line of communication of the Germans at Stalingrad. The Red Army in Stalingrad would increase its activity so as to draw attention in that direction. In the south Yeremenko's mobile forces would strike to the northwest, cut the Kotelnikov-Stalingrad railroad, and drive on to Kalach to establish contact with Rokossovsky's divisions.

Luftflotte IV had been weakened considerably by months of intensive combat. By October, the Red Air Force had wrested air superiority from the Germans as both more and newer aircraft arrived. In addition,

▲ ***The Romanians managed to halt the first attack of Soviet infantry, seen here, but were cut to pieces when the Soviets sent in their tanks*** **en masse.**

as the Germans captured more and more of Stalingrad, the Red Air Force could more easily bomb the city. The Stavka dispatched General A.A. Novikov, Commander of the Red Army Air Force, to help coordinate air operations for Uranus. He became such a valued team member that when he stated that the air forces were not yet prepared, Zhukov delayed the opening of the offensive.

Timing was critical for the counteroffensive. Zhukov and Vasilevsky waited for the German Sixth Army to expend its combat power in Stalingrad. They also waited for the Allied offensives to succeed in North Africa. By waiting until November 19, they allowed the ground to freeze, giving their armour greater mobility.

The Soviets' artillery preparation was short but powerful, after which the offensive launched at 08:50 hours. Three armoured and three cavalry corps of the Don Front broke out of the Serafimovich bridgehead after an artillery bombardment. On the 20th, two motorized and one cavalry corps of the Stalingrad Front broke through the lightly held German positions south of Stalingrad and reached the railroad the next day. Over the next few days these two attacks overran the disorganized Romanians and closed the ring by joining forces at Kalach on the 23d. During the next week the Soviets exploited their breakthroughs and by December 1 they had taken 65,000 prisoners and captured or destroyed 1000 tanks. They had already cleared the area of the Don bend northeast of the Chir and had reached the Don in the south. The headquarters of the Fourth Panzer Army and a few Romanian divisions managed to escape, but the Sixth Army was firmly trapped at Stalingrad.

The tactics of this Russian offensive were typical of all their subsequent operations. The attack was launched by surprise, in several directions simultaneously (seven in all). Thanks to the breakthroughs achieved at different points, and to the rapid drive of mobile units of opportunity through these breaches, the German reserves were speedily isolated from one another and defeated separately. The intervals between adjacent breakthroughs were 16–24km (10–15 miles), permitting the attack groups, after they had broken the German position, to join up with each other by the second day.

▼ *One thing that aided the Soviet attack was the weather. November 19 was a day of snow and mist, which prevented Luftwaffe ground-support missions.*

Red Army tactics

The attack, organized in depth, consisted of two echelons. In the forefront, charged with the execution of the breakthrough, were units of all arms, heavily supported by artillery and by tanks. A second echelon, essentially of armoured and motorized units, had the mission of transforming the tactical into a strategic success. The mobile forces had to reach the rear and the communications of the enemy as rapidly as possible. They were to bypass at once, without stopping, all resistance found, leaving it to be reduced by the units of combined arms following in their wake.

In the Stalingrad battle of encirclement, the depth to which Soviet mobile units reached was 120km (75 miles) for the units of the Don Front and 96km (60 miles) for those of the Stalingrad Front. Their junction was effected in less than five days at a speed of advance of 32km (20 miles) and more per

▲ *A charging Red Army infantryman races past a dead Romanian. Many Romanian soldiers threw down their weapons and surrendered without a fight.*

day, reaching as high as 56km (35 miles) per day in some directions. The infantry's speed of advance was 4.8-9.6km (3-6 miles) per day during the breakthrough and averaged 19.2km (12 miles) in the later advance.

The Romanian defence broke rather easily, allowing Soviet armour to begin the exploitation at about 14:00 hours. Both Romanian armies collapsed, and there were no Axis reserves to stem the tide. The Soviet forces continued their advance nearly unopposed and on November 22 met at Kalach. Some Soviet forces wheeled in against Stalingrad, while others expanded the advance westwards to limit any Axis relief efforts.

German defensive measures

When the Soviet offensive broke, the Germans flung in units in a desperate attempt to stem the Red Army tide. Typical of these efforts was the 2nd Battalion of the German 132nd Infantry Regiment, which in November 1942 occupied defensive positions on the bluffs along the west bank of the Don River near Sirotinskaya. The battalion's three rifle companies averaged 50-60 men, while the strength of the heavy weapons company was 100 men. The combat efficiency and morale of the battalion, which had been fighting in Russia since the beginning of the campaign in June 1941, were high.

The 1st and 2nd Battalions arrived at Verkhne-Buzinovka on the evening of November 19. At the time of their arrival, weak German elements were defending the northern and northwestern outskirts of the village in the face of heavy enemy pressure.

At dawn on November 20 the two battalions launched a counterattack, which was preceded by a heavy artillery preparation. The 2nd Battalion, on the right, was to thrust to the north across a wide, overgrown ravine, while the 1st Battalion was to drive along the road leading northwest towards Platonov. The 1st Battalion's attack was to be supported by assault guns.

As always when they were on the defensive, the Russians proved to be tough opponents. Small detachments forming nests of resistance in the numerous depressions and recesses of the ravine were so well dispersed and concealed that German artillery fire had little effect. As a result, the 2nd Battalion had to form small assault detachments to get the attack under way. The German machine-gun and mortar teams worked together systematically. First, the high trajectory fire of the mortars drove the Russian soldiers from their concealment, then the machine guns pinned them down, and finally the men armed with submachine guns and hand grenades finished them off. As soon as a nest of resistance on one side of the ravine was neutralized, a Russian position on the other side was taken under flanking fire. Simultaneously, other German assault detachments worked their way forward across the bottom of the ravine, where the defenders were pinned down. By alternating punches, as does a boxer, the Germans pushed their opponents back. Towards noon the Russians abandoned the ravine altogether and withdrew northwards. Their casualties had been heavy, and no less than 80 men had been taken prisoner. The enemy forces opposing the 1st Battalion joined the withdrawal, giving way to German pressure.

▲ ***Georgi Zhukov, mastermind behind Uranus, who by November 1942 was deputy supreme commander-in-chief of the Red Army, second only to Stalin.***

This incident was typical of the first phase of the Russian counteroffensive west of Stalingrad, during which higher headquarters, both German and Soviet, often lost contact with their subordinate units.

Caught in the tidal wave of Red Army forces converging upon Kalach from the northwest, individual German units were still launching local counterattacks. They acted according to orders that were long superseded, ignorant of the fact that enemy forces had driven past them and that they were cut off. On the other hand, the Soviets, equally ignorant of the general situation and of the exact frontline demarcations, advanced in the general direction of the northern arm of the pincers in massed columns without security or reconnaissance detachments, apparently under the impression that they were crossing territory that had already been mopped up by their predecessors.

At this time Sixth Army headquarters attempted to tighten its control over all German units in the Stalingrad Pocket. In its effort to direct the employment of every unit, Sixth Army occasionally issued orders that went into too much detail and did not take the local situation sufficiently into account. The commander of the 2nd Battalion, for example, had selected the gently ascending hill west of Verkhne-Golubaya for establishing a defensive position. Higher headquarters, however, ordered him to move his unit to the east bank of Golubaya Creek, as unfavourable a line for setting up a defence position as could be found in that area. The section of the village west of the creek obstructed the battalion's field of fire. The manoeuvring space between the houses lining the east bank of the river and the steep slope adjacent was very narrow. Also disadvantageous was the large gap between the 2nd Battalion and the nearest German unit, which was committed northeast of the village. By noon of 23 November reconnaissance patrols had established contact with that unit, but the gap remained open.

A Russian force, consisting of two infantry battalions, 10 T-34 tanks, and two troops of cavalry approached Verkhne-Golubaya around noon. The 2nd Battalion was exhausted from the recent fighting and hasty withdrawal and, despite the firepower delivered by its heavy weapons emplaced on the

▼ ***Germans captured during the early phases of Uranus. Many were held in special camps and were later used to try to convince their Sixth Army comrades to surrender.***

hills to the east, was unable to prevent the Russian infantry from gradually infiltrating the western section of the village. At 15:00 hours the 10 T-34 tanks emerged from behind the hill situated west of Verkhne-Golubaya and drove straight towards the village. The Germans destroyed four, but the other six managed to penetrate the western section. In the bitter struggle that followed the 2nd Battalion sustained extremely heavy losses. Only a desperate counterattack saved the battalion from destruction.

During the second phase of the Soviet encirclement Sixth Army headquarters made many mistakes. It decided to shorten the defence perimeter in accordance with an integrated plan. During this phase, isolated units which had been fighting at outposts within the pocket gradually established contact with their neighbours. The defence lines solidified, even though the front was far from continuous. In many instances, however, the planning was too hasty and superficial; units were ordered to occupy sectors as if the front were a continuous line. At Verkhne-Golubaya, for example, higher headquarters made the mistake of designating a sector from a map without on-the-spot reconnaissance, thus denying the lower-echelon commanders any

▲ ***While fighting raged to the north and south of Stalingrad, in the city itself the Germans continued to battle the Soviet Sixty-Second Army.***

exercise of initiative. Moreover, since every man would be needed for the defence of the pocket, battalion commanders and below should have been allowed to use their judgement regarding holding specific locations in order to keep casualties low.

The last week of November was marked by several minor engagements similar to the one at Verkhne-Golubaya. During their gradual eastwards withdrawal across the Don towards Stalingrad, German units repeatedly became involved in bitter fighting that flared up suddenly. In the process they slowly drew closer to one another and began to form a continuous front. The troops were subjected to extreme hardships, spending cold nights without sleep, making difficult marches without adequate rations, and fighting without sufficient ammunition against an enemy superior in firepower and tanks.

▼ ***A Red Army truck drives past the bodies of dead Germans to the west of Stalingrad in late November 1942. The Sixth Army was now trapped in the city.***

Often the soil was frozen so solid that the men were unable to dig in. This difficult period was the acid test of whether or not a unit had *esprit de corps* and discipline. Some newly organized divisions, which had recently arrived from Germany, showed early signs of disintegration. Men who lost their leaders discarded their weapons, plundered ration dumps, stole alcoholic beverages and staggered aimlessly over the snow-covered paths. Stragglers and isolated service troops roamed around as fugitives without discipline. On the other hand, the older, seasoned regiments - and they represented the majority - continued to give a good account of themselves, even after their officers had become casualties. Those noncommissioned officers (NCOs) who had participated in innumerable engagements since the crossing of the Bug River in June 1941 formed the backbone of resistance.

In units that still had their officers, the comradeship between officers and enlisted men became closer than ever. The company commanders did their best to provide the men with food and shelter and set an example of endurance and courage. Once the Sixth Army assumed control over all personnel in the pocket, it disbanded those units whose combat value was doubtful and distributed their personnel, as well as any excess service troops and stragglers, to reliable regiments, where high morale and strict discipline prevailed. Even so, the Red Army had achieved a stunning victory and by the end of November 1942 Sixth Army was trapped.

▲ ***A shattered factory in Stalingrad. Despite the great success of Operation Uranus, Soviet troops in the city itself were still very much on the defensive.***

▼ *Ju 52 transport aircraft under Soviet artillery fire at Tatsinskaya airfield. The airfield was finally abandoned in January 1943.*

Phase VI: Relief Efforts Fail

With his army trapped inside a ring of Soviet steel, General Paulus informed Hitler that he only had six days of food for his troops. His men were also suffering from similar shortages of fuel, ammunition and clothing. The Führer assured Paulus that his soldiers would be supplied by air prior to being rescued by a ground assault, but the Luftwaffe proved incapable of supplying the Sixth Army with even a fraction of its needs. In addition, Manstein's relief effort in December 1942 failed. With no hope of relief and forbidden to surrender, the troops of the Sixth Army faced certain death from the enemy, starvation, disease and exposure.

December 3

SOUTHERN USSR, *LAND WAR*

The Soviet Fifth Tank Army has established a bridgehead on the Chir at Nizhne Kalinovski, and the Fifty-First Army assaults the railway at Kotelnikovo, the launch pad of the German Stalingrad relief operation. Units of LVII Panzer Corps (6th Panzer Division) detrain and counterattack, throwing the Soviets back.

December 7

CENTRAL USSR, *LAND WAR*

The Soviet Forty-First Army near Belyi is being encircled, the 19th Panzer Division having cut off the 1st Mechanized and 6th Rifle Corps.

SOUTHERN USSR, *LAND WAR*

The 11th Panzer Division halts the advance of the Soviet Fifth Tank Army near Surovikino. Meanwhile, the Soviet Fifth Shock Army moves up to the Chir Front.

December 9

CENTRAL USSR, *LAND WAR*

The Soviet 1st Mechanized and 6th Rifle Corps are surrounded at Belyi.

SOUTHERN USSR, *LAND WAR*

On the Chir the 11th Panzer Division destroys an enemy bridgehead at Oblivskoye. The Soviet Fifth Tank Army has sustained heavy casualties. Red Army probes against the Stalingrad Pocket have revealed a larger number of trapped Axis troops than was estimated. This forces the Stavka to amend its Operation Saturn, the objective of which is now the destruction of the Italian Eighth Army and isolation of Group Hollidt. Its codename is Little Saturn.

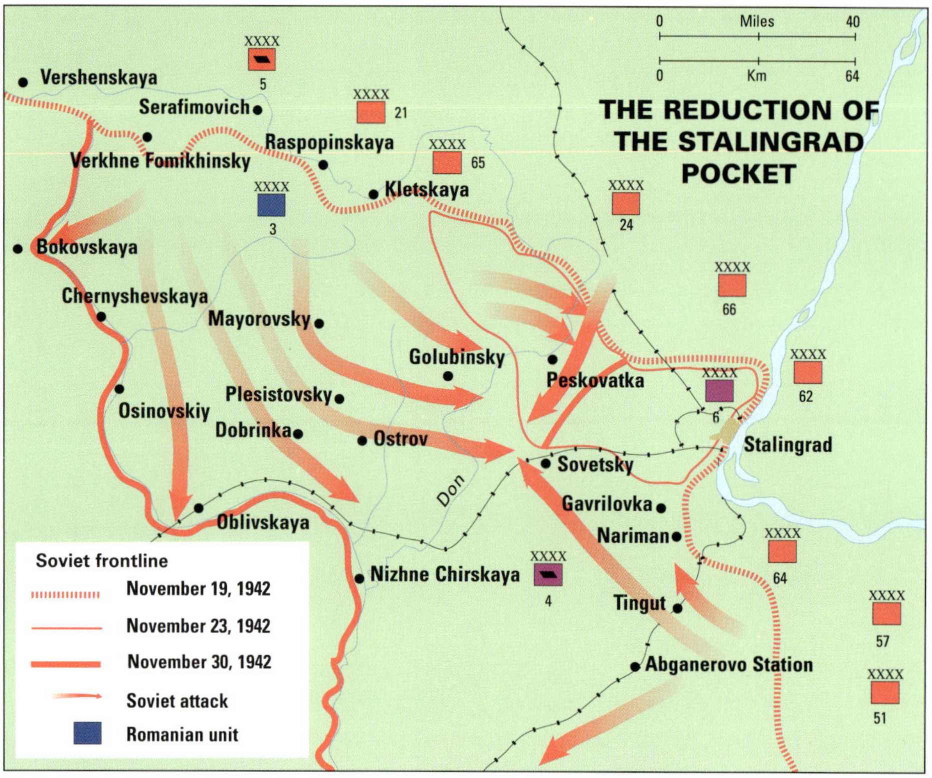

▼ ***Ju 87 dive-bombers in the Caucasus, December 18, 1942. The Luftwaffe had 495 aircraft in the Caucasus in mid-October. This had fallen to 240 by January 1943 due to the demands of the Don sector.***

December 12

SOUTHERN USSR, *LAND WAR*

The 11th Panzer Division continues its fire-fighting role along the Chir, destroying a Soviet bridgehead at Lissinski and containing another at Nizhne Kalinovski. Meanwhile, Manstein's attempt to relieve the Sixth Army, codenamed Winter Storm, gets under way. LVII Panzer Corps (23rd Panzer Division, 6th Panzer Division and the Romanian VI and VII Corps) – 30,000 troops and 190 tanks and 40 self-propelled guns – smashes through the Soviet Fifty-First Army at Kotelnikovo. The weather results in an advance of only 19km (12 miles), and Eremenko deploys the Soviet 13th Tank Corps and 4th Mechanized Corps to reinforce the Fifty-First Army.

December 14

CENTRAL USSR, *LAND WAR*

The Soviet Third Shock Army continues to make gains around Velikiye Luki.

SOUTHERN USSR, *LAND WAR*

On the Chir the Soviet Fifth Shock and Fifth Tank Armies continue to pin down XXXXVIII Panzer Corps. The advance of LVII Panzer Corps is slowing as the Soviet 4th Mechanized and 13th Tank Corps enter the fray.

SOUTHERN USSR, *AIR WAR*

The Luftwaffe has delivered only 152 tonnes (150 tons) of supplies thus far to the trapped Sixth Army.

December 16

SOUTHERN USSR, *LAND WAR*

The Stavka launches Operation Little Saturn, involving 425,000 Red Army troops and 5000 artillery pieces. The Soviet First Guards and Sixth Armies attack the Italian Eighth Army (216,000 troops) but make only limited gains, their units encountering minefields and effective resistance from the Axis reserve (27th Panzer Division). The Soviet Third Guards Army makes good initial progress but is then forced back by the 22nd Panzer Division. Meanwhile, the Soviet Fifty-First Army gives ground grudgingly to the painfully slow-moving LVII Panzer Corps.

GERMANY, *STRATEGY*

Hitler issues an order on how to deal with partisans on the Eastern Front: "If the repression of bandits in the East, as well as in the Balkans, is not pursued by the most brutal means, the forces at our disposal will, before long, be insufficient to exterminate this plague. The troops, therefore, have the right and the duty to use any means, even against women and children, provided they are conducive to success. Scruples of any sort are a crime against the German people and against the German soldiers."

DECEMBER 19

SOUTHERN USSR, *LAND WAR*
Little Saturn continues to make progress, with the Italian Eighth Army on the verge of collapse: 15,000 Italians are surrounded at Vertyakhovski. The Romanian I Corps on Hollidt's left flank has collapsed, endangering the rear of the Chir line and Army Group Don. The 11th Panzer Division continues to fend off Soviet attacks, knocking out large numbers of Red Army tanks at Nizhne Kalinovski. Hoth's 6th Panzer Division reaches the River Myshkova, 48km (30 miles) from the Sixth Army. Manstein signals the codeword Thunderclap, ordering Paulus to break out and link up with his force. Hitler, however, orders Paulus to stand firm.

The 15th Panzer Regiment, 11th Panzer Division, attacks a force of Soviet tanks of the Fifth Tank Army in the rear 8km (5 miles) south of Oblivskaya, south of the Chir. In the engagement the Germans destroy 65 Red Army tanks.

Soviet tank tactics are still poor, the formation going into battle without coordination, and without the cooperation of numerous infantry divisions.

▲ ***The Italian Eighth Army on the retreat from the Don. Lacking tanks and anti-tanks guns and having hardly any motor transport, the Italians suffered greatly from incessant Soviet attacks.***

DECEMBER 20

SOUTHERN USSR, *LAND WAR*
As Manstein tries to get Hitler to agree to a breakout, Group Hoth is attacked on the Myshkova by the Second Guards Army. The 17th Panzer Division (which was transferred to the relief force because Hoth had lost the 11th Panzer Division) is down to just eight tanks.

DECEMBER 24

SOUTHERN USSR, *LAND WAR*
The German line on the Chir is falling apart, the Soviet 25th Tanks Corps and 1st Guards Mechanized Corps surrounding Morozovsk and the 24th Tanks Corps capturing Tatsinskaya and its airfield (a Luftwaffe base for relief flights to Stalingrad). Some 56 Luftwaffe aircraft are destroyed attempting to take off from the airfield. The 6th Panzer Division completes its switch to Group Hollidt, leaving LVII Panzer Corps with only the weak 17th and 23rd Panzer Divisions – 28 tanks and 20,000 troops. Facing them are the Fifty-First and Second Guards Armies – 149,000 troops and 635 tanks. The latter now counterattack, forcing the Germans back, a situation made worse by the annihilation of the Romanian VI and VII Corps on the flanks. Operation Winter Storm is over.

DECEMBER 29

SOUTHERN USSR, *LAND WAR*
The 2nd Guards Tank Corps breaks out of Tatsinskaya, being pursued by the 6th and 11th Panzer Divisions. Over the next 24 hours the two panzer divisions will inflict heavy losses on the forces of the Third Guards Army.

DECEMBER 31

SOUTHERN USSR, *LAND WAR*
The Soviet Fifth Shock Army recaptures Tomorsin as the Germans recreate XXIX Corps around Morozovsk. Operations Uranus and Little Saturn have compelled Hitler to order an evacuation from the Caucasus, with XXXX Panzer Corps withdrawing from the Terek.

The Red Army has achieved much since November 19. However, it has paid a high price in blood for its successes: Southwestern Front, 64,600 killed and missing; Stalingrad Front, 43,000 killed and missing; Northern and Black Sea Groups, 132,000 killed and missing.

There has also been operational shortcomings, especially with regard to coordinating infantry and armoured units: as the tank corps advanced, the infantry fell behind and were unable to catch up once German forces moved in. Such was the fate of the 24th Tank Corps at Tatsinskaya, for example. In addition, poor coordination between the tanks corps allowed the Germans to engage them in a piecemeal fashion and inflict heavy casualties.

▼ ***Soviet troops advance on the Don Front in late 1942. Their somewhat bulky appearance is due to the layers of clothing worn under their camouflage smocks, including padded trousers.***

JANUARY 1

CENTRAL USSR, *LAND WAR*
With the Germans besieged in the citadel at Velikiye Luki, officers of the Soviet Third Shock Army demand their surrender, an offer that is rejected.

USSR, *ARMED FORCES*
At Stalingrad the Stalingrad Front (Eremenko) is moved to the outer ring, leaving the Don Front (Rokossovsky) to surround the pocket.

JANUARY 2

SOUTHERN USSR, *LAND WAR*
Another airfield falls to the Soviets as the Third Guards Army recaptures the one at Morozovsk, further reducing the number of Luftwaffe relief flights to Stalingrad. Farther south, the First Panzer Army falls back from the Terek.

JANUARY 4

CENTRAL USSR, *LAND WAR*
The German LIX Corps and Group Wohler attempt to relieve Velikiye Luki, resulting in fierce fighting with the Third Shock Army.

JANUARY 8

SOUTHERN USSR, *LAND WAR*
Rokossovsky offers surrender terms to Paulus at Stalingrad. His terms are generous on paper: "We guarantee the safety of all officers and men who cease to resist, and their return after the end of the war to Germany or to any other country to which these prisoners of war may wish to go. All personnel who surrender may retain their military uniforms, badges of rank, decorations, personal belongings and valuables and, in the case of high-ranking officers, their swords. All officers, noncommissioned officers and men who surrender will receive normal rations." Hitler forbids any surrender. Those Germans who did surrender after the fall of the city would find their captors in a less generous mood.

▼ Axis allies in retreat: frozen troops of the Italian Eighth Army on their way west. By mid-January the army had ceased to exist.

◀ *Men of the Soviet Volkhov and Leningrad Fronts meet near Workers' Settlement No 5 on January 18, 1943, thus creating a narrow corridor to Leningrad.*

JANUARY 10

SOUTHERN USSR, *LAND WAR*
The Don Front (281,000 troops, 257 tanks and 10,000 artillery pieces) commences Operation Ring, the destruction of the German Sixth Army at Stalingrad. Facing this force are the freezing 191,000 troops of the Sixth Army, with 7700 artillery pieces and 60 fuel-starved tanks. The Twenty-First, Twenty-Fourth, Fifty-Seventh and Sixty-Fifth Armies, supported by the Sixteenth Air Army, launch a series of blistering attacks.

JANUARY 11

SOUTHERN USSR, *LAND WAR*
The Sixth Army at Stalingrad is being torn apart, although Paulus is reminded by OKH that surrender is out of the question. To the west the Soviet Second Guards and Fifty-First Armies are approaching Rostov and, in the Caucasus, the German Army Group A continues its withdrawal.

JANUARY 12

NORTHERN USSR, *LAND WAR*
The Red Army launches Operation Iskra, designed to push the German Eighteenth Army out of the Schlusselburg-Mga salient and thus reopen a supply line to the besieged city of Leningrad. The Sixty-Seventh Army (130,000 troops) attacks from south of the city, and the Second Shock Army (114,000 troops) assaults from the Volkhov. In between lie German troops in well-entrenched positions.
SOUTHERN USSR, *LAND WAR*
The Don Front's attack at Stalingrad has incurred 26,000 casualties, but Paulus has lost 60,000 troops and massive stocks of weapons. In the Caucasus, attacks by the Soviet Eighteenth and Forty-Sixth Armies encounter heavy resistance.

JANUARY 13

NORTHERN USSR, *LAND WAR*
As the Second and Sixty-Seventh Armies continue to attack on the Neva and Volkhov, the Soviet Eighth Army joins the assault. The result is that the German XXVI and XXVIII Corps suffer heavy losses.
SOUTHERN USSR, *LAND WAR*
The offensive by the Soviet Fortieth Army against the Hungarian Second Army – part of a larger Red Army offensive involving the Voronezh, Bryansk and Southwestern Fronts along a 480km (300-mile) front – begins. The Hungarian 7th Division is soon destroyed.

JANUARY 15

CENTRAL USSR, *LAND WAR*
The Soviet Third Shock Army captures Velikiye Luki. It is a great success for Operation Mars, although bought at a heavy price: 31,600 Red Army troops killed and missing and 72,300 wounded. The Germans have lost 17,000 troops in and around the town.
SOUTHERN USSR, *LAND WAR*
Trapped Axis troops in Chertkovo attempt to break out. At Stalingrad, Pitomnik airfield, one of only two remaining

▶ *German wounded being evacuated from Stalingrad. Inside the aircraft the men were laid on straw. Nearly 850 aircraft were used in the German airlift.*

German air bases in the pocket, comes under Red Army artillery fire.

JANUARY 16

SOUTHERN USSR, *LAND WAR*
The Hungarian Second Army falls apart, allowing Soviet units to drive west. At Stalingrad the Red Army captures Pitomnik airfield; only Gumrak air base remains.

JANUARY 18

NORTHERN USSR, *LAND WAR*
Schlusselburg is recaptured by the Soviet Second Shock and Sixty-Seventh Armies. With a narrow corridor created through German lines south of Lake Ladoga, Leningrad can now be supplied.

SOUTHERN USSR, *LAND WAR*
As the Soviet Third Tank and Fortieth Armies link up at Alexievka, three Hungarian corps and the Italian Alpine Corps are encircled. Gumrak airfield is now under Red Army attack.

USSR, *ARMED FORCES*
Notwithstanding the failure of Mars, Zhukov is promoted to Marshal of the Soviet Union and Deputy Supreme Commander of the Soviet Armed Forces. Considering the losses incurred during what was his brainchild, his promotion is perhaps somewhat surprising. Mars cost the Red Army nearly 500,000 troops killed, wounded or captured (German casualties were around 40,000). The Twentieth Army lost 58,524 troops out of its original strength of more than 114,000. The 1st Mechanized Corps lost 8100 of its 12,000 troops and all of its 220 tanks, and the accompanying 6th Stalin Rifle Corps lost more than 20,000 of its 30,000 men. At lower levels the cost was even higher. Red Army tank losses during the operation amounted to 1700.

JANUARY 19

SOUTHERN USSR, *LAND WAR*
What is left of the Hungarian Second Army surrenders at Ostrogozh (50,000 men) as the Soviet Voronezh Front develops its assaults against Army Group B. The 7th Cavalry Corps races into Vayluki and annihilates the Italian garrison. At Stalingrad, Gumrak airfield is now being pounded by Red Army artillery.

JANUARY 20

YUGOSLAVIA, *PARTISAN WAR*
In response to increasing partisan activity, the Germans launch Operation Weiss headed by General Lueters, Commander of German Troops in Croatia. Cooperating with Italian forces, its objective is the annihilation of partisan units west and northwest of Sarajevo. German units include the 7th SS Mountain, 369th and 717th Infantry Divisions, and a regiment of the 187th Infantry Division. The Italian contingent is V Corps of the Second Army. In the first attack the Axis troops inflict 8500 casualties on the partisans and capture a further 2010. German losses are 335 dead and 101 missing. Weiss will conclude on February 18, 1943.

▲ ***A 105mm le FH18 howitzer of the German Eighteenth Army in action near Leningrad at the end of January 1943.***

JANUARY 23

SOUTHERN USSR, *LAND WAR*
At Stalingrad Gumrak falls to the Soviet Twenty-First Army. The Soviet bridgehead on the River Manych, which was established by the Soviet Southern

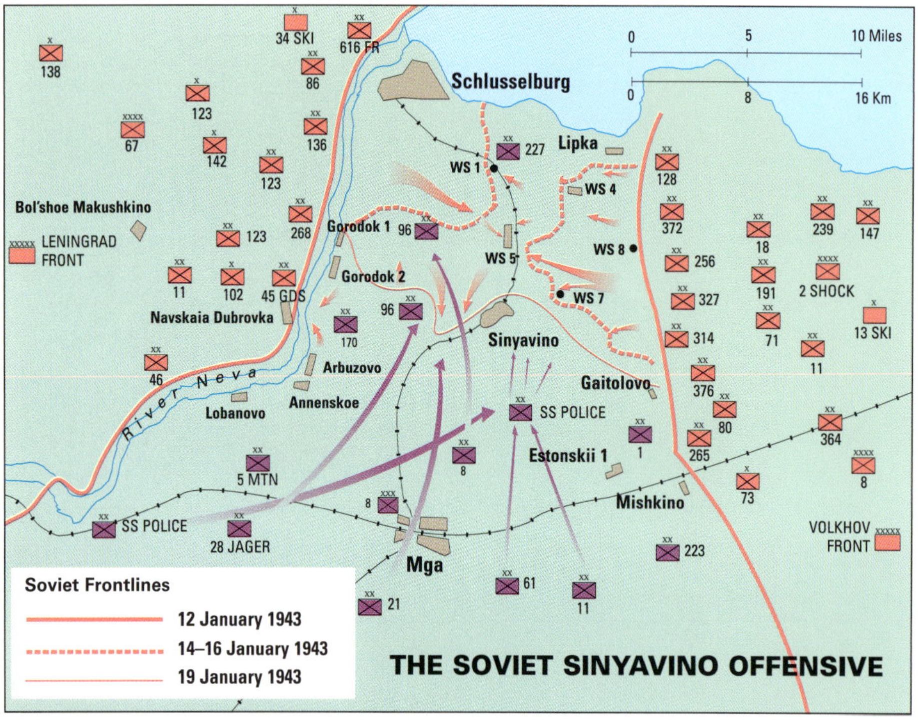

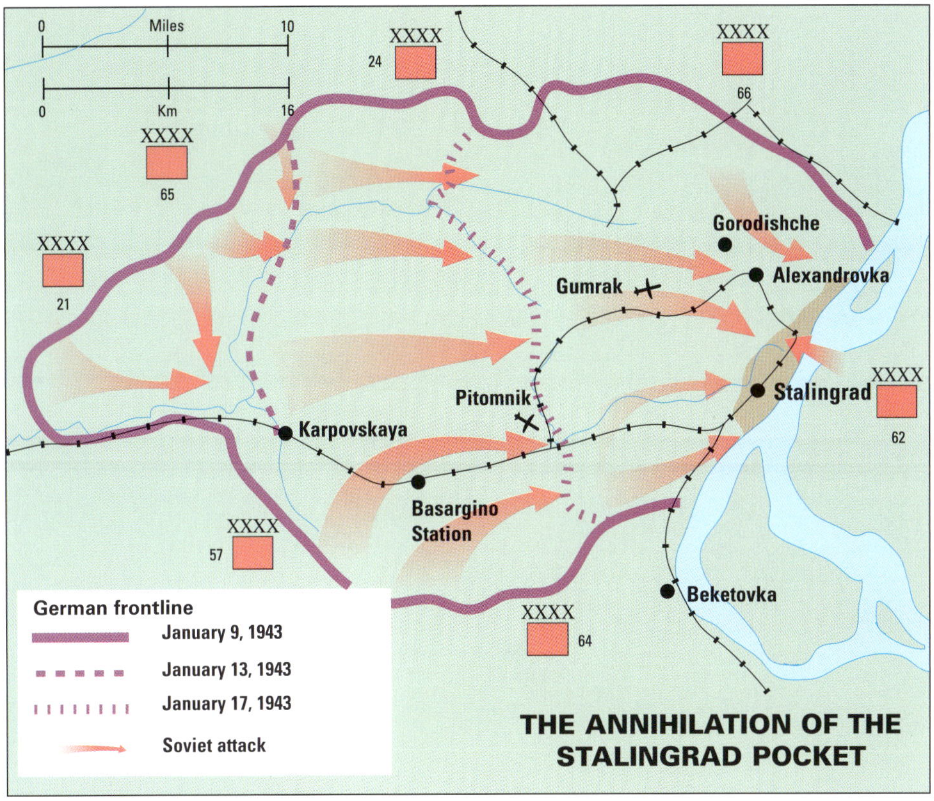

▲ *A sick Field Marshal Paulus meets Soviet commanders at Stalingrad to negotiate the surrender of the Sixth Army.*

Front's Second Guards Army, is destroyed by two German divisions.

JANUARY 24

SOUTHERN USSR, *LAND WAR*

The Soviet offensive continues to score successes, with the Sixtieth Army recapturing Voronezh and the Fortieth Army cracking open the southern flank of the German Second Army.

In the Kuban the Stavka orders that the German Seventeenth Army is to be surrounded by the Southern Front; the Forty-Fourth and Fifty-Eighth Armies will assault Bataisk; and the Ninth and Thirty-Seventh Armies will cooperate with the Black Sea Group. Hitler orders Paulus at Stalingrad to fight to the end: "Surrender is forbidden. Sixth Army will hold their positions to the last man and the last round and by their heroic endurance will make an unforgettable contribution towards the establishment of a defensive front and the salvation of the Western world."

◀ *Yugoslav partisans retreat with their wounded following the German*

JANUARY 26

SOUTHERN USSR, *LAND WAR*

In the Stalingrad Pocket the survivors of the German 297th Infantry Division surrender to the 38th Guards Rifle Division, the Sixty-Fifth Army links up with the Sixty-Second Army between Mamayev Kurgan and the Red October factory, and the Twenty-First and Sixty-Fourth Armies link up with the Sixty-Second Army. What is left of the Sixth Army is now trapped in two small pockets.

JANUARY 29

NORTHERN USSR, *LAND WAR*

The fighting calms down around Leningrad. The Soviet armies have suffered substantial losses: Sixty-Seventh Army, 12,000 killed and missing and 28,700 wounded; Second Shock Army, 19,000 killed and 46,000 wounded; and Eighth Army, 2500 killed and 5800 wounded.

SOUTHERN USSR, *LAND WAR*

The Soviet Southwestern Front commences its operation to outflank the German Army Group Don as enemy units retreat towards Izyum.

JANUARY 30

SOUTHERN USSR, *LAND WAR*

Hitler promotes Paulus to field marshal, a cynical move to prompt the commander at Stalingrad to commit suicide rather than surrender (no German field marshal has yet surrendered to the enemy).

In a radio broadcast Hermann Göring proclaims to the nation: "A thousand years hence Germans will speak of this battle with reverence and awe, and that in spite of everything Germany's ultimate victory was decided there. In years to come it will be said of the heroic battle on the Volga: when you come to Germany, say you have seen us lying at Stalingrad, as our honour and our leaders ordained that we should, for the greater glory of Germany!"

JANUARY 31

SOUTHERN USSR, *LAND WAR*

Paulus surrenders at Stalingrad. Now only XI Corps in the northern pocket in the city continues to hold out. Hitler is disgusted, stating: "Here is a man who can look on while fifty or sixty thousand are dying and defending themselves with courage to the end – how can he give himself up to the Bolsheviks?"

South of Izyum, at Slavyansk, the 3rd and 7th Panzer Divisions move into the frontline in an effort to halt the Red Army's advance.

The Stalingrad Airlift

Luftwaffe chief Hermann Göring assured Hitler that his aircraft could supply the trapped Sixth Army at Stalingrad, but such a boast was beyond the means of the Luftwaffe's airlift capacity.

Events that precipitated the Stalingrad airlift were twofold: the Russian winter and a Soviet counterattack. In late 1942, General Paulus's Sixth Army was fighting to capture Stalingrad. Seven-eighths of the city was already in German hands when the onset of winter coincided with the Soviet counterattack of November 19. Two days later the Sixth Army found itself on the horns of a dilemma. It could make a fighting retreat or allow itself to become separated from the main German front and trapped between the Don and the Volga. Paulus was not inclined to retreat, concerned that he did not possess enough fuel to succeed. However, his misgivings became irrelevant once Hitler decreed that the Sixth Army was to defend Stalingrad under any circumstances. With the Sixth Army aware of the pincer movement being formed around it by Soviet tanks, Lieutenant-General Martin Fiebig, commander of VIII Air Corps during the Stalingrad operations on November 21, telephoned the Sixth Army's chief of staff, Major-General Arthur Schmidt. With Paulus himself listening to the conversation, Fiebig asked Schmidt what the army's plans were:

"The C-in-C", answered Schmidt, "proposes to defend himself at Stalingrad."

"And how do you intend to keep the army supplied?"

"That will have to be done from the air."

The Luftwaffe general was flabbergasted. "A whole army? But it's quite impossible! Just now our transport planes are heavily committed in North Africa. I advise you not to be so optimistic!"

Fiebig promptly reported the news to his chief, General Wolfram von Richthofen, whose telephone call in turn woke up the chief of general staff, Jeschonnek, at Goldap.

"You've got to stop it!" Richthofen shouted. "In the filthy weather we have here there's not a hope of supplying an army of 250,000 men from the air. It's stark staring madness!"

But the memories of the airlift successes at Demyansk and Cholm still resonated strongly and fate took its course.

◀ The extreme cold required special "heating wagons" to pump hot air around each Ju 52's engine cowlings so the powerplants could be started.

A disastrous decision

Historians have argued the soundness of the decision to execute the airlift, as well as who really is to blame for making that decision. Since there was no German air transport fleet, there were no high-ranking airlift experts to advise the decision makers on the soundness of any decision regarding large-scale airlifts, nor to present cost-benefit analyses from previous airlifts to predict the risks associated with subsequent efforts under different circumstances. Weather conditions, enemy strength and activity, pre-existing airlift infrastructure and other factors can all pose challenges and increase the risks for different operations. For the Stalingrad airlift, the status quo since Demyansk and Cholm had changed.

In hindsight, the order to execute the Stalingrad airlift was disastrous. Hitler was the ultimate authority and the primary responsibility rests with him. However, there were three people to blame: Hitler, Göring and Jeschonnek. Jeschonnek, initially believing that the supply would be a temporary operation to allow Paulus to break out, rashly promised Hitler that the Luftwaffe was capable of meeting the army's needs, before he had consulted with airlift experts, made his own calculations or spoken with General von Richthofen (commander of the Fourth Air Fleet) and the other air force and army commanders at the front. Had he taken any of these actions, he might have cautioned Hitler as to the possibility of failure of an airlift. Later, when he learned the airlift was to be considerably longer and that Richthofen and Fiebig were strongly opposed to it, he admitted his mistake and attempted to dissuade Hitler and Göring.

However, there are several reasons that Hitler's blame is greater than Jeschonnek's. Only four will be discussed here. First, his egotism caused him to believe that his iron will is what had saved the Eastern armies the previous winter and would do so again. He did not look objectively at the situation facing the Sixth Army. Second, he would lose face if he allowed a withdrawal after publicly promising to keep the city. Third, he turned a deaf ear to the repeated pleas and warnings of his frontline army and air force commanders, calling them defeatists for questioning the stand-fast solution that he had elevated to doctrine. Fourth, he did not fire Göring and replace him with someone competent despite the Reichsmarschall's poor track record and the negligence of his command the previous year or even insist that Göring act responsibly during this crucial period, rather than in the haphazard fashion for which he was known.

Göring's responsibility for the airlift decision was equal to Hitler's. When the Nazi leader asked him if the Luftwaffe could meet the Sixth Army's needs as Jeschonnek had promised, he should not have blindly agreed. He should have first consulted his airlift experts; sought the opinions of Richthofen and his other commanders; and thoroughly acquainted himself with the conditions at Stalingrad to include the enemy order of battle, size and needs of trapped forces, weather patterns and conditions and operational readiness of Fourth Air Fleet. Göring did none of these things. His assurances to Hitler may have been nothing more than an attempt to restore his importance and influence with the Führer.

The Luftwaffe's airlift deficiencies

Luftwaffe commanders in the field were united in their belief that the air force could not supply the entire Sixth Army and expressed their objection to the idea to local army commanders and the High Command itself. Fiebig's thoughts on the airlift's feasibility have already been mentioned. Richthofen urged an immediate breakout. He noted in his diary on November 21, "Sixth Army believes that it will be supplied by the air fleet in its hedgehog positions. I made every effort to convince it that this cannot be accomplished, because the necessary transport resources are not available."

The next day Major-General Wolfgang Pickert, the 9th Flak Division commander, repeated these same thoughts to Paulus and Schmidt during a conference. Pickert insisted a breakout was the only option. When Schmidt asked him what he would do, he replied: "I would gather together all the forces I could and break out to the southwest." Schmidt replied that the Sixth Army would not attempt a breakout. Hitler had expressly forbidden a breakout and the enemy held the high ground to the west, thus exposing the Sixth Army to Soviet guns if they did attempt a breakout. The Sixth Army would remain in the pocket and defend itself as Hitler had

◀ *Kurt Wendt, one of the Luftwaffe pilots who flew supplies into the Stalingrad Pocket. He flew a total of 39 supply missions and lived to tell the tale.*

▲ ***November 19, 1942: German vehicles flee east towards Stalingrad following the Soviet breakthrough on the northern Don flank.***

ordered. Now decisions had to be made for the organization and leadership of the airlift.

Officers in charge of the airlift

German leaders placed responsibility for the airlift with the Fourth Air Fleet. Major-General Wolfgang Pickert was the senior Luftwaffe officer inside the pocket and was responsible for the effort to receive the supplies and defend the airspace around the city. Initially, Fourth Air Fleet appointed Major-General Victor Carganico, Commander of the Airfield Area Tatsinskaya, as the Stalingrad Air Supply Chief. It soon became apparent that General Carganico and his staff were in over their heads, having insufficient airlift experience. On November 29, Fourth Air Fleet relieved Lieutenant-General Martin Fiebig, commander of VIII Air Corps, of his combat-mission responsibilities and directed him to assume responsibility as the Stalingrad Air Supply Chief. He possessed an experienced command staff as well as communication and weather facilities, and fighter and bomber units for escorts. Colonel Foerster took command of the air transport units then assigned to the Air Fleet at Tatsinskaya.

Fiebig's assignment resulted in the use of bombers for airlift, but those same aircraft were also desperately needed for bombing missions to support the fighting along the front. At this time, Colonel Ernst Kuehl received command of the He 111 units, stationed at Morozovsk, and became Air Transport Chief (Morozovsk). Colonel Foerster retained command of the Ju 52 units at Tatsinskaya, but was later replaced by Colonel Morzik. Major Willers became Air Transport Chief (Stalino) and

▲ ***On return flights the Ju 52s brought back the wounded from Stalingrad. The casualties had to endure a flight lying on a mattress of straw.***

assumed command of all the long-range aircraft stationed there.

The Quartermaster General of the Sixth Army at Morozovsk submitted his requests for provisions to Army Group Don. The army group then arranged for the transportation and rigging of the required items. An army group liaison officer at each airfield ran a supply detail charged with packing and loading the aircraft, and also assisted the medical staff with evacuation. Eventually, coordination among these agencies was good.

Sources vary, but estimates to sustain a fighting force of 250,000 men were initially established at 680 tonnes (750 tons) per day, but later reduced to 453 tonnes (500 tons) per day. The required aircraft and crews for the Stalingrad airlift assembled on short notice from the advanced flight training school. Sending many of the Luftwaffe's most experienced instructor-pilots contributed to degradation in the quality of new pilots being trained. If the best instructors were removed from flight training and deployed to the front, who was left to train future aviators to allow sustained operations and maintain combat effectiveness?

Every single available aircraft was mobilized for the airlift. On November 23, Lieutenant-General Hans-Georg von Seidel, the Quartermaster-General of the Luftwaffe, ordered all Ju 52s (transport aircraft); Ju 86s (trainer; completely inappropriate as a transport); FW 200s and Ju 90s (long-range reconnaissance aircraft); and He 111s (long-range bomber) from every unit, staff, ministry and the Office of the Chief of Training. Six hundred aircraft, along with some of the best flight instructors, were stripped away from the training facilities. Specialized training schools were closed due to the ruthless efforts taken to ensure the success of the airlift. By early December, Fourth Air Fleet had approximately 500 aircraft at its disposal, with more becoming available as the operations progressed. Germany's military leaders were convinced that the number of aircraft now dedicated to the operations was sufficient to meet the logistical needs of the Sixth Army.

Faulty preparations

Military leaders were incorrect if they assumed that the requisition order of November 23 would mean the miraculous arrival of all available Ju 52s a mere 24 hours later. Kirovograd and Zaporozhye airfields were supposed to winterize the aircraft. However, personnel assigned to these bases were more concerned with reporting turnaround statistics than with properly preparing the aircraft for the Russian snow and ice. Accordingly, the aircraft arrived at Tatsinskaya ill prepared for winter employment and choked the airfield awaiting proper equipment. Lack of winter preparation for the transports was only one problem the Luftwaffe faced in an effort to maximize throughput to Stalingrad; the human dimension was also overlooked.

Aircrews did not have a certification programme, local area familiarization or any other method of adapting to the exigencies present at Stalingrad. They were fully employed upon their arrival. The bitter cold; perilous approach and return flights facing enemy fighters and anti-aircraft artillery; steady shelling of the home and offload bases; ground operations within the enclave while facing constant artillery fire and grenades; and the ubiquitous danger of icing and the mechanical hazards caused by the severe cold presented difficult challenges. Crews also had to confront the psychological depression inherent when dealing with starving troops and countless wounded, many of whom were left behind owing to lack of space. These young and inexperienced crews were disturbed by their experiences.

The only two acceptable airlift bases, Tatsinskaya and Morozovskaya, were located 256km (160 miles) and 165km (130 miles) (60 and 50 minutes' flying time) respectively from the encircled airfield of Pitomnik, a distance that did not allow the aircraft to trade much fuel for freight. The Ju 52 could carry about 2.26 tonnes (2.5 tons), and the He 111 could carry only 1.8 tonnes (2 tons). Spread between Tatsinskaya and Morozovskaya, a total of 350 Ju 52 and Ju 86 transports and 190 He 111 bombers were available for the airlift.

Despite this ostensibly adequate airlift fleet, other factors proved to be far more significant in determining the Sixth Army's fate than simply the sheer number of aircraft. An army requirement of 680 tonnes (750 tons) per day would require 240 to 300 missions per day. These numbers are based on the assumptions that the airlift could and would operate nonstop, day and night, with no allowance for airfield capabilities, mechanical difficulties, or other conditions that would affect operational readiness rates and delivery amounts; that aircraft would be able to carry their maximum designed cargo weight, with no consideration for fuel-versus-cargo

▶ ***In the early stages of the airlift Russian prisoners were used to load supplies into the Ju 52s, under the watchful eyes of German guards.***

limitations; that the enemy would not interfere; and that the Russian winter would not hinder operations. The 240 to 300 missions per day numbers are based on the cargo capacity of the Ju 52. Considering that a majority of the airlift aircraft were less capable than the Ju-52, the mission was doomed before it started. Even if adequate delivery platforms were available, the Germans could not begin to keep up with the offloading operations, because 240 missions per day would equate to one aircraft every six minutes, assuming the Germans could maintain 24-hour operations; 300 missions equals one landing every 4.8 minutes. Under ideal conditions, this is possible. However, taking into account the Russian weather and Luftwaffe counter-tactics to mitigate the Soviet threats, many times the transports were forced to arrive in large numbers, hopelessly overwhelming offloading ground crews and their equipment. The chaos on the ground was probably equal to the chaos created once additional inbound aircraft discovered they were unable to land due to a clogged runway and airfield, and were forced to return to their home base. Thus, without the ability to maintain a consistent, sequential and predictable (at least to the Germans) airlift flow, the operation was doomed before it even started, regardless of the number of aircraft dedicated to the airlift.

There were six airfields available in the pocket; but Pitomnik and Basargino were the only significant ones. Only Pitomnik was capable of handling large-

▲ ***Inside the pocket many Ju 52s were damaged by enemy artillery and air attacks. In addition, other transports were damaged when they landed on holed runways.***

scale operations, in addition to being the only airfield in the pocket with night capability. The others were nothing more than bare-grass landing strips, lacking the necessary radio and air traffic control equipment. Several of those fields had been used previously to supply the Sixth Army, but the weather had been better, and the loads smaller.

The Germans at Stalingrad would have needed 25 airfields to effectively resupply the besieged troops. Their conclusion also suggests that a protracted combat operation demands at least one runway per 10,000 combat personnel. Granted, at Stalingrad, there were two runways, but Gumrak was too small to be of any practical use.

In addition to the inadequate number of airfields in the pocket, the Germans failed to account for the atrocious and bitterly cold weather conditions, as well as the uncertainties and hazards associated with operating airlift aircraft in a war zone. The Volga is a "meteorological frontier", marking the boundary where cold, Siberian air from the steppes of Asia collides with warm, moist air from the Black and Caspian Seas. In addition to the seemingly endless days of snow, clouds and fog generated from this clash of weather patterns, the Luftwaffe had to endure brutal temperatures as low as 50 degrees Fahrenheit below zero. Brigadier-General Wolfgang Pickert, the flak commander and senior Luftwaffe officer trapped in the pocket, later recalled: "The cold caused unimaginable difficulties in starting aircraft engines, as well as engine maintenance, despite the already proven 'cold starting' procedures. Without any protection against the cold and the snowstorms, ground support personnel worked unceasingly to the point where their hands became frozen. Fog, icing and snowstorms caused increasing difficulties, which were compounded at night."

In addition to the bitter cold, Luftwaffe forces were forced to stand down for days on end due to ice, fog, heavy snow and other weather factors making flight impossible. There was no respite for the crews and ground personnel. Many times delays were unavoidable. If Ju 52s were packed for an airland mission and the unpredictable weather changed to preclude landing in the encircled area, then standby ground crews would have to rig the supplies for airdrop. They had to be ready to go at a moment's notice to take advantage of any favourable weather.

Enemy aircraft

When the weather did allow airlift operations, there was always the threat of Russian flak and fighters. Initially, Russian fighters were surprisingly acquiescent towards the German transports, but as the weeks passed fighters became more and more active. Russian fighters forced the transports to fly in groups of 40 or 50 to maximize the efficiency of German fighter escort. Simultaneously, ground operations required the use of German fighters and bombers to repel heavy Soviet ground attacks. All these factors continued to add to the attrition toll.

At the beginning of the airlift, with good weather and high ceilings, supply units flew in squadrons or in groups of five aircraft with a fighter escort. During times of low visibility or low cloud ceilings, only crews fully proficient with instrument flying flew in groups of five; the rest flew in groups of two or three. Night missions were always flown singly, necessitating carefully coordinated take-off schedules between Morozovskaya and Tatsinskaya.

Throughout the entire operation the Russians attacked the transports from the air and the ground. Pitomnik possessed relatively strong anti-aircraft artillery, yet these weapons did not deter Russian attacks. Personnel and aircraft losses were high, particularly when the attacks came during take-off and landing operations, or when the transports were being loaded or unloaded. The relentless bombs, artillery fire and even grenade attacks took considerable tolls on the operation and even brought it to a standstill at times.

▼ The view from a Ju 52 cockpit as it flies over the River Don towards Stalingrad. Note the smashed bridge and the aircraft's low altitude.

Tatsinskaya and Morozovskaya were the largest and best-equipped airfields in the region, as well as the principal supply bases for Stalingrad; their loss would be a tremendous setback to the airlift and, accordingly, Soviet bombers attacked them repeatedly. On December 21, two Soviet armies had broken through Axis defences and were heading south toward Rostov. The 24th Tank Corps had advanced to within 20km (12.5 miles) of Tatsinskaya, while Soviet bombers were pounding Morozovskaya. The whole German southern front was in danger, but the immediate objectives were Tatsinksaya and Morozovskaya. General Fiebig had requested permission to evacuate before the Red Army was in a position to fire upon it. At first, Richthofen told him to stand fast. He would seek clarification from the High Command. A day later the latter had still given him no reply. Acting on his own accord, he ordered Fiebig to prepare both Tatsinskaya and Morozovskaya for immediate evacuation should enemy forces threaten the airfields. Early evacuation was essential to ensure the availability of important equipment for future missions. He could not afford to lose fuel tankers, engine-warming equipment and spare parts.

On December 23, Göring himself finally stepped in and flatly refused to allow the 180 Ju 52s to retreat until they were under direct fire. An entire transport fleet was at stake. Fiebig accepted the orders with the same reticent acquiescence shown by Paulus at Stalingrad. That evening Fiebig wrote in his diary: "I see that we're rushing headlong into disaster, but orders are orders!" As a result, Fiebig refused to allow the evacuation even after Soviet artillery batteries and tanks began shelling the field. A tank shell destroyed the signals centre. Artillery and tank gunfire destroyed several transports on the ground, but this did not prevent other aircraft from taking off. Bekker describes the event that finally made Fiebig relent and order the evacuation on his own authority. Colonel Herhudt von Rohden, Fourth Air Fleet's Chief of Staff, stood beside Fiebig in his shelter, up to this time remaining silent as to what was unfolding before him. An hour and a half after the shelling began, Fiebig's chief of staff, Lieutenant-Colonel Lothar von Heinemann, burst into Fiebig's shelter after witnessing the pandemonium breaking out among the crews:

"Herr General," he panted, "you must take action! You must give permission to take off!"

"For that I need Luftflotte authority cancelling existing orders," Fiebig countered. "In any case it's impossible to take off in this fog!"

Drawing himself up, Heinemann stated flatly: "Either you take that risk or every unit on the airfield will be wiped out. All the transport units for Stalingrad, Herr General. The last hope of the surrounded Sixth Army!"

Colonel von Rohden then spoke. "I'm of the same opinion," he said.

Fiebig yielded. "Right!" he said turning to the Gruppen commanders. "Permission to take off. Try to withdraw in the direction of Novocherkassk."

Saving the air fleet

Aircraft took off in all directions. Two collided directly over the field. Others taxied into each other, bumped wings on take-off, or damaged their tail assemblies. The aircraft, those that were still flyable, scattered. On December 28 the Germans recaptured the airfield, but only for several days as their time was now running out.

Fiebig's disobedience saved the transport fleet from certain annihilation. Some 108 Ju 52s and 16 of his Ju 86s made it to various airfields, but he lost

▲ ***The Soviets also lost aircraft over Stalingrad. This German intelligence officer in the pocket is sitting on the remains of a shot-down Tupolev bomber.***

nearly one-third of his operational aircraft. Aircraft operational readiness rates sank to less than 25 percent. Perhaps just as significant was the loss of vital ground equipment to ensure the surviving aircraft would remain operational at their new base, because Göring's decision to forbid a pre-emptive evacuation meant that when the moment to escape arrived, the aircraft were still heavily loaded with boxes of ammunition and canisters of fuel for the trapped forces at Stalingrad.

To the east, Morozovskaya was under the same threat. Colonel Ernst Kuehl realized the danger and did not hesitate. When he received news that Tatsinskaya had been overrun, he ordered his He 111s and Stukas to depart for Novocherkassk. He remained behind and hoped for flying weather that would allow his bombers to keep the Red Army in check. On Christmas Day the weather cleared; Colonel Kuehl's forces returned to Morozovskaya and turned back the Soviet spearheads. The airfield was safe for the time being, but the fair weather gave way to ice and fog, allowing the Soviet armour to resume the attack. By early January 1943, both Tatsinskaya and Morozovskaya were finally abandoned.

The loss of Tatsinskaya and Morozovskaya forced the Luftwaffe to operate from bases 96km (60 miles) farther from the pocket, which retarded the delivery rate and used up precious fuel intended for the Sixth Army. The Ju 52s resettled at airfields in Salsk, located in the northern Caucasus, 400km (250 miles) from Stalingrad. This distance was very close to the maximum range of the transports. The He 111s now operated from Novocherkassk and were hampered by the same distance problems as the Ju 52s. The new distance was 328km (205 miles), an increase of 128km (80 miles). The longer routings correspondingly cut even deeper into the supplies available to those depending upon them for their survival. But the Russians also had some tricks up their sleeves to further complicate transport efforts.

Soviet anti-aircraft measures

Capitalizing on the increased flight distance, the Russians set up a continuous line of flak sites along the Pitomnik radio beam, forcing the transports to take longer routings to avoid the deadly ground fire. These necessary detours exacerbated an already critical fuel shortage. By the end of December, only 375 German single-engine fighters existed along the entire Eastern Front, forcing them to be thinly spread and unable to bring any concentration to bear. Meanwhile, Russian fighters grew stronger and stronger as the operation progressed. As the German line was forced farther and farther back from Stalingrad, the city fell beyond the effective range of the fighters. The paucity of German fighters available for escort forced the transports to fly in groups of 40 or 50 to counteract the resurgent Red Air Force. Regardless of these measures, the longer distances meant the fighters were unable to escort the airlifters the entire distance, leaving them vulnerable to enemy fighter attack as they approached the pocket. Another tactic to minimize detection and destruction from enemy fighters was to approach the airfields with large waves of transports arriving simultaneously from different directions. This method usually started with two or three Ju 52s under fighter escort approaching the field from a different direction than the main body of transports.

But the losses of German aircraft and personnel continued. The rate of attrition always exceeded the rate of replacement, regardless of the additional transport aircraft and personnel robbed from the schools and training installations.

In an effort to prevent unnecessary bloodshed, on January 8 the Soviets issued an ultimatum to the Sixth Army to surrender. Paulus, still maintaining blind obedience to Hitler, refused.

▼ ***Pilot fatigue, improperly trained aircrews, ice and Soviet fighters soon left a trail of downed aircraft strewn across the steppe on the approaches to Stalingrad.***

▲ ***Despite the desperate situation in which the Sixth Army found itself, useless items were flown into the pocket, such as crates of condoms.***

The Russians continued to attack with ever-stronger forces. It seemed only a matter of time before Salsk would be overrun. On January 18, Soviet bombardment and strafing attacks damaged 30 Ju 52s. This attack precipitated the move from Salsk to Zverevo. Under the direction of Colonel Morzik, the leader of the Demyansk airlift of the previous winter, the Ju 52s began operations from Zverevo. However, within 24-hours, Russian bombers attacked Zverevo as well. Morzik lost 52 aircraft.

The loss of Pitomnik

With the Red Air Force becoming more active as each day passed, the transports were obligated to fly in groups. Ground crews at Pitomnik would sit around for hours with nothing to do, then suddenly they would be overwhelmed with 40 or 50 aircraft, all desperate to be unloaded immediately, which was not possible, and precious time was wasted.

To make matters worse, the Soviets overran Pitomnik on January 16. Now the Russians had free access to the Pitomnik landing apparatus: German airfield lighting and direction-finding equipment. They set-up a decoy installation and tricked several German pilots into landing in enemy territory.

The fighters assigned to Pitomnik had performed remarkably, not allowing Russian fighter or ground-attack aircraft to stop the arrival of supplies or the evacuation of the wounded. With the Russians at the doorstep and destruction imminent, the six Stukas and six Bf 109s stationed there were ordered to evacuate to Gumrak. But the Sixth Army had not prepared the airfield at Gumrak, despite the requests of VIII Air Corps since the beginning of the airlift. The airfield was in such poor condition, with bomb craters and snow drifts, that five of the six Bf 109s were destroyed in their attempts to land. From this point the Luftwaffe lost air superiority over Stalingrad and its approaches.

Gumrak had been a Russian Army airstrip. Richthofen actually wanted it improved and enlarged several weeks earlier and had ordered Luftwaffe

▲ ***The severity of the Russian winter made flying impossible on some days, and often transports would crash while attempting to land, blocking the airstrip.***

personnel within the pocket to prepare it for the airlift operations, but Sixth Army refused permission.

By mid-January, the aircraft reliability rate was critical. On January 18, less than 7 percent of Ju 52s were available, 33 percent of the He 111s, 0 percent of the Fw 200s and 35 percent of the He 177s.

The situation grew more desperate. Before Pitomnik fell, the Sixth Army had already appealed to Berlin for help, which only increased Hitler's nervousness. In an attempt to salvage something, Hitler sent Field Marshal Erhard Milch to Fourth Air Fleet to take over the airlift and gave him special powers and authority to issue orders and take any action he deemed necessary for the armed forces in the region.

Milch discovered upon arriving at Richthofen's headquarters at Taganrog that he possessed 15 operable Ju 52s out of 140, and 41 operational He 111s out of 140, and one operational FW 200 out of 20. Of VIII Corps' 300 aircraft, he had 57 that could fly, or 19 percent. At the time of his arrival, Ju 52s were unable to land within the cauldron. They had resorted instead to airdropping supplies, and even to flying past the troops and merely pushing the supplies out of the open doors. He raised operational ready rates and supplies for the suffering troops to 30 percent, which was still too low to save Paulus's army, but the cost was additional losses of Ju 52s and He 111s, as well as the irreplaceable instructor pilots who were shot down with their aircraft. Milch even planned to use gliders, but slowly changed his mind after realizing that Richthofen and Fiebig were right. Gliders were not suitable for the conditions at Stalingrad.

Even though the Luftwaffe assessed conditions at Gumrak as unsuitable, Sixth Army radio messages claimed that the airfield was "day-and-night operational." Many transport pilots were convinced the airfield was too dangerous to land and had resorted to merely throwing out supply canisters.

Aircrews also had to unload their own aircraft. Determined to discover the true status of thc field, on January 19 VIII Air Corps sent their representative, Major Erich Thiel, commander of an He 111 bomber group that had been converted to an improvised transport role, into Gumrak. He landed in an He 111 to assess the condition of the runway and offload operations and then report his findings back to his superiors. Milch wanted him to contact Paulus in an effort to convince the latter to improve the conditions at the airfield. The army leader refused to accept any criticism for the ground operations, even when Thiel reminded him that aircraft turnaround time had slipped to around five hours; even when Thiel pointed out that the airfield, including the runway, was littered with wrecks, Paulus still claimed that it was not his responsibility.

Death trap at Gumrak

Thiel's report concluded that aircraft were cleared for landing during the day despite the 13 aircraft wrecks littering the field, but only the most experienced crews could land at night. Of particular concern for heavily laden transports attempting a night landing was the wreckage of a Bf 109 at the end of the runway. The field was exposed to enemy fighters, which circled the field when the weather was clear. Ju 52 landings would be impossible when enemy fighters were present unless the weather was bad. Enemy artillery also threatened safe operations. The airfield was also strewn with unrecovered airdrop canisters half-buried in snow. Regarding the offloading procedures, Thiel added that he landed at 11:00 hours; by 20:00 hours he had not even seen an offload team. By 22:00 hours, his aircraft still had not been unloaded or defuelled, despite the fact his aircraft was carrying excess petrol for the fuel-starved army. Airfield personnel claimed the reason was the constant shelling. Other aircraft were unloaded by their own crews, where the supplies were left unguarded and then stolen by passing soldiers.

Major Thiel reported his conclusions to Paulus who, in the presence of several staff officers, then replied: "When [aircraft] don't land, it means the army's death. It is too late now, anyway. Every machine that lands saves the lives of 1000 men. Dropping [supplies] is no use to us. Many supply canisters ['bombs' in Paulus's original text] are not found, because we have no fuel with which to retrieve them. Today is the fourth day in which my troops have had nothing to eat. We could not recover our heavy weapons [during recent withdrawals], because no fuel was available. They are now lost. The last horses have been eaten. Can you imagine it: soldiers diving on an old horse cadaver, breaking open its head and devouring its brain raw? What should I say, as supreme commander of an army, when a man comes to me, begging: 'Herr Generaloberst, a crust of bread?' Why did the Luftwaffe say that it could carry out the supply mission? Who is the man responsible for mentioning the possibility? If someone had told me that it was not possible, I would not have reproached the Luftwaffe. I would have broken out."

Responding to criticism that aircraft were landing only half-full and at other times with useless supplies, Milch himself ordered that some of the supply containers be opened and inspected before departure. To his horror he discovered many of the containers contained only fish meal, whereupon he

▶ ***Many Ju 52s came from North Africa and the Mediterranean, and were delayed before they took part in the airlift due to refitting at Kirovograd and Zaporozhye.***

returned them and asked the army to hang the victualling officer. Pickert himself pointed out many years later that, "the fact that transport aircraft and para-dropped goods now and then contained foolish and unnecessary items is undisputed, but this was an exception which should not be overestimated." Nevertheless, Milch wanted it stopped.

Situation at Gumrak

Milch did improve conditions at Gumrak. To enable his pilots to fly into Gumrak at night, he ordered lighting equipment, smoke pots and radio detecting equipment, and sent signals and air traffic experts into the cauldron. Then he assured Paulus, Manstein and the High Command that on the night of the 18th, his aircraft would fly into Gumrak. He did not disappoint them. On January 18, six He 111s and one FW 200 landed at Gumrak and offloaded critical supplies. Despite the improvements, the airfield was still more dangerous at night than during the day. Some 25 percent of the He 111s destined for the field either crashed or sustained damage during landing or take-off, but the airlift into Gumrak continued steadily. On the night of January 21/22, the last night Gumrak was to be in German hands, 21 He 111s and four Ju 52s landed fully laden.

The Red Army overran Gumrak on January 23. This was a tremendous blow to the Sixth Army, which now was totally cut off from the outside world except for airdrops. The problem with airdrop missions is that they are inherently less efficient than airland missions. Airdrop loads require more time to pack, load and rig the cargo for the airdrop. An airdrop mission, no matter how expert the crew, will seldom drop the supplies exactly where the customer (the Sixth Army in this case) demands, whereas an airland mission can put the cargo literally at the customer's feet. Airdrop missions result in more damaged cargo due to the impact velocity. It does an army no good to receive water they cannot drink, food they cannot eat and bullets they cannot shoot. Airdrop has no provision for backhaul; there is no way to evacuate the wounded and sick.

When the fall of Gumrak appeared imminent, the Sixth Army had initiated a repair and construction programme at Stalingradskiy, a lesser airfield further within the pocket. It was operational on the 22nd, but Stalingradskiy fell only hours after Gumrak.

▲ ***Inside the pocket a Luftwaffe crew larks around while their transport is prepared for the return flight back to friendly territory, through enemy flak and fighters.***

The Soviets continued their thrust through the Sixth Army, dividing it into two pockets and contracting the perimeters. All the Luftwaffe could provide now were just a few insignificant airdrops from the He 111s and Ju 52s. The situation was hopeless. On the 24th, Paulus, trapped in the southern pocket, sent an urgent request to the High Command: "Troops without ammunition and food. Collapse inevitable. Army requests immediate permission to surrender in order to save the lives of remaining troops." Hitler refused.

Many of the airdrop loads were irretrievable by the army; the emaciated troops simply lacked the strength to dig them out of the snow and there was no fuel left to transport them. To make matters worse, the transports were not able to identify the locations of the German soldiers and scattered the canisters all over the pocket in an attempt to get something to them. Consequently, many of the supplies intended for Sixth Army troops never made it to them. The supplies may have been dropped in the wrong area, lost in the city ruins or snow, blown out of reach, or simply landed in enemy sectors. In an attempt to improve the accuracy of the drops, on the evening of January 25 Major Freudenfeld, senior Luftwaffe signals officer, finished creating a drop site in the southern pocket. On January 28, he created a drop zone in the northern pocket.

On January 26, Paulus requested that the Luftwaffe drop only food. Ammunition was no longer needed since there were not enough guns.

By dawn on January 31, the southern pocket no longer existed; Paulus, having been promoted to field marshal the day prior, capitulated, becoming the first German field marshal ever to be taken prisoner. The Germans in the northern pocket, though, continued fighting.

Army and air force leaders monitored their radios for further messages. The Luftwaffe refused to abandon the German soldiers. On February 2, Milch ordered the aircraft to fly over the Stalingrad Pocket and airdrop supplies to any clearly identifiable German troops. When the aircraft returned, Fiebig reported to Milch that it was hopeless. "The outline of the pocket can no longer be recognized. No artillery fire was seen. An enemy vehicle column with headlights blazing is advancing from the northwest into what was formerly the northern pocket. The front of that column is almost at our former drop site." These aircrew observations, combined with the lack of any radio transmissions from the ground, signified that the battle for Stalingrad was finally over.

▼ ***These Russian prisoners inside the Stalingrad Pocket were used to unload transport aircraft after they had landed at Pitomnik airfield.***

Winter Storm

In December 1942 the Germans launched a relief operation, codenamed Winter Storm, to save the Sixth Army in Stalingrad. But the route to the city was barred by strong Soviet forces.

Hitler had based his decision to keep Sixth Army at Stalingrad on two assumptions: that sufficient forces to conduct a successful relief operation could be assembled, and that the Sixth Army could be sustained as a viable fighting force by air supply until the relief was accomplished. The air supply problem appeared to be one of simple arithmetic: matching the number of planes to the required tonnages. Such was not the case, but even if it had been, the problem would still have been beyond solution. In late November 1942, the German Air Force was undergoing its greatest strain since the start of the war. At Stalingrad and in North Africa, it was fighting a two-front war in earnest. By the end of November, 400 combat aircraft had been transferred from the Eastern Front to North Africa, reducing the front's numerical strength by a sixth and its effective strength by nearly a third. Moreover, of 2000 aircraft left on the Eastern Front, OKW estimated that no more than 1120 were operational on November 29, 1942. As the previous chapter illustrated, the aerial relief operation failed. Now it was the turn of the ground forces to attempt to relieve the Sixth Army

Planning Winter Storm

On December 1, Army Group Don began preparing the relief, under the codename Winter Storm. The main effort went to Fourth Panzer Army's LVII Panzer Corps, which, with two fresh panzer divisions (6th and 23rd) then on the way, would push northeastwards from the vicinity of Kotelnikovo towards Stalingrad. The Romanian VI and VII Corps would cover its flanks. For a secondary effort towards Kalach, out of a small German bridgehead on the lower Chir, Fourth Panzer Army was given XXXXVIII Panzer Corps. Headquarters, XXXXVIII Panzer Corps, left its two original divisions, 22nd Panzer Division and 1st Romanian Armoured Division, in the front on the Chir and assumed command in the bridgehead of three divisions coming in - the 11th Panzer Division, 336th Infantry Division and 7th Air Force Field Division. General Paulus, head of Sixth Army, was to bring together all of his armour on the southwest rim of the Stalingrad Pocket and to be ready to strike towards LVII Panzer Corps if ordered. He was also to be prepared to break out towards Kalach, but was at the same time to hold his fronts to the north and in Stalingrad. Field Marshal von Manstein, commander of Army Group Don, wanted to be ready to start the relief operation anytime after daybreak on December 8.

The outlook for Winter Storm was not auspicious from the first and grew less promising with each passing day. The Sixth Army shifted two motorized divisions and a panzer division to the southwest as ordered, but after December 2, the Soviet Don and Stalingrad Fronts hit the pocket hard for a week and tied the three divisions down in defensive fighting. On December 3, the Southwest Front again became active along the Chir, in the Romanian Third Army sector, forcing Manstein to commit the three divisions of XXXXVIII Panzer Corps there and, in effect, to drop the corps out of Winter Storm. In addition, the two divisions of LVII Corps were slow in arriving, and OKH instructed Manstein to use the air force field divisions, of which he had two, for defensive missions only.

By December 9, Winter Storm had dwindled to a two-division operation. Nevertheless, the next day Manstein decided to go ahead, and he set the start date for the morning of December 12. Any more

◀ There were some heavy Tiger tanks on the Eastern Front in late 1942, such as this one, but Manstein was not allocated any for the Stalingrad relief operation.

▲ ***Soldiers of the 6th Panzer Division just prior to their participation in Winter Storm. The division would lose half its tanks during the operation.***

delay, he believed, could not be tolerated because supplies were running short and because Soviet armour had been detected moving in opposite Fourth Panzer Army. Sixth Army reported that an average of only 63 tonnes (70 tons) of supplies a day were being flown in, and rations, except for odds and ends, would run out by December 19.

Hitler was still confident. On December 3, answering a gloomy Army Group Don report, he cautioned Manstein to bear in mind that Soviet divisions were always smaller and weaker than they at first appeared to be, and that the Soviet commands were probably thrown off balance by their own success. A week later his confidence had grown. Concluding that the first phase of the Soviet winter offensive could be considered ended without having achieved a decisive success, he returned to the idea of retaking the line on the Don. By December 10, he was at the point of planning to deploy the 7th and 17th Panzer Divisions on the Army Group Don left flank and to use them to spearhead an advance from the Chir to the Don. The next day he ordered Manstein to station 17th Panzer Division in XVII Corps' sector on the Chir, thereby, for the time being, ending the possibility of its being used in Operation Winter Storm.

Winter Storm begins

After jumping off on time on the morning of the 12th, LVII Panzer Corps made good, though not spectacular, progress. During the afternoon situation conference at Führer Headquarters, General Zeitzler, the Chief of the General Staff, tried to persuade Hitler to release the 17th Panzer Division for Winter Storm, but Hitler refused because a threat appeared to be developing on the Army Group Don left flank, where it joined the right of the Italian Eighth Army. In the conference, he restated his position on Stalingrad, saying, "I have reached one conclusion, Zeitzler. We cannot, under any circumstances, give that [pointing to Stalingrad] up. We will not retake it. And we know what that means. If we give that up we sacrifice the whole sense of this campaign. To imagine that I will get there again next time is insanity."

On the second day, LVII Panzer Corps reached the Aksai River and captured a bridge at Saliwski; but on the Chir and at the Don–Chir bridgehead, XXXXVIII Panzer Corps barely held its own against the Soviet Fifth Tank and Fifth Shock Armies, which were trying to tighten the grip on the Sixth Army by enlarging the buffer zone in the west. Fifth Shock Army was newly formed out of two rifle divisions and a tank corps from the Stavka reserves. Before 12:00 hours, Manstein told Hitler that the trouble on the Chir had eliminated every chance of XXXXVIII Panzer Corps' freeing forces for a thrust out of the bridgehead and that, without such help, LVII Panzer Corps could not get through to the Sixth Army.

Manstein asked for the 17th Panzer Division, to take over the attack from the bridgehead, and for the 16th Motorized Infantry Division (then stationed at Elista, between the Army Group Don and Army Group A flanks) to reinforce LVII Panzer Corps. Hitler released the 17th Panzer Division but not the 16th Motorized Infantry Division. The decision about 17th Panzer Division was made easier by a growing impression at OKH that the Russians were only simulating a build-up on the Army Group Don left flank.

For another four days, Winter Storm went ahead without gathering enough momentum to ensure an early success. On the 14th, however, the part of the Don–Chir bridgehead east of the Don had to be evacuated. The attack out of the bridgehead would have been abandoned in any case, since the 17th Panzer Division was having to be sent to LVII Panzer Corps. On the 17th and 18th, LVII Panzer Corps, increased to three divisions by the 17th Panzer Division, became tied down in fighting around Kumskiy, halfway between the Aksai and Mishkova rivers.

Oberfeldwebel Friedrich Bösch was a company section commander in the 1st Company, Panzerjäger, or Tank Hunter, Battalion 41, part of the 6th Panzer Division. In December 1942 the division was part of the forces that were desperately trying to relieve the Sixth Army that was encircled at Stalingrad. However, in the panzer army's way were hundreds

▼ ***Halftracks of the 6th Panzer Division just prior to commencing Operation Winter Storm. In their way were hundreds of Soviet tanks and tens of thousands of troops.***

of Russian tanks and tens of thousands of Red Army infantry. In mid-December Bösch and his men were defending crossings over the River Aksai against ferocious Red Army attacks.

"During the night of December 13 to 14, the 1st Company had been attached to Battle Group Remlinger, which was protecting the Saliwski bridgehead, where the enemy had assembled strong forces (prisoners we had taken reported 20 to 30 enemy tanks) in order to attack Saliwski itself.Therefore the company had been moved from height 56.3 to Saliwski. The attack of Battle Group Remlinger in the morning hours of December 14 against Wodanksi had been pinned down by strong Russian fire from tanks, anti-tank guns, mortars and Stalin's Organ rocket launchers as soon as it had reached open ground on the western edge of Saliwski. The crews of 1st Company, Panzerjäger Battalion 41, which were taking part in the attack, suffered losses.

"By 10:00 hours Oberfeldwebel Bergner, one of my closest friends since before the war, when I had served in the 1st Company, was brought back dead to the company command post, as was Unteroffizer Hüsken. Both had been killed by mortar shells that had landed behind their vehicles. Furthermore, Gefreiter Mentrup from Dortmund was wounded in the hand.

"I receive an order from the company commander: 'Take over Bergner's platoon straight away and secure the western edge of Saliwski against enemy tanks. Not one step back! Saliwski bridgehead has to be held, because otherwise it will be a catastrophe for the whole division!' Observing the Russian attacks, this becomes very apparent.

Under enemy fire

"In the meantime Battle Group von Hünersdorff has become involved in what was probably the biggest tank battle of World War II, at a place called Werchne-Kumsky. In the face of this overall situation, I am well aware of the importance of my task. The three Marder tank destroyers belonging to the

▼ ***6th Panzer Division halftracks, part of LVII Panzer Corps, on the road to Stalingrad. The going was slow due to the adverse weather and enemy resistance.***

▲ ***The spearhead of LVII Corps was its Panzer IV tanks. During Winter Storm the 6th Panzer Division started with 24 Panzer IVs, while the 23rd Panzer Division had 32.***

platoon with their well-trained crews, each one armed with a 76.2mm cannon, take up well-camouflaged positions behind some small huts, which here in the seemingly endless steppe have been built half into the ground to provide shelter from the weather. Distances are established. To our right and left our machine guns, mortars and infantry field guns have found good fields of fire and cover. And a big, flat clay hollow provides good cover for our infantrymen.

"We get great moral support from a self-propelled 88mm flak gun, which has taken up position 300 metres (330yds) on the left to ward off tanks from the direction of Wodjanski. Furthermore, about 400 metres (440yds) behind us in Saliwski I can clearly make out the mounted periscope of the battalion command post, where Captain Neckenauer, Oberleutnant Dr. Timm and Oberleutnant Dr. Middendorf are located. That also steels our nerves.

"Around us the Russians are getting more and more lively. Their fire from tanks, anti-tank guns, mortars and Stalin's Organs grows continuously. The accursed Stalin's Organs shell us severely, their nerve-shattering rockets falling on our positions and on Saliwski.

"In the afternoon I send out two men of the platoon with a food container to get dinner (today there is pea or bean soup) for the three tank destroyers that are lying in ambush positions. Returning very slowly and using all available cover, both men approach our positions with the food containers and place them on the ground. Suddenly the rumble and gurgle of Stalin's Organs can be heard coming from Wodjanski. We see the smoke of the launchers on the edge of Wodjanski, then 36 rockets hit us in a chessboard formation. Pressed against the wall of a hut I see one of the rockets hit a food container and rip it to shreds. The precious soup splashes everywhere and sinks into the ground. At the same time some infantrymen are wounded and an Unteroffizer on one of the tank destroyers is shot through the elbow. They are sent to the aid station in Saliwski.

"A radio message arrives: 'One tank destroyer to the bridge at Saliwski, as it is under threat!' This as well. Now I only have two tank destroyers at my disposal. The Russians are shelling us with their artillery to wear us down. I can't concern myself with that. I have to study the terrain in front of us through the large binoculars and observe the edge of the enemy-held village of Wodjanski, around 1500 metres away. The ground is covered with a light dusting of snow, broken up here and there by long steppe grass

"Suddenly there is movement. Three, no, four, five, six Russian tanks, probably T-34s, slowly advance on our position echeloned to the rear. I sound the alarm for my two remaining tank destroyers. Their crews huddle behind the thinly armoured gun shields as the barrels turn towards the enemy. Apart from this there is no movement on our side. Across no-man's land the slowly advancing tanks are followed by several waves of Russian infantry wearing thick brown greatcoats that stand out against the snow. More and more Russian infantry - like ants - burst forth from Wodjanski and follow the tanks. Slowly the ground in front of us becomes black with these infantry masses. In the meantime the six Russian tanks have closed to a range of 1000 metres (1100yds). What is their plan? They are difficult to spot in the rolling terrain. Then they all stop and take up hull-down positions so only their turrets are visible. Then the barrels of the six T-34s flash. They shell our positions in Saliwski, and several rounds fly over Saliwski towards the supply vehicles that are driving to the rear over open terrain.

"What to do? Should I order 'open fire' against these small turret targets? What is the penetration of our 76.2mm rounds at this distance? Until now we have no way of knowing the answers to these questions. So it is better to wait. The tank destroyer

crews sit behind their gun shields motionless. This takes a lot of guts. Suddenly, the 88mm flak fires from its position, which is hidden from our view by a hut. Damn, what's going on there? With my binoculars I can make out three, then five tanks that are driving across the steppe on our left at high speed towards Saliwski. Are these our own tanks that are coming to reinforce the Saliwski bridgehead? One is already burning - hit by the 88mm flak gun. Ah, so they're Russians. The four remaining tanks charge toward the southern edge of Saliwski. Two reach the first houses, but they have had to make a wide detour towards the right to avoid the 88mm shells.

"My heart is pounding and my head is throbbing. What are the six tanks in front of our position doing? They are still firing on Saliwski from their hull-down positions. Now there is an order for the tank destroyer on the left: 'Change front towards the left and take up a new position.' Two T-34s are now burning after being hit by the 88mm gun. But the other two T-34s that pressed on have gone past the flak position and are roaring around at the edge of the village. They will be taken care of by the tank destroyer that now has changed position. It has a good field of fire and a range of only 300-350 metres (330-385yds). Then, disaster. I see the tank destroyer that is driving into a new position disappear into a crater that was made by a heavy shell or bomb. The barrel of the 76.2mm anti-tank gun drills into earth. Disabled. My knees are trembling as I race and stumble towards my last tank destroyer.

A field of burning T-34s

"All around me erupt explosions from shells fired by the six hull-down T-34s from Wodjanski. I shout to the last tank destroyer: 'Left turn, engage enemy tanks at edge of Saliwski, fire at will.' With a shock the tank destroyer, commanded by Unteroffizer Münnich, turns around and drives a few metres forward to a favourable firing position between a hut and a pile of peat. 'Range: 200 metres. Fire. A hit!' The T-34 starts to burn straight away. Next! 'Range 250 metres. Fire!' I observe the course of the projectile while standing next to the tank destroyer. Miss. Damn! 'Aim a little farther to the left,' I shout at the commander, who at the same time acts as gun aimer. He again aims at the T-34, eyes to the gun sight and presses the firing switch. No shot is fired! What's wrong now? The loader opens the breech block. The shell casing flies out the rear, but the shell is missing. It has got loose from the shell casing and is stuck in the barrel! It is a matter of seconds before the barrel can be lowered. On the track cover on the side of the vehicle are the three parts of the barrel cleaning rod. In a flying hurry I assemble the three parts then race to the front in front of the muzzle, and from there I push the projectile backwards out of the barrel and the breech block. Then there is a rattle - the loader has chambered a new round.

◀ As Manstein's relief force approached Stalingrad, inside the pocket many of Paulus' vehicles had been abandoned due to crippling shortages of fuel.

"I run back. Suddenly there is a hissing, an explosion, a flash and a shock wave that nearly knocks me out. The right half of my face is burning like fire, my hearing is nearly gone. The Russians have spotted our position and are firing on us. Luckily they have mistaken the nearby pile of peat for a tank. So this first T-34 round has missed its target – lucky for me. Now our gun roars, a tracer shows the path of the shell. A hit! Smoke pours from the T-34 and shortly it begins to burn on the edge of Saliwski. All is now quiet. A lucky break. It now becomes clear to me that the hairs on the right side of my head have been singed, and my eardrum has been shattered. That explains the deaf feeling in my head. But the dance isn't over yet.

"The six dug-in T-34s are now rolling towards Saliwski, and us, from the direction of Wodjanski. Already the 88mm gun has opened fire. The tank destroyer drives back to its starting position and also fires shells towards the enemy attacking from Wodjanski. It is almost as if we are on the firing range. We have good fields of fire, good cover and bore-sighted distances. We fire round after round and after a few minutes all six T-34s are burning. After a while they burst into flame when the shells and machine-gun rounds stowed inside their hulls explode. The Russian infantry which has followed the tanks like a herd is fired on by the infantry with machine guns and mortars. The infantrymen must be almost despairing, as again and again new waves of Russians, massed in their hundreds, rise from behind sunken ground and hollows and attack. So I order the tank destroyer to change the kind of rounds it is firing. Instead of armour-piercing shells, high-explosive rounds are loaded into the barrel and the Russian infantry is attacked with these, pinning some down and forcing others to withdraw. Slowly the firing dies down on both sides and stops at 14:30 hours, when dusk begins to envelop the steppe. Occasionally a machine-gun burst sweeps the area, though without hitting anything."

Nearing the pocket

On the 19th, LVII Panzer Corps shook itself loose and drove to the Mishkova, 56km (35 miles) from the pocket. Manstein, however, told Hitler that LVII Panzer Corps, because of its own losses and stiffening enemy resistance, probably could not get through to Sixth Army and certainly could not open a permanent corridor to the pocket. He had, he added, sent his intelligence officer into the pocket, who had reported that the Sixth Army only had rations for another three days. Consequently, Manstein said, he believed the only answer was to order Sixth Army to break out, gradually pulling back its fronts in the north and in Stalingrad as it pushed towards LVII Panzer Corps in the south. That, he maintained, would at least save most of the troops and whatever equipment could still be hauled.

To Paulus, Manstein sent notice to get ready for Operation Thunderbolt, which would be the breakout. The army's mission, Manstein said, would have to include an initial push to the Mishkova. There, after contact with LVII Corps was made, truck convoys, which were bringing up 3048 tonnes (3000 tons) of supplies behind the corps, would be sluiced through to the pocket. Subsequently, the Sixth Army, taking along what equipment it could, would evacuate the pocket and withdraw southwestwards. Paulus was to get ready but was not to start until ordered.

Hitler, encouraged by LVII Panzer Corps' getting to the Mishkova, refused to approve Thunderbolt. Instead, he ordered the 5th SS Panzer Division *Wiking* transferred from Army Group A to the Fourth Panzer Army. Sixth Army, he insisted, was to

◀ Manstein's forces included the Marder II self-propelled anti-tank gun, which was armed with a captured Soviet 76.2mm gun rechambered to accept German ammunition.

▲ ***A knocked-out T-34 tank in the Kotelnikovo area in December 1942. The turret has been torn off, probably after being hit by an 88mm shell.***

stay put until firm contact was established with LVII Panzer Corps and a complete, orderly withdrawal could be undertaken. In the meantime, enough supplies were to be flown in, particularly of motor fuel, to give the army 48km (30 miles) of mobility (Hitler had heard that the army had only enough fuel to advance 29km [18 miles]).

On December 21, after LVII Panzer Corps had failed to get beyond the Mishkova in two more days of hard fighting, Generalmajor Friedrich Schulz, Manstein's chief of staff, conferred with General Schmidt, Paulus' chief of staff, by means of a newly installed high-frequency telecommunications system. Schulz asked whether the Sixth Army could execute Thunderbolt. The operation had not been approved, he added, but Manstein wanted to be ready to go ahead as soon as possible because of the unlikelihood of LVII Panzer Corps getting any closer to the pocket. Schmidt replied that the army could start on December 24, but he did not believe it could continue to hold the pocket for any length of time thereafter if the first losses were heavy. If Stalingrad were to be held, he said, it would be better to fly in supplies and replacements, in which case the army could defend itself indefinitely. In the case of Operation Thunderbolt, he and Paulus thought the chances for success would be better if the evacuation followed immediately upon the breakout, but they regarded evacuation under any circumstances as an act of desperation to be avoided until it became absolutely necessary. The conference ended on that indeterminate note.

Manstein transmitted the results of the exchange to OKH. He could give no assurance, he added, that if Sixth Army held out, contact with LVII Panzer Corps could be re-established, since further gains by the panzer corps were not to be expected. In effect Winter Storm had failed, and both Manstein and Paulus had sidestepped the responsibility for Thunderbolt, which neither could order without Hitler's approval. Later in the day, on the 21st, Hitler talked at length with the chiefs of the army and air force general staffs, but to those present, "the Führer seemed no longer capable of making a decision".

Surrender is Forbidden!

The failure of the airlift and Manstein's relief attempt condemned the Sixth Army to annihilation. It was now merely a question of when, not if, Paulus would capitulate.

Ordered to stand fast and repeatedly assured by Hitler that Sixth Army would be relieved, General Paulus swiftly put his forces into a giant hedgehog defensive posture.

Establishing an effective defensive perimeter at Stalingrad was doubly difficult due to a desperate shortage of infantrymen (the bulk of whom had fallen in the earlier street fighting) and the lack of prepared positions. On the eastern face of the pocket, German troops continued to occupy the defensive positions built up during the previous fighting for the city. However, the southern and western portions of the perimeter lay almost completely on shelterless steppe, and the hasty defences there never amounted to more than a few bunkers and shallow connecting trenches. (Because the steppe was almost treeless, no lumber was available for building fires for heat or for constructing covered defensive positions.) Significantly, the subsequent Soviet attacks to liquidate the surrounded Sixth Army came almost exclusively from the south and west against the least well-established portions of the German defences. On November 23, well-built positions to the north of Stalingrad were rashly abandoned without orders by the German LI Corps commander, General Walter von Seydlitz-Kurzbach, who had hoped thereby to provoke an immediate breakout order from Paulus. This action sacrificed the 94th Infantry Division, which was overrun and annihilated by Red Army forces during the movement to the rear, and also gave up the only well-constructed defensive positions within the pocket.

Sixth Army had difficulty in defending itself because of insufficient resources. Lack of fuel prevented the use of Paulus' three panzer and three motorized divisions as mobile reserves. Hoarding its meagre fuel supplies for a possible breakout attempt, Sixth Army wound up employing most of its tanks and assault guns in static roles. Likewise, shortages of artillery ammunition and fortification materials hindered the defence. The Luftwaffe's heroic attempts to airlift supplies into Stalingrad were hopelessly inadequate: since daily deliveries never exceeded consumption, the overall supply problem grew steadily worse in all areas. In some ways the aerial resupply effort was counterproductive. Scores of medium bombers were diverted from ground support and interdiction missions to serve as additional cargo carriers, a move that emptied the skies of much-needed German combat air power at an extremely critical period.

◀ A German machine gunner in his frozen foxhole on the edge of the Stalingrad Pocket in January 1943, now without hope of any relief.

The fortress myth

For both tactical and logistical reasons, then, what the Nazi press dramatically called "Fortress Stalingrad" was, in reality, no fortress at all. Surrounded by no fewer than seven Soviet armies, the Sixth Army was marooned on poor defensive ground without adequate forces, prepared positions or stockpiles of essential supplies. Forbidden by Hitler to cut its way out of the encirclement, Sixth Army's eventual destruction was a foregone conclusion unless a relief attack could re-establish contact.

The second problem shackling German operations was the Germans' own Byzantine command arrangements. Afield in the southern portion of the Eastern Front were three autonomous army groups (Army Groups A, B and Don). No single commander or headquarters coordinated the efforts of these army groups save for the Führer himself. From his East Prussian headquarters, Hitler continued to render his own dubious brand of command guidance.

Inspired by the success of his stand-fast methods the previous winter, the Führer now balked at ordering the timely withdrawal and re-assembly of the far-flung German armies, even truculently resisting the transfer of divisions from the lightly engaged Army Group A to the mortally beset Army Group Don. Hitler's opening response to the new Soviet offensive against the rear of the German southern wing was to decree a succession of meaningless halt lines, ordering the overmatched German forces to hold position after position "to the last man".

For those in the pocket, such orders amounted to a death sentence. Typical of those units trying to survive was the 2nd Battalion of the German 132nd Infantry Regiment. In early December 1942, the 2nd Battalion reached the Kergachi Hill area, where it was to remain until the end of the Stalingrad Pocket. Although available maps indicated that the Kergachi Hills dominated the area, the terrain was actually fairly level, thereby exposing the battalion to enemy observation. The hills, whose elevation averaged 122m (400ft), did not appear very prominent on the vast plateau west of the Volga. There were no trees, shrubs or inhabited localities which might have provided a defending force with adequate cover or concealment. The battalion's situation with regard to strength is illustrated by Company G. Of the 55 men who had departed from Verkhne-Buzinovka, only 25 remained fit for combat. The company was subsequently reinforced by 30 men from a veterinary unit, a few riflemen from the disbanded 376th Infantry Division and 26 Romanians, so that its strength in early December was 90 men. Company G was committed on the 2nd Battalion's right flank and ordered to defend a 457m (500yd) sector. The German line was established as an almost straight row of foxholes. Each squad, consisting of 6–10 men, occupied 3–4 foxholes situated close to one another for mutual support. Each centre of resistance had a machine gun, of which Company G had a total

▼ ***A starving and lice-infested member of the Sixth Army captured in January 1943. By the middle of the month the Germans were virtually out of fuel and ammunition.***

▲ *Soviet infantry fight their way into the diminishing Stalingrad Pocket in January 1943. The white camouflage suits were reserved mainly for reconnaissance companies and snipers.*

◀ *Red Army infantry in the rubble of Stalingrad. By the end of January there were an estimated 100,000 German soldiers crowded into the ruined city, many wounded and without weapons.*

▲ ***The crew of this 37mm anti-aircraft gun, probably from the 9th Flak Division, fell victim to Soviet forces which overran Gumrak airfield in late January 1943. Note their lack of winter clothing.***

of six. Approximately 55m (60yds) behind the line the company commander emplaced his three light mortars. Ammunition was a critical item. During the first week of December each man was allotted 400 rounds, but this allowance had to be cut to 80 rounds during the following week.

The 2nd Battalion occupied a particularly important sector since the Kergachi Hills blocked access to the Rossoshka Valley from the northwest. By driving through this valley the Russians could split the pocket in two. It was therefore not surprising that the battalion soon became involved in some of the bitterest fighting in the pocket.

The first day

During the night of December 3/4, the noise of engines and tracked vehicles coming from the valley north of Hill 440 betrayed the assembly of a Russian armoured force. Ammunition shortage limited the German artillery's interference with the enemy concentration to only weak harassing fire. At dawn the following morning, while a dense fog blanketed the area, 40 T-34s accompanied by a few KV-1s were seen driving directly towards the 2nd Battalion's position. From then on things began to happen with incredible speed. Within a few minutes the Russian tanks overran Company G's line and drove adjacent Company E from its positions. Some Russian infantrymen, moving up behind the armour, occupied the foxholes formerly held by Company E and fired into Company G's flank, while others made a frontal attack against Company G's frontline. The Russian armoured force fanned out and broke through the German lines in massed formation. About 10 tanks drove to the 2nd Battalion's CP, overran the heavy weapons of Company H emplaced in the vicinity, smashed the battalion's communication centre located in a bunker and took up positions in a depression east of the road leading to Bolshaya Rossoshka. Ten other tanks stopped near Company E's former CP and kept the terrain west of the road under fire. Another group of 10 tanks roved across the depth of Company G's position, while the remaining tanks tried to annihilate this company by rolling over the foxholes and firing at everything in sight.

Company G was in an extremely precarious situation, with enemy armour and infantry to its front, on its left flank and in its rear. A steady stream of fire poured from the tanks as they crisscrossed over the foxholes. Only on its right did the company still maintain contact with friendly elements. Despite the many adverse factors, the company held out until evening. This was possible because the ground around the narrow, carefully dug foxholes had frozen so hard that the walls withstood the pressure of the Russian tanks. Soviet infantry, advancing hesitantly and half-heartedly, was pinned down at a distance of 183m (200yds) by bursts of machine-gun, aimed carbine and well-placed artillery fire from the 1st Battalion sector on the right. Two of the T-34s were destroyed by German riflemen who fired

▼ Abandoned German vehicles at Stalingrad. The lack of fuel meant that the Germans could not move their armoured vehicles to counter Soviet attacks.

shaped charges at the tanks just after they had rolled over a group of foxholes. As a result, the other Russian tanks became more cautious in their forward movements.

German counterattacks

Despite the tremendous superiority of the Russian forces, Company G still held its position at 15:00 hours, as darkness was settling over the area. The majority of the Russians withdrew to Hill 440 and established a hedgehog defence. During the night the left-wing platoon of Company G emerged from its foxholes and attacked the Russian detachment that was occupying the foxholes formerly held by Company E. Without firing a shot the German platoon took the vodka-happy Russians by surprise, overwhelmed them and re-occupied 183m (200yds) of the former German line. In the early hours of December 5, a German reserve battalion which had shrunk to only 80 infantrymen and 8 Panzer IV tanks moved up and assembled approximately 1188m (1300yds) south of Hill 440. At dawn that

German force counterattacked northwards astride the road leading from Bolshaya Rossochka to Samofalovka. This counterattack was no less successful than the Russian operation of the preceding day. At the very outset six T-34s were put out of action. The Soviets on Hill 440 withdrew to the north and the 2nd Battalion reoccupied all its former positions. Some hundred prisoners and a sizeable quantity of supplies and equipment fell into German hands.

Thus ended the first engagement near Hill 440. Once again an experienced infantry unit had demonstrated that a seemingly hopeless situation can be mastered provided the men do not give way to panic.

On December 8 the Russians launched another powerful attack at the same point, but this time they announced their intentions with a large artillery preparation. The situation developed in a fashion similar to that of December 4–5. Again a strong combined-arms team, this time with infantry mounted on tanks, penetrated the weakly held German line south of Hill 440. Although accurate German small-arms fire did inflict heavy casualties on the tank-mounted Russian infantry, the 2nd Battalion was overrun and isolated, except for one contact point on the right wing. Despite heavy odds the battalion held out until nightfall brought an end to the enemy attack. The German counterattack the next morning jumped off from the ravine near the 1st Battalion's CP and drove the Russians from the former German positions. Five Russian tanks were destroyed during this action.

The final phases of the battle

On December 11 weaker Russian forces launched one more attack against the 2nd Battalion's line, but during their approach they were stopped by two German tank destroyers stationed at the exit of the ravine in the 1st Battalion sector. The situation then remained unchanged until after Christmas.

In the 2nd Battalion's sector the Russians limited their operations to minor diversionary attacks, their main effort being directed against the 1st Battalion. Their repeated attempts to break through the German positions were, however, unsuccessful, even though on many occasions the Germans averted disaster by only a narrow margin.

The third and final phase of the operations along the periphery of the Stalingrad Pocket began immediately after Christmas 1942. At that time the pocket had a diameter of approximately 35km (22 miles). The life expectancy of the encircled Sixth Army depended on its ability to defend this perimeter. If the Russians succeeded in breaking through the German ring at any point, they would split the

◄ *A Red Army artillery unit closing in on Stalingrad in January 1943. The gun is a 76mm ZiS-3 divisional piece, which was introduced in 1942.*

▶ Friedrich Paulus photographed on the day of his surrender to the Red Army. At the time he was suffering from depression and dysentery.

encircled army into smaller pockets, capture the remaining airfields, and thus cut off the supply by airlift. Ration and ammunition dumps would fall into their hands, and German resistance would crumble. Although sporadic fighting might continue, such isolated German resistance would merely have nuisance value and could be eliminated in the course of mopping-up operations.

This explains the ferocity with which both sides fought to gain a decision. The stakes were high, and the Germans needed cool-headed leaders. Whereas German unit commanders could envisage the possibility of a voluntary withdrawal during the first and second phases of the encirclement, defence in place was mandatory during the third. At this stage Russian frontline propaganda took over. On New Year's Day Russian psychological warfare teams went to work. Night after night loudspeakers blared forth speeches by German refugees speaking from a studio in Moscow, who read appeals, ostensibly from German mothers and wives, imploring their loved ones to give up the fight. German prisoners, who had been confined in model Russian camps, were sent back across the lines to their former units to report the excellent treatment they had received.

The end at Stalingrad

The prospect of relief from the outside had meanwhile grown dimmer. Nevertheless, the men in the pocket refused to give up hope, even though there was every indication that the Sixth Army was doomed. Living conditions in the pocket went from bad to worse. The German infantrymen had to stay in their foxholes, exposed to snow and rain, extreme cold and sudden thaw. Again and again the rations had to be cut. At first every man was issued one-third of a loaf of bread per day, then a quarter and later a fifth. This monotonous diet was occasionally supplemented by a few slices of sausage and a meat broth obtained by boiling horse meat. Only the wounded were given half a bar of chocolate and some brandy immediately after the evacuation to revive their spirits.

Constant Russian pressure resulted in a steadily growing number of casualties. The 2nd Battalion's combat strength diminished gradually. When the Russians resumed their large-scale attacks early in January 1943, the battalion had only 3 officers and about 160 men left. In mid-January, the executive officer was killed in close combat during a German counterattack. On the following day the battalion commander committed suicide as the result of a nervous breakdown. On January 19 the battalion's last remaining officer, a platoon commander from Company G, launched a final, desperate counterthrust and led the last 13 men of the battalion to their deaths. A few days later, at the beginning of February 1943, the Battle of Stalingrad came to an end when the remnants of the garrison surrendered.

▶ Some of the 91,000 German prisoners that fell into Soviet hands after the fall of Stalingrad. Weak from weeks of inadequate rations and most suffering from frostbite, half would be dead by the spring of 1943. Some prisoners, such as those who could not walk, were shot on the spot.

The Turning Point of the War?

The Axis never recovered from the losses in men and hardware suffered at Stalingrad, while a rejuvenated Red Army stood poised to take the strategic initiative on the Eastern Front.

The Germans were never able to replace their own and allied formations lost at Stalingrad, signalling that Germany would no longer be able to achieve outright military victory on the Eastern Front. And with Axis forces reeling in southern Russia, the Stavka ordered the Red Army's offensives to continue. In late January 1943, the Southwestern and Voronezh Fronts advanced towards Kharkov and into the Donbass region (the eastern Ukraine). At first they achieved spectacular successes, capturing Kursk, Kharkov and Belgorod. Stalin, believing that the Germans were on the verge of collapse in southern Russia, ordered the offensive to continue, ignoring the fact that his forces were becoming overextended, exhausted and short of supplies. German forces in the Donbass, though weakened, were actually regrouping under the able leadership of Field Marshal Manstein. Using forces withdrawn from the Caucasus and fresh units from Western Europe, Manstein struck the vulnerable flanks of the Red Army on February 20, 1943.

Within days the entire Soviet front collapsed, and by mid-March Manstein had recaptured Kharkov and Belgorod. The Stavka, thoroughly alarmed, poured fresh forces into the Kursk and Belgorod regions in expectation of a further German attack. However, the spring thaw brought thick mud and operations ground to a halt.

However, though the line had been stablized, the Germans had many reasons to worry about the Eastern Front, not least their ability to retain influence over the neutral powers of Europe.

The defeat at Stalingrad had lost Germany the tungsten of Portugal and the chrome of Turkey, both vital elements in munitions production and thus a highly significant factor in Hitler's strategic thinking

▶ *While Hitler boasted that the men of the Sixth Army had died "shoulder to shoulder", on the Volga tens of thousands of Germans trudged into captivity.*

(which placed the possession of such raw materials at the top of his military agenda). Furthermore Sweden, a major supplier of iron ore which had until this point pursued a policy of "benevolent neutrality", now adopted a less compliant stance. Indeed, such was Hitler's concern in respect of Swedish raw materials that reinforcements were sent to Norway in case the situation should require the occupation of Sweden. Hitler had hoped that Turkey would invade the Soviet Union through the Caucasus. In the aftermath of Stalingrad, Germany's recovery notwithstanding, it became clear that this would not happen. The support of Germany's partners on the Eastern Front was also becoming less than wholehearted. Both Italian confidence in Germany's ability to win the war and Mussolini's faith in Hitler had been seriously eroded. Finland, regarding itself as Germany's ally more by chance than choice, was in need of peace and now made no secret of that fact. Romania, having sustained heavy casualties as a result of the Soviet breakthroughs around Stalingrad, requested that its remaining troops in Russia be withdrawn from the frontline. The Hungarian forces became less amenable to following German orders and their role was restricted to security duties in the rear. Finally, Japan was now highly unlikely to violate the non-aggression pact with Stalin and move into the Soviet Far Eastern provinces and Siberia. Therefore it was with a sense of increasing urgency that the German High Command began planning the summer campaign.

The 1942 campaign not only marked a turning point in the fortunes of the German Army; it also indicated that the Red Army was becoming more competent. The success of the November 1942 Uranus counterstroke, for example, demonstrated not only that it had outfought the German Army during late 1942 in tactical and operational terms, but also that it had planned unfolding operations more effectively at the strategic level. Unlike Blue, Uranus

pursued modest goals – a shallow double envelopment – that remained achievable despite the still quite modest offensive capabilities that the Red Army had managed to establish by this stage of the war. Clearly, the Soviets had learned from earlier mistakes, particularly the premature over-expansion of the initially successful winter 1941–42 counteroffensive. The success of Soviet operations during late 1942, therefore, owed much to their ability to learn from previous mistakes.

This, though, was a skill that Hitler and his High Command seemed less able to master in 1942. In Blue, for example, the Germans repeated the mistakes they made during Barbarossa. As an overambitious offensive initiated too late in the year, Blue failed to translate tactical success into strategic triumph, extended the German front beyond that logistically sustainable, and left vulnerable flanks that invited a Soviet counterthrust. And in Uranus the Red Army gratefully accepted – with devastating results – the invitation inadvertently issued by the Germans. The failure of the Germans to defeat the Soviets in 1942 did not result from less effective all-arms cooperation, or a slower tempo of exploitation, or ineffective junior leadership, or even declining troop morale, all

▲ ***A field of Axis corpses on the outskirts of Stalingrad. Many of the bodies were stripped of their clothing by civilians before they arrived here.***

of which remained reasonably close to their previous 1941 standards. Rather, improving Soviet capabilities exploited German weaknesses at the strategic and operational levels. And unfortunately for the hard-pressed ordinary German soldier, Operation Uranus was just the start of a coordinated Soviet strategic riposte across the Eastern Front. The Soviets intended Uranus to be a classic double

envelopment that pitted Soviet strength against Axis weakness. However, unlike the "cauldron battles" attempted by the Germans, the Soviets pursued geographically limited objectives to ensure these aims remained achievable.

1943: year of decision

In northern Russia during early 1943, the Germans abandoned their Demyansk and Rzhev salients and withdrew west to create a more defensible front. Thus by the spring of 1943 the Red Army was in control of a huge salient in the central sector of the front that bulged into German-held territory: the Kursk salient.

Both sides recognized that the summer of 1943 would be a critical period on the Eastern Front. Having failed to defeat the Red Army in 1941 and 1942, Hitler realized that 1943 was his last chance to avoid defeat in the East, a position made more urgent by the recent defeat of Axis forces in North Africa, U-boat losses in the Atlantic and the threat of an Allied invasion of Western Europe. Thus Germany's ultimate fate depended on a favourable outcome on the Eastern Front in 1943. If the Soviets could be exhausted, then they would be more likely to negotiate a separate peace (or so the Nazis believed). To achieve this Hitler decided to launch an offensive to destroy enemy forces in the Kursk salient.

For Stalin, too, 1943 was to be a year of decision. Although the Red Army had inflicted major defeats on the Wehrmacht (German armed forces), the Germans still possessed large areas of Russian territory. If they were to be driven from the soil of Mother Russia, the Red Army would have to inflict a major defeat on the enemy in the summer of 1943. The strategy Stalin and the Stavka agreed upon to achieve this was divided into three parts. First, the Red Army would conduct a deliberate defence of the Kursk salient to wear down enemy forces in a so-called battle of attrition. Second, once the Germans were exhausted the Red Army would launch a series of offensives in the Kursk region. Finally, these offensives would be expanded to the flanks with the aim of reaching the River Dnieper and, if possible, advancing into Belorussia and the Ukraine.

German defeat at Kursk

The Kursk salient thus became the focus of both sides in the spring of 1943, and a strange lull descended on the Eastern Front as they rebuilt their forces after a winter of heavy fighting. If the Germans could eradicate the salient in a battle of encirclement, they would shorten the front and destroy those enemy forces in the area. Unfortunately for the Wehrmacht, this strategy was also apparent to the Soviets, who had received prior intelligence of Germany's intentions through their own spies inside the Wehrmacht and British intelligence intercepts. Thus the Red Army poured 2.5 million troops into the salient and constructed five defence lines, backed by 3000 tanks, to meet the enemy attack.

The German offensive at Kursk failed, and the defeat triggered a series of Red Army offensives that forced the Germans west during the summer and autumn of 1943. By the end of the year it was clear that Germany would not only lose the war on the Eastern Front but would also lose World War II. Only one question remained to be answered: how long would the war last?

◀ *German prisoners walk across the frozen Volga on their way to captivity. Later in the year prisoners were used to raise vessels that had been sunk by the Luftwaffe.*

INDEX

Page numbers in *italics* indicate illustrations.